Caveat Emptor

People Named Smith

BOOKS BY

H. ALLEN SMITH

PEOPLE NAMED SMITH
WE WENT THATAWAY
LARKS IN THE POPCORN
LO, THE FORMER EGYPTIAN!
THREE SMITHS IN THE WIND
RHUBARB
LOST IN THE HORSE LATITUDES
LIFE IN A PUTTY KNIFE FACTORY
LOW MAN ON A TOTEM POLE

DESERT ISLAND DECAMERON
(SELECTED BY H. ALLEN SMITH)

LOW AND INSIDE
(WITH IRA L. SMITH)

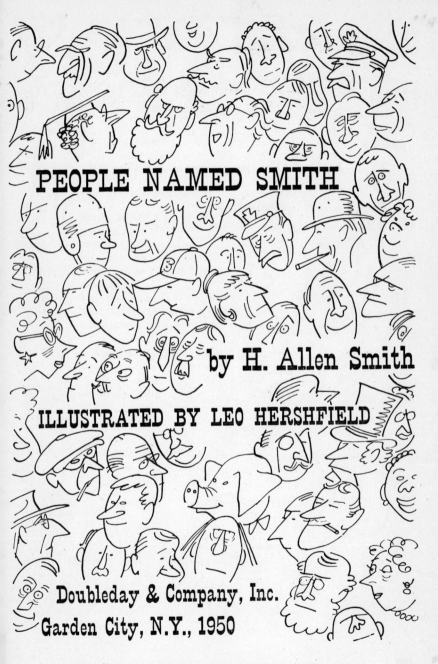

PEOPLE NAMED SMITH

by H. Allen Smith

ILLUSTRATED BY LEO HERSHFIELD

Doubleday & Company, Inc.
Garden City, N.Y., 1950

Warning

Anyone named Johnson, Brown, Williams, Miller, or Jones caught in the act of borrowing this book will be prosecuted to the full extent of the law.

Acknowledgments

Hundreds of books, magazines, and newspapers were consulted during the preparation of this volume, and it would be foolish for me to attempt a listing of them. Credit is given in the text wherever it seems proper that it should be given. And special acknowledgments include the following:

Esquire, for extract from "The Main Currents of Jazz," by Eduard Miller and James Crenshaw, from *Esquire's 1945 Jazz Book*, copyright, 1945, by Esquire, Inc.

Doubleday & Company, Inc., for "The Quest," from *Trivia*, by Logan Pearsall Smith.

Heath Cranton Limited, for extract from *Prisoner at the Bar*, by Anthony L. Ellis.

Harper & Brothers, for dedication from *The Jumping Frog*, by Mark Twain.

John Lane the Bodley Head, Ltd., for "Essay on Kipling," from *Heretics*, by Gilbert Chesterton.

Max Lerner for an extract from his column.

Little, Brown & Company, for lines from "Pride Goes Before a Raise," from *Many Long Years Ago*, copyright, 1933, by Ogden Nash.

Macmillan & Co., Ltd., and the Trustees of the Hardy Estate, for lines from "Epitaph on a Pessimist," by Thomas Hardy.

H. L. Mencken, for extract from his *Supplement II to The American Language*.

Henry F. Pringle, for extract from his *Biography of Alfred L. Smith*.

Frank Sullivan, for extract from an article by him.

Contents

People Named Smith

We, The Smiths

*Robert Ripley once reported that Albert J. Smith
of Dedham, Massachusetts, was a man with one
arm, a paper hanger by trade, and that he suffered from wheals of urticaria, popularly called
the hives.*

One morning near the mid-mark of the twentieth century a girl
named Polly O'Connor arrived at the side of a large plane which
was being loaded at LaGuardia Field. Miss O'Connor was present
for the purpose of making a routine check of the ship's personnel
before the take-off for Puerto Rico. Such matters are generally carried off with a dignified precision borrowed from the military. The
uniformed members of the crew stood at attention and Miss O'Connor, pencil poised above her check sheet, sang out:

"Captain?"

"Clifford Smith," said the captain.

"First Officer?" said Miss O'Connor.

"Harry Smith," came the response.

"Second Officer?"

"Ben Smith," said the second officer.

"Purser?"

"Gulie Smith."

"Stewardess?"

"Priscilla Smith," answered the stewardess.

"Sakes!" exclaimed Miss O'Connor, departing slightly from rou-

LIGHT GREEN
SMITH

1ST
PRIZE

tine, for such a concatenation of Smiths had never happened before, at least in her experience.

Along about this same time a news dispatch concerned with another Smith came out of Chicago. A professional ukulele player living in the heart of the meat metropolis was revealed as the owner of a pig which he had raised in the yard back of his house. When the International Livestock Show opened the ukulele player hauled his pig over to the exposition and a few days later walked off with a ribbon. The pig's name was Light Green Smith.

A couple of months after the triumph of the pig named Smith, Superior Court Judge William A. Smith mounted to the bench in Newark and examined the papers in the case before him. Mrs. Anna Smith was suing on behalf of her son, Robert Smith, who had been struck by an automobile. Judge Smith summoned counsel to the bench and after a conference announced: "There are too many Smiths in this case. By consent of counsel I excuse the four Smiths on the jury panel."

These incidents—a mighty plane roaring down to Rico with a crew made up exclusively of Smiths; a pig named Smith winning an award at the nation's greatest livestock show; seven Smiths brought together in a New Jersey courtroom because an automobile hit a boy—were closely related in time and illustrate the vast range of the Smiths upon our earth. Only the most ignorant of all the inhabitants of this planet (possibly a Smith) needs to be told that we excel in numbers. Our lead is so commanding, our procreative instincts so sharply developed, that it is unlikely that any of the other family groups will ever catch up to us. There have been times in the past when the Johnsons or the Browns or the Millers or the Joneses have taken to their mattresses and tried to make a fight of it, and some of these have actually shown slight gains, but in the end they faded and gave up.

We, the Smiths, are far and away the largest family group in the United States. We hold an easy lead, too, in the British Isles. The Smiths are predominant in England, and it is a fact that in Scotland there are many more Smiths than there are MacDonalds. In some sections of Scotland one out of every fifty persons is named Smith. Please keep in mind that we are dealing here with straightaway Smiths—people having the name Ess-Em-Eye-Tee-Aitch. Not Smythe, or Schmidt, or Smitt, or Smid, or Smed, or Kovacs, or Kowalski, or Gowan, or Taliaferro, or Haddad, or all the multitude of other versions and variations of the name.

No field of human endeavor is without its share of Smiths, from the arts and government down to highway robbery and indecent exposure. There is nothing we can't do and nothing we don't do. It could easily have been a Smith who kidnaped Charley Ross. A Smith, perhaps, was responsible for the presence of overalls in Mrs. Murphy's chowder. A Smith very likely ate the first oyster. It may have been a Smith who wrote Shakespeare's plays.

Our concern in this book is mainly with the Smiths of the United States, though we cannot ignore all the others scattered across the world. We represent a perfect cross section of the population. A few years ago a New York City newspaper made a custom of telephoning Smiths at random whenever a symposium of public opinion was wanted. The answers of the Smiths were, generally speaking, just as wise as if the newspaper had called Browns or Johnsons or Cohens.

We are Black Republicans and Communists and we are anarchists; we are Baptists and Catholics and Jews and Christian Scientists and Pillar of Fireites and Presbyterians and Jehovah's Witnesses and atheists. We are black and white and pink and red and brown and even yellow. We are rich and well off and just getting by and starving to death. We are titled lords and honorable sirs and we inhabit the hobo jungles. We are male and we are female and some of us—well, you wouldn't quite be able to tell for sure. We are bishops at the baptismal font and we are diggers of graves. We have not as yet produced a President, but one of ours, Abigail Smith, married a man before there ever was such a thing as the United States, and he became its first Vice-President and its second President; and this same Abigail, with the not inconsiderable assistance of her famous husband, produced from her womb another man who was to become the sixth President of the new nation.

If it would appear that we are a heterogeneous brotherhood of mixed beliefs and clashing passions, the picture is true enough; yet we are capable of unity and dangerous when aroused. The oldest maxim associated with our family, handed down from one of our ancient Scottish clans, is: *Touch not the cat without a glove.* We are a minority and, like all other minorities, we have certain inalienable rights—including the right to impose our will on the non-Smiths of this country. Woe betide the Hollywood producer who calls a scoundrel by our blessed name! Let no comic, by the utterance of stale and stereotyped jokes, caricature the Smiths! Warn the Southerner to cease insulting the race of Smiths by calling us "Smitty"! And woe again to the perverted scribbler who would ridicule us by putting the Smith manner of speech into the mouths of his characters! Touch not the cat without a glove! Best touch 'er not at all!

I have before me a magnificent book just recently published. It is titled *The Complete Button Book* (one of its two authors was formerly a Smith) and it is a beautiful specimen of the book designer's art. It sells for ten dollars. And what is it about? Buttons. This splendidly fashioned volume is of interest only to people who make a hobby of collecting old buttons. It is by no means the first book ever written about buttons. There are fat books about Cree Indians, and glass blowers, and bird watchers, and outfielders, and able-bodied seamen, and cloud seeders—but where is there a book about the Smiths? There are shelfloads of books about other families, from the Jukes and the Kallikaks to the Adamses of Boston. No one but an Adams of Boston would contend that his dynasty is greater than that of the Smiths, and we can quickly quell him by pointing out that the Queen Mother of his tribe was a Smith. Even granting that the Adamses are entitled to have whole libraries of books written about them and the Smiths none, are the Smiths of this world less important than buttons?

I have found but two alleged books purporting to be about the Smiths. One of these is a little volume called *Origin and History of the Name of Smith,* published in Chicago in 1902 and written, apparently, by a retarded eighth-grader. This pamphlet contains about fifty pages and only five or six of these pages are given to a consideration of the name Smith—a subject about which the anonymous author knew close to nothing. The second book is called *The Clan of Fire and Forge, or The Ancient and Honorable Smiths.* It came out in 1910 and, notwithstanding its pretty title, is of somewhat lesser stature than the other.

After an examination of these two essays I believe I can safely say that no book has ever, up to now, been written about the Smiths. I have been doing casual research on the subject for years and as a preliminary to the writing of this volume devoted several months to earnest digging, interviewing, and correspondence. Yet the book you hold in your hand is a modest endeavor, a simple prospectus, a mere sampling of the subject. Its purpose is to demonstrate something of the adventure that goes with being named Smith, and to show that the Smiths of this world are common only in the sense that they are numerous. It is a large subject— as large, perhaps, as vinyl plastics, nervous tension, or Moral Rearmament.

The great Mark Twain had his first book published in 1867—a

small volume titled *The Celebrated Jumping Frog*. It contained the famous frog story and a handful of humorous sketches written originally for newspapers. The dedication by the author follows:

To

JOHN SMITH,

Whom I Have Known in Divers and Sundry Places
About the World, and Whose Many and
Manifold Virtues Did Always
Command My Esteem, I

DEDICATE THIS BOOK.

It is said that the man to whom a volume is dedicated, always buys a copy. If this prove true in the present instance, a princely affluence is about to burst upon

THE AUTHOR

In the same mood, it would be my hope that this volume will find its way into the hands of all the Smiths who can read. I expect to hear from many of them. I have already found out that they can be as proud and as sensitive as Cuban college professors or English servants. They will howl after my blood for neglecting certain Smiths, for overlooking others. They will blast me because of some of the swinish Smiths whose attainments are included herein. No doubt they will catch me in error. All of this will be welcomed by me because someday, I should think, this book will need to be enlarged and revised. Whether I do the job or not is of no consequence; it will have to be done. The person or persons who ultimately write the final and definitive story of the Smiths will range much farther than I have, taking in all the variations of the clan name at home and abroad, for they are all Smiths. The Kuznetzovs of Soviet Russia are the Smiths of that country, but they are not the first family—that distinction belongs to the Ivanovs, or Johnsons. I have a strong conviction that if the situation were reversed—if the Smiths were as proportionately strong as they are in Britain and the United States—things would be different in the Kremlin.

The Red Badge of Smith

*In Columbus, Georgia, there is a monument to a
Negro named Bragg Smith, hero of a disaster involving a collapsing trench.*

When the Wandering Duke was the Prince of Wales he made
a pilgrimage to the United States, and that visitation, bordering
on the divine, helped fill out the picture of that great period in
our history called the Era of Wonderful Nonsense. In Philadelphia the young prince grew curious about a word which was
repeated again and again in polite company.

"Tell me," he finally asked, "just what is a biddle?"

I would like to enlarge upon his question. What, indeed, is a
Biddle alongside a Smith? The answer lies in that mysterious
fragment of gristle attached to the human brain which compels its
owner to dwell upon the quality of his ancestors. Biddles have it
and Smiths have it and Kallikaks have it. Says the conscience-rid-
den grandee: "No one of our line ever before was caught kissing
an upstairs maid." And says the disconsolate serf, shoving up to the
trough: "Nobody in our family ever et slop with the pigs before,
and I wouldn't do it if I wasn't starvin' to death."

Shortly before he died in New Orleans, Roark Bradford and I
had a long evening of talk, and one of the stories Brad told concerned a train ride he had taken through northern Mississippi. He
was about to get to sleep in a berth when a violent quarrel erupted
in the aisle of the car. Brad poked his head through the curtains

and saw two angry men facing each other in the aisle. At that instant one of them roared: "Nobody can say that to an Abernathy and get away with it!" Whereupon he clouted his opponent to the floor. The fallen one got to his feet and shouted: "No Abernathy can hit a Tolliver and live to tell the tale!" Whereupon he, Tolliver, belted Abernathy to the carpet. Abernathy got up screaming that no Abernathy had ever tasted dust before, most particularly at the instigation of a Tolliver, and went at Tolliver again. The battle raged on, and from his Pullman berth Brad noticed that the train conductor was standing in the vestibule watching the proceedings with an air of resignation and boredom.

After Abernathy and Tolliver had slugged each other half senseless they dragged themselves away and the conductor came down the aisle. Brad stopped him. "How come," he said, "you didn't stop those two men?"

"Listen," said the conductor, "my name happens to be Dabney. I wouldn't give a damn if trash like that kilt each other."

Idolatry of family has not been a strong characteristic of the Smiths as a whole, though it has existed in a virulent form among certain small branches of the clan. The generality of Smiths, in fact, have had a tendency to lower their eyes and blush slightly at mention of their tribal affiliation; as if the name were a burden, an embarrassment, almost a shame. Somerset Maugham, in *A Writer's Notebook,* quotes a certain Annandale as having said: "I often think life must be quite different to a man called Smith; it can have neither poetry nor distinction." This book is, in a sense, a refutation of that statement. And as a direct challenge to this bird Annandale, I offer herewith perhaps the greatest tribute ever penned to the Smiths of the world. It was written by G. K. Chesterton, as follows:

> In the case of Smith, the name is so poetical that it must be an arduous and heroic matter for the man to live up to it. The name of Smith is the name of the one trade that even kings respected; it could claim half the glory of that *arma virumque* which all epics acclaimed. The spirit of the smithy is so close to the spirit of song that it has mixed in a

million poems, and every blacksmith is a harmonious blacksmith.

Even the village children feel that in some dim way the smith is poetic, as the grocer and the cobbler are not poetic, when they feast on the dancing sparks and deafening blows in the cavern of that creative violence. The brute repose of Nature, the passionate cunning of man, the strongest of earthly metals, the weirdest of earthly elements, the unconquerable iron subdued by its only conqueror, the wheel and the ploughshare, the sword and the steam-hammer, the arraying of armies and the whole legend of arms, all these things are written, briefly indeed, but quite legibly, on the visiting-card of Mr. Smith. Yet our novelists call their hero "Aylmer Valence," which means nothing, or "Vernon Raymond," which means nothing, when it is within their power to give him this sacred name of Smith— this name made of iron and flame. It would be very natural if a certain hauteur, a certain carriage of the head, a certain curl of the lip, distinguished everyone whose name is Smith. Perhaps it does; I trust so. Whoever else are parvenus, the Smiths are not parvenus. From the darkest dawn of history this clan has gone forth to battle; its trophies are on every hand; its name is everywhere; it is older than the nations, and its sign is the Hammer of Thor.

As a Smith I bow to the shade of Chesterton and make but one small curl of the lip: why did he give *his* most famous hero the name of Father Brown?

People named Smith have always had to contend with certain annoyances because of the commonness of their name. Every Smith has the usual story to tell of the smirking hotel clerk. Another cliché involves the confusion attending the paging of a Mr. Smith in a public place. Far back in my youth I can remember seeing a two-panel cartoon on this subject. In the first panel a bell-boy stands in the center of a hotel lobby and is crying, "Paging Mr. Smith!" In the second panel he has disappeared beneath a great pile of struggling men.

The cough-drop gambit has been with us for many decades.

"Meet Mr. Smith," someone says, performing a routine introduction.

"Trade or Mark?" comes the inevitable question, with perhaps the addition of, "I see you've shaved off your whiskers."

The Smiths themselves have a favorite cliché when it comes to discussing the origin of their name. I never knew a Smith who didn't, at one time or another, spring it on me; and I in turn have sprung it on others. Here, in 1950, it pops up on an advertising postal card addressed to a John J. Smith in the Bronx. Printed on the back of the card is this message:

DEAR MR. SMITH:
A long time ago everyone was named Smith. As each committed a sin, he was compelled to take another name. Today only a few of us Smiths are left. See Roy C. Smith for your new Chevrolet.

Among other fables dealing with the origin of our name is the one which says we are lineal descendants of Noah, by way of his eldest son Shem. The name went from Shem to Shemit to Shmit to Smith. And a lady named Sara Payson Willis Parton, who called herself Fanny Fern, once wrote: "When Adam got tired of naming his numerous descendants he said, 'Let all the rest be called Smith.'"

The most readable single volume dealing with the origin of personal names which I have encountered was published early in 1950 under the title, *The Story of Our Names*. It is the work of a Chicago lawyer who has spent more than twenty-five years studying onomatology, the science of names. And what do you suppose *his* name is? Smith. Elsdon C. Smith. He explains that people did not begin acquiring surnames until about the year 1000 and that these names derived generally from four sources: localities, occupations, fathers' names, and descriptive or personal traits. Smith is almost but not quite purely occupational in origin. There are a few Smiths whose ancestors had nothing whatever to do with working in metals; their name derives from the fact that in Old England they lived near a smooth field, which was called a *smeeth* field. The famous Smithfield region of London, where knights of old slew one another in tournaments and where heretics were burned, got its name not from any member of our family but from the fact that as a field it was smeeth. Meaning not bumpy.

The occupational origin of the name Smith has always been obvious, but there is a point which helps explain how the Smiths happened to become a multitude. Most people assume that a smith is a shoer of horses, a blacksmith; or at most they broaden the definition only so far as to include all workers in metals. Actually, in the olden times a smith was any man who worked with a hammer, whether in metals, in wood, or in stone. Hence there were more smiths around than anything else. The present-day lexicography of *smith* takes in a wide territory. First, a smith is "one who forges with the hammer; a worker in metals." But secondly, a smith is "one who fabricates a thing; especially one who writes, paints, etc., as though forging." Under this latter definition I am, at the moment, a Smith at work as a smith. The big Webster lists thirty-nine different types of smiths as belonging in our modern language. Most of these have obvious connotations: anvilsmith, axlesmith, blacksmith, bladesmith, boilersmith, boltsmith, brass-smith, bronze-smith, carriagesmith, clocksmith, coachsmith, coppersmith, goldsmith, gunsmith, ironsmith, jobsmith, jokesmith, lock-smith, pansmith, platinumsmith, sawsmith, scalesmith, scissors-smith, scythesmith, silversmith, stonesmith, swordsmith, tinsmith, tiresmith, toolsmith, and wiresmith. A hedgesmith is defined as an itinerant smith or tinker, while a housesmith is a smith who helps in constructing the steel framework of a building. There is some dispute about the origin of the modern surname of Naismith or Nasmyth—it comes either from knifesmith or nailsmith—and it is important to us in case we want to boast that a Smith gave the world the game of basketball (Dr. James Naismith). A jawsmith is a professional talker, or demagogue. A picksmith is a drop-forger who makes heads of picks. A runesmith is "one who writes in or deciphers runes," and a rune is a sort of mysterious magical writing in an alphabet known as the futhark. A whitesmith is one who works in galvanized iron, although a whitesmith is also a kind of light-colored gooseberry.

It should be clear by now that our remote ancestors did not necessarily follow the trade of shoeing horses. Back when it all began every man who used a hammer in his work was called a smith. Anything that could be hammered—iron, gold, pewter, sod, harpoons, hickory nuts—produced its own smith. And don't forget that with everyone hammering like mad there had to be special hammerers to hammer hammers, creating them and keeping them

in repair, and these were called hammersmiths, and there were probably more of them than there were of actual blacksmiths.

In the time when every warrior and his horse had to be encased in armor, the smith was the man who served as tailor. Usually, too, he had to travel along with his clients, for when they ripped their coats or split their pants the damage couldn't be repaired with a needle; a soldering iron was needed.

In the Revolutionary War novel *Drums,* by James Boyd, there is a character named Dr. Clapton, an absent-minded old clergyman who is engaged on a large writing project which he calls "The Work." It develops that Dr. Clapton is trying to write, in heroic couplets, a masterpiece to be titled *The Sminthiad, or The Cosmopolis of Smiths.* When I first heard of this matter I assumed that Dr. Clapton was trying to write what I was trying to write; but when I got the book it developed that he was interested in the trade of the smith, and he spoke of notes he had accumulated on famous smiths, notably Tubal-cain, Apollo Smintheus, Vulcan, Wayland Smith, and Basil the Macedonian. I can only hope that my Cosmopolis of Smiths is more accurate than Dr. Clapton's. Tubal-cain fits, being described in the Bible as the first worker in brass and iron. Apollo Smintheus had nothing to do with smithing; he was the mouse god and his assignment was to get rid of mice— his statue was put out in the field to frighten the mice away. Vulcan was the Roman fire god whose main business was to keep houses from burning down (his Greek counterpart, Hephaestus, was more in the nature of a smith). Vulcan's last name was Mulciber, though few people called him by it. Wayland Smith, or Wayland the Smith, was a hero in Teutonic mythology and was a worker in metals. He was captured by a Swedish king named Nidudr and put to work as a smith on a small island after the sinews of his knees had been cut. He got back at Nidudr, however. He killed the King's two sons, then gold-plated their skulls and sent them as a present to their father. He then raped Nidudr's daughter and escaped by flying away on a pair of wings he had fashioned for himself. As for Dr. Clapton's final candidate, Basil the Macedonian, he was a ruthless Byzantine emperor who, so far as I can determine, didn't know an anvil from his elbow.

An interesting theory about ancient smiths comes to me from a George Groskritz who lives in Connecticut, and who chafes under the knowledge that there are so many Smiths and so few Groskritzes. He writes:

"While the Smiths shoed our horses, the members of the Groskritz (Greatcross) family rode off and fought the battles. All the Groskritzes fought and died except one, and he was captured and tortured, but his winsome smile saved his life. But for him there would be no Groskritzes left at all. We did the fighting and you Smiths stayed at home and married our daughters, and that is the reason why today so many Groskritzes bear the name of Smith. The Browns were cooks and did the same, so many Browns today are really Groskritzes."

Among some savage tribes of Africa the craft of the smith is sacred and only the chiefs may meddle with it. So in more civilized climes the smith was respected and honored. In Wales he sat beside his master the King at table and was entitled to take a drink of every wine that was brought into the hall, even before the most important guests were served. He fashioned the iron collar which bound the serf (O evil smith!) and he wrought and installed the chastity belt which secured the charms of Queen and Lady (O enviable smith!). The rest of the time he just smote whatever needed smiting—for the name of his trade derives from the Saxon word which means *to smite*.

The average Smith looks with considerable distaste on anyone bearing the name Smyth, or Smythe. A Smith can tolerate a person with any one of the many foreign variants of his surname, but he is somehow contemptuous of Smyths, just as he is inclined to be antagonistic toward Hyphenated Smiths. It appears to be almost inherent in a Smith to believe that a Smyth was originally a Smith and changed the spelling for the sake of haughtiness. This cleavage between Smith and Smyth becomes all the more curious when we consider that many Smyths will snarl at you if you address them as Smith. There exists a lovely illustration of this latter point. Because Smyth and Smith are antithetical, Notre Dame once unexpectedly beat the Army at football.

The year 1923 was the first year in which the famous backfield called the Four Horsemen played together as a unit for Notre Dame. That year found the Army riding high, unbeaten in two seasons. Then into New York came Notre Dame and the Four Horsemen (not yet known by that name), and the experts gave them little or no chance against the power of the West Pointers. Harry Stuhldreher, quarterback for the Horsemen, has recounted the story of what happened that afternoon.

One of the backfield stars for the Army was George Smythe, and George Smythe needed to be stopped if Notre Dame was to get anywhere at all.

Just before the game started someone told Stuhldreher that George Smythe of the Army hated to be called Smith—that he had been known to assault people who addressed him as Smith. Stuhldreher had a quiet conference with some of the boys who played the line in front of the Horsemen. Joe Bach was given the key assignment. Joe was to lead the strategic heckling of George Smythe.

The throng in the stands wasn't aware of it, but all through that game the Notre Dame players were calling the West Point star "Mr. Smith." Smythe would drop back to punt and Joe Bach would call across the line: "Why, Mr. Smith, you going to kick it now?" Or one of the other Notre Dame boys would speak in mock politeness to the whole Army team: "Why don't you fellas give the ball to Mr. Smith now?" As had been anticipated, George Smythe grew both furious and wild. He began to flub important plays and get off sorry punts. The final score was Notre Dame 13, Army 0.

There are some excellent people in the world named Smyth. Among them is a man we would dearly love to have using an *i* instead of a *y* in the middle of his surname—Henry DeWolf Smyth, the physics professor out of Princeton who is sometimes called "Mr. Atom." He is, at this writing, the top scientist involved in the atomic energy program and he was picked to write the first official history of the Manhattan District wartime atomic bomb project. His book was released a few days after the big egg was dropped on Hiroshima and was widely known as the Smyth Report.

I wrote to Professor Smyth seeking his thoughts on the subject of Smith versus Smyth. I am informed that he carried the letter around in his coat pocket for a month. Now and then he'd drag it out and look at it again and compose himself for some deep thinking, but always a film of heavy hydrogen would choose that moment to envelop his mind. At last he handed the letter over to Mrs. Smyth and asked her to answer it. In a way I'm glad he did, for her letter contained the following eloquent paragraph:

> The sad truth is that we cannot think of anything
> of the slightest use to you in this dismal business of
> being called Smyth. From our lonely island we look
> across at all the happy, carefree people called Smith
> cavorting on the mainland, untroubled by those who
> misunderstand and misspell. It must be a wonderful
> life.

There is at least one other Smyth whose career suggests that she was operating under a disguise and actually belonged to us—Dame Ethel Smyth, who died in 1944 and who was one of England's top composers. She was famous as a violent suffragette, smoked cigars, and was jailed once for throwing a brick through the Home Secretary's window when the Home Secretary was home.

The Smyths, however, must wait for their own book, as must the Schmidts and the Goldsmiths and the Chilingirians and the Schmids. I drop that last one in deliberately in order that I might mention a particular Schmid. A man of that name is deserving of wide recognition for a single achievement. He wrote a dictionary of the language used by hens. I have not seen his book, but I shall not rest until I have my copy. There are so many questions I want to ask hens.

The percentage of Smiths who Hyphenate is quite small in the United States, but not so in England.

There are 209 Smiths listed in the British Who's Who and fifty-one of these are Hyphenates. Among them are Lucie-Smith, Heathcote-Smith, Broke-Smith, Shrapnell-Smith, Hammersley-

Smith, Rivers-Smith, Lumley-Smith, Protheroe-Smith, Grafftey-Smith, Babington-Smith and Tottenham-Smith. Ogden Nash once wrote a little poem touching on this practice as follows:

> In the phalanx of hy-
> Phenated names!
> (Have you ever observed
> That the name of Smith
> Is the oftenest hy-
> Phenated with?)

It has been calculated that half the Smiths in the United States can trace their ancestry to the British Isles. Most of the remainder are Germanic Smiths, originally called Schmidt, Schmid, Schmitt, Smitt, or Smit. The rest are people whose names in their native languages were the literal equivalent of smith and who changed to the more convenient form when they settled in the United States. Some changed, that is, but some did not. For example, the Hungarian for smith is *kovács*. There are many Hungarians bearing the name Kovacs. Some of them, when they came to the United States, translated themselves and became Smiths. Others retained the original form (Sandor Kovacs is a name familiar to present-day wrestling addicts).

It needs to be pointed out that there are many Smiths in the United States who acquired the name not through choice but through a sort of compulsion. In earlier days, when the flow of immigration was heavy, many of our minor public officials were impatient, rude, and stupid, just as they are in these more advanced times. The newcomers to America had to deal with whole platoons of these bureaucrats, who in turn were angered whenever they came upon a foreign name that was long and difficult to spell. A man named, say, Kolodziejcak would appear before one of these public servants and utter the name and try to spell it, and the American official, in high disgust, would snort and sputter and then write on the card, "Smith." Mr. Kolodziejcak would then go away with a new name, an American name, and in a great number of cases it stayed with him for the remainder of his life and was passed on to his children.

Some of the foreign equivalents of Smith are:

FRENCH: LeFevre, or Taillefer, or Forgeron
SCANDINAVIAN: Smed
POLISH: Kowalczyks, or Kowalski
CZECH: Kovác
ITALIAN: Fabro
UKRAINIAN: Zhinchak
PORTUGUESE: Ferreira
SPANISH: Herrero
ARMENIAN: Chilingirian, or Darbinian
FINNISH: Seppänen
SYRIAN: Haddad
RUMANIAN: Covaciu
GYPSY: Petulengro

Some Smiths among my correspondents insist that the Greek equivalent of Smith is Pappas. It is the equivalent of Smith only in the sense that it is a common surname in Greece. According to one authority, pappas means priest; according to another, it means grandfather. The whole business of Smith in Greek is in a state of utterable confusion. In an attempt to clear it up I have made overtures to the head of the Greek Department in a big university. He says that originally the Greeks had no word meaning blacksmith. Apparently they felt very silly about this because they had blacksmiths and no way of calling them anything. So they eventually took the word for bronze maker and applied it to blacksmiths, that word being *chalceus*. Pronounced cal-cuss. The learned professor doesn't know of any Greek people named Chalceus or Cal-cuss; it is his belief, in fact, that there is no such thing as a Greek Smith.

We have noted that Scotland probably has more Smiths in proportion to the total population than any other country. There are, in addition to the straightaway Smiths, many Scots named Gow, or McGow, or MacGowan, and all these are actually Smiths; in Gaelic the word *gow* means *smith*.

Coming now to the Smiths of French origin, we find ourselves in a position to play a little game which suggests itself whenever you get to dabbling in the foreign variations of the name. You say to me challengingly: "After all, there are no Smiths in the Hall of Fame up there on the campus of New York University. Seventy-seven famous Americans, and not a Smith among them." And I come back at you: "The hell there ain't!" You check through the list again and make sure, and then say: "Show me a Smith on that list." And I point to the name of Booker T. Washington.

Now, to prove my point. Booker T. Washington was born in slavery and during his early childhood had no name other than "Booker." When his mother was questioned about his origin, she said that his father was a certain white plantation owner. The time came, in school, when Booker had need of a last name, so he chose one for himself—Washington. And so he went through life. The "T" was for the name of the man who was his father—Taliaferro. And Taliaferro is Smith.

We can go back to the time of the Conquest and the Battle of Hastings to find a Variant Smith (possibly an ancestor of Booker T. Washington) performing great deeds. The first man to draw blood in that historic battle was a Norman knight and troubadour who charged into the English lines, singing as he slashed. His name was Taillefer, meaning Smith, and his name is perpetuated in several variations today in the United States, notably in the South, where there are many Tollfers and Taillifers and Taliaferros and Tollivers and Telfairs.

There are American Indians named Smith. There are a multitude of Negro Smiths, though the name is not in the first place among them. There are more Negroes named Johnson and Brown than are named Smith. And there is at least one Chinese Smith. H. R. (Bud) Ekins, the former war correspondent who served many years in the Far East, reports to me that he met a Chinese Smith on the Pa Pao Shan golf course near Peiping. When Mr. Ekins asked his caddy to identify himself, the boy replied that he was Smith Hu. Mr. Ekins was curious, and the caddy, a bright boy, explained his name. Some of the important people in China, he said, had made it fashionable to assume English names. He mentioned Wellington Koo and Victor Hu and Hollington Tong

among others. "Smith Hu told me," says Mr. Ekins, "that he decided to follow suit and to adopt the most distinguished of all foreign names for himself."

The Bureau of the Census does not count Smiths as Smiths and doesn't bother with a breakdown of the population according to family name. Extensive samplings, however, tell us approximately how many Smiths there are in the United States. One out of every one hundred persons in this country is a Smith. Actually it is slightly over this—the percentage is usually a trifle above one per cent. This figure obtains in almost every list available for examination—military rolls, Social Security files, telephone directories, the frightening archives of the Federal Bureau of Investigation, social registers, federations of chinchilla breeders, and compendiums of Important People. One out of every hundred. That adds up to at least 1,500,000 Smiths in the United States alone.

These million and a half are, let me repeat, straightaway Smiths. The figure does not take into account the numerous female Smiths who by marriage have become Johnsons and Terwilligers and Adamses and Sullivans and Biddups. Add to them the thousands of Almost Smiths—the sons and daughters of mothers who were named Smith. Then add to that the names of Sugar Ray Robinson and Mary Pickford. Before you know it you've got yourself a mess of Smiths.

The Johnsons rank second in the United States with a mere million. The first twenty most numerous surnames in the country are:

1.	Smith	11.	Thomas
2.	Johnson	12.	Moore
3.	Brown	13.	White
4.	Williams	14.	Martin
5.	Miller	15.	Thompson
6.	Jones	16.	Jackson
7.	Davis	17.	Harris
8.	Anderson	18.	Lewis
9.	Wilson	19.	Allen
10.	Taylor	20.	Nelson

There are more Cohens than Smiths in New York City, but that doesn't mean there are not many Smiths. There are hordes of them. Almost from the beginning New York has had Smiths to throw away. In 1786 a local newspaper carried this item: "Col. William Smith, late of Red Mill, Dutchess County, informs his friends and the public that having moved into New York, and finding so many of his name, to distinguish himself from them, has added the letter M. as a middle initial."

Running second to the Cohens in New York, the Smiths also have been nosed out by the Johnsons in Chicago. And in Minneapolis and St. Paul the Smiths have been overwhelmed by Johnsons, Andersons, Nelsons, and Petersons. In almost all other large cities, however, the Smiths occupy first place.

Who's Who in America recognizes 363 Smiths. Ninety of these are college professors; thirty-three are lawyers; twenty-eight are clergymen; fifteen are army officers; seventeen are bankers; fourteen are manufacturers; another fourteen are newspapermen, and thirteen are authors. Scattered among the others are doctors, architects, economists, engineers, politicians, railroad officials, judges, musicians, insurance men, ranchers, artists, librarians, a critic, a cartoonist, a shipbuilder, a livestock specialist, a temperance leader, a geographer, a director of cinematography, a farmer, and a Christian Science practitioner. There is one Smith on the honor roll of those who have been in Who's Who for half a century or longer: Professor Charles Lee Smith, an educator of Raleigh, North Carolina.

Anthony L. Ellis, in *Prisoner at the Bar,* wrote: "In all the wide vocabulary of the English language are there two words which, conjointly, suggest a finer guarantee of simple faith than the name of John Smith? The words are the embodiment of honesty of purpose, the epitome of rugged sincerity and truth."

Perhaps so. But there are some people in this world who must yearn at times for a society rendered completely John Smithless. The clerical help, for example, in the Veterans Administration, where the rolls contain thirteen thousand John Smiths—eight thousand of them with no middle initial.

And concluding this brief statistical section of our book, let us consider just one more fascinating figure:

Every day in the United States nineteen Smiths die.

The Brothers Kuznetzov

*Eli Smith was the first man in all history to
cast a font of type in the Arabic language.*

Because of the diversity of their creeds and the disparate bulk of
their pocketbooks, the Smiths of the earth will never be organized
into a single unit for any real serious purpose—save only to resist
an attack made upon them solely because they are named Smith.
They would unite for that, and send a powerful lobby to Congress,
and parade behind defiant brass bands, and bomb the homes of
Johnsons and Joneses. Otherwise, trying to organize people named
Smith would be as foolish as trying to organize People.

It is likely that when Alfred E. Smith ran for President of the
United States in 1928 more Smiths voted against him than voted
for him. The Revolt of the South was a salient factor in that election, and it is worth noting that a renegade Smith was one of its
leaders—Dean Leon Perdue Smith of Wesleyan College was chairman of the convention of "Hoover Democrats" in Georgia that
year.

Any brotherhood of Smiths, even when united by close ties of
consanguinity, is subject to the same strains and stresses that exist
in all human confederations. A few years ago an old-fashioned
Smith Family Reunion was held at the picnic grounds on the edge
of a Midwestern town, with nearly a thousand Smiths and their
kin attending, drawn together by feelings of fellowship from all
over the United States. Late in the afternoon a male Smith from a

distant state was observed pinching the rear fatty tissue of a lady who was the wife of his cousin-german. The cousin-german hit the trifler with "an empty bottle of Old Grand-dad." Within seconds Smiths were smiting Smiths with legs ripped off the picnic tables, and by evening every bed in the town hospital was occupied and additional wounded were groaning on the floors of the corridors. Touch not the cat without a glove.

There have been and there are organizations made up of Smiths, but their purposes are frivolous in the way that the purposes of the Society for the Preservation and Encouragement of Barber Shop Quartet Singing in America, the Guild of Former Pipe Organ Pumpers, the Society for the Prevention of Disparaging Remarks about Brooklyn, and the Association for the Promotion of International Understanding are frivolous. Back in the olden times— the middle 1930s—an organization calling itself the Benevolent and Protective and Completely Universal Order of Fred Smiths of America held a convention in New York City. At that time I was a newspaper reporter, and because my name was Smith I was assigned to cover the convention. The by-line over my stories was: "By H. Allen (Call Me Fred) Smith." There must have been a hidden gimmick in that convention, but at this late date I don't know what it was. There were forty or fifty delegates from all over the country, the sole qualification for membership being possession of the name Fred Smith. Among them was the head of a dissenting branch of the Mormon Church, and the headmaster of a boys' school, and an executive of the Lily Cup Company, and a radio announcer named Smith who, I learned, had conveniently given himself Fred for a middle name in order to add point to his broadcast of the proceedings. The thing was gagged up from beginning to end, and a man named Smith Frederick who sought admission to the banquet hall was permitted to enter walking backward and it was required that he eat his dinner out of his lap, with his back turned to the table.

Groups of Smiths are sometimes assembled by the movie-company publicity wizards when they have a picture in which the central character is named Smith. When the film *Mr. Smith Goes to Washington* was given its première showing in Washington, special invitations were issued to people named Smith. Enough of them turned up to load the galleries (the main auditorium was given over to Washington dignitaries), and Ira L. Smith, who attended as a journalist, recalls: "I happened to be backstage and I remember peeping out of the wings to get a look at that audience. There they were, the Smiths, looking like rows of clucking pigeons perched up under the eaves. I had a feeling that at any moment they would all take off and swoop down onto the stage and start hollering for peanuts."

Another movie, possibly *Joe Smith, American,* was scheduled into one of Broadway's leading picture palaces some years ago. The theater's press agent came up with the usual colossal scheme. Why not, he suggested, announce in the newspapers that authenticated Smiths would be admitted free to the first performance? The idea was accepted as great by the manager of the theater. The first showing of the picture was to be around eleven o'clock in the morning, and the announcement of the stunt was published in the press.

By ten-thirty on the appointed day there was a mob of Smiths on the sidewalk in front of the theater. The manager, however, was not happy. He was, in fact, in great distress because fully half the Smiths out front were Negroes. His theater had always maintained a policy of gentle discouragement when it came to Negro customers. But this time he was stuck with them—there was nothing he could do but fix his face in a smile, reserve his curses for the press agent, and invite them all inside. When the thing was over the manager hastened to the office of the press agent, who braced himself for the assault.

"You know something?" said the manager. "I've been thinking. There wasn't a bit of trouble with that Smith crowd. The blacks and the whites were all mixed together and everybody had a good time. Not a single argument. From now on, any colored people want to come in this theater, they're welcome."

Now and then the newspapers carry reports concerning the activities of the Organized Smiths of America. Early in each year the president of the organization, Colonel Larry Smith of Hollywood, announces a series of awards to outstanding Smiths of the nation. I have found my name on the list a couple of times, but until now I never knew exactly what it was all about. Recently I have been in communication with Colonel Larry Smith, who is in the radio business, and now I have the answer.

Back in 1945 Colonel Smith was approached by a friend, Bill Hendricks of the Warner Brothers publicity department. Mr. Hendricks had a problem. He was seeking some means of calling the public's attention to a comparatively new actress on the Warner lot—Miss Alexis Smith. He needed to get Miss Smith's name in the papers. Over scotch and puddle water he and Colonel Smith dreamed up the Organized Smiths of America, and Colonel Smith was forthwith elected president by a unanimous vote of two. He then announced the first annual OSA awards to Smiths of achievement and among them, of course, was the award for acting, given to Miss Alexis Smith. Colonel Smith was agreeably surprised to find that the story of the awards was used on front pages all over the country. The following year he got up a new batch of Smith awards and phoned the list in to the press associations with the same happy result. The third year the press services were *asking* for the list and Colonel Smith accommodated them, leading off with an award in military science to General Holland M. (Howlin' Mad) Smith. Imagine Colonel Larry's surprise when, a short time later, old "Howlin' Mad" himself arrived in Hollywood for the purpose of collecting his honors. Some sort of certificate was rigged up and the general was taken out to Warner's, where he had lunch with Alexis Smith, and he seemed quite thrilled by the whole thing.

Colonel Smith informs me that the Organized Smiths of America, in spite of its rather shabby beginning, is today a going concern and that he receives much mail from assorted Smiths all over the land. "This year," he reports, "we are applying for a charter. We are going to make the world understand that the Smiths are an old, established, and honorable people, notwithstanding the fact that you and I belong to the clan."

There remains one more organization of Smiths, and I would like to introduce it with a story I picked up a couple of years ago while traveling in Arkansas. In the Lum and Abner country I had a session with Hal L. Norwood, former attorney general for Arkansas, and Mr. Norwood told the story of John Smith and the wolf scalps.

Years ago there was a certain justice of the peace who held office in a township near Mena. At that time the state of Arkansas had a law providing a bounty for the killing of wolves and wildcats. The county courts were authorized to pay five dollars for each such animal slain.

One day this justice of the peace notified the county court that John Smith had killed a wolf, had brought in the wolf's scalp, and had assigned the certificate for collection of the bounty to the justice, who was promptly given the money. A few days later John Smith killed another wolf, and the justice collected the five dollars. Before long John Smith was slaughtering wolves and wildcats at a prodigious rate and the bounty money was flowing from the county court to the justice of the peace. At last some meddlesome crank grew suspicious and the grand jury began an investigation. The justice of the peace was summoned for examination.

"Who is this John Smith who killed a wolf on such and such a date?" he was asked.

"Well," said the country jurist, "I didn't know him personally. He was a stranger, just passing through, and he happened to kill this wolf. He couldn't stay around, had to be in Texas, so he sold me his certificate at a ten-per-cent discount."

Additional certificates were produced, and in each case the justice said that this particular John Smith also was a stranger, passing through, killing a wolf in transit. The justice was now asked why the signature of John Smith on each of the certificates and his own signature were in the same handwriting. Well, he said, these fellas named John Smith were all old men and couldn't write so good with a pen and had asked him to sign for them.

For some queer reason the grand jury didn't believe his story and indicted the justice for obtaining a whole series of bounty warrants under false pretenses. He was convicted of the charge and on the day for sentencing was called to the bar and asked if he had anything to say.

"You damn right I got something to say," he retorted with passion. "You go ahead and send me to the pen and leave the damn wolves and wildcats take the country and go to hell with it!"

The court obliged him with a penitentiary sentence, and his misfortune serves here to illustrate how misappropriation of the name Smith can be a dangerous thing.

The National Society to Discourage Use of the Name Smith for Purposes of Hypothetical Illustration, called TNSDUNSPHI for short, had its birth in 1942 at the University of Minnesota—a strange locality for the event, when we consider that Minnesota is one of the few states where Smiths are not the first family.

The idea for TNSDUNSPHI was born in the mind of a young man named Glenn E. Smith, who was taking a graduate course in labor relations under Dale Yoder. This Glenn E. Smith is one of the Super Smiths, from the fact that his father, a Smith, married a Smith, so that all of Glenn's grandparents were named Smith. To distinguish between them, as a youngster Glenn called them "little grandma and little grandpa" and "big grandma and big grandpa." He grew up, to be sure, with a special sort of self-consciousness about his name.

During that summer course at Minnesota, Glenn Smith had only one complaint to make against his teacher, Dale Yoder. He recognized Yoder as a master of his job who used anecdote liberally to illustrate his lectures, but he resented the fact that the principal character in every Yoder anecdote was a hypothetical "James Smith." Day after day this James Smith appeared in the professor's stories, and Glenn Smith took to brooding about it. In the end he thought up TNSDUNSPHI. At his own expense he had elaborate letterheads printed so he could solicit members, and an artist named Harrison Smith Hartley donated his services in designing a membership card. The printer, a non-Smith, wanted sixteen dollars for five hundred of the cards, so Glenn Smith wrote to his cousin, C. Lowell Smith, in California. Glenn said he would make C. Lowell Smith chairman of the board of directors of the new organization for eight dollars cash. C. Lowell Smith, a radio newscaster in Los Angeles, kicked in with the money and in a few days was over at Warner Brothers having his picture taken handing Alexis Smith a membership card in TNSDUNSPHI. The newspapers made quite a to-do about it and the organization was well launched.

Glenn E. Smith is now chief of the Guidance Services Division in the Michigan State Department of Public Instruction. He has seen the organization he founded grow almost out of hand. Hundreds of Smiths, many of them prominent, have written to him accepting membership in TNSDUNSPHI, pledging themselves to the common cause. Kenneth G. Smith, head of the Pepsodent Company, contributed a couplet which serves as the organization's official motto. It goes:

> *A guy named Smith*
> *Must be reckoned with.*

Members are required to carry their handsomely embossed cards with them at all times, and whenever they hear someone use the name Smith for hypothetical illustration, they are honor bound to get up and hand the offender the card, which describes the clan's battle cry as: "When you think of Smith, say John Doe!" One New England Smith, in accepting membership, wrote to President Glenn: "I fear I may not always be able to use the battle cry. My secretary's name is Doe."

TNSDUNSPHI has traffic only with what its president calls "pure Smiths." A pure Smith is described as one who eschews spelling his name Smyth or Smythe and who would rather die than hyphenate. The society has its own version of the origin of our name. This bit of legend appears on the back of the membership card. It says that when Adam was first privileged to look upon Eve he blurted: "It's a myth!" The remark was overheard by the Serpent, who thought Adam had said, "It's Smith." Thus the family name had its beginning in the Garden of Eden, and Eve was the first human to bear it.

As president of the organization Glenn Smith keeps a file of correspondence he has had from assorted Smiths, ranging from a voodoo enchantress in Harlem to the late Harold D. Smith, who was Director of the Budget under Roosevelt and president of all Smiths in the District of Columbia.

Arthur G. Smith, senior member of an important law firm in Honolulu, accepted membership in the society and became president for Hawaii. He voiced an objection to the Garden of Eden legend. He recalled having spent some time in the Egyptian Room of the British Museum, where he inspected an obsidian statue of a hippopotamus rampant. Lawyer Smith reported that, despite an alderman's paunch, the hippo was a rather dignified-looking chap, and the plate at the base of the figure was inscribed: "Smithis, or Smithicus, the River God of Egypt."

"I have never," wrote Lawyer Smith, "thought an awful lot of Adam and his antics in the Garden of Eden and I was very much pleased to learn that we Smiths do not need to admit him as an ancestor, but that we can go back beyond him and claim a direct descent from this deity, even though he be a minor one."

Lawyer Smith made no specific charge against Adam, so I don't know what was in his mind; he must have had some private information of a shocking character, inasmuch as it led him to prefer descent from a Smith who was a dead ringer for a hippopotamus.

Warren Storey Smith, music critic for the Boston *Post*, wrote a confession, admitting that at one time in his career as a composer he had succumbed to temptation and become a hyphenate, signing himself Warren Storey-Smith. "However," he added, "the real renegade in our branch of the family is my second cousin, Edmund Ware Smith, who writes short stories under the pen name of Edmund Ware. That, thank God, I would never do!"

Named president of TNSDUNSPHI for Florida was the late Thomas W. Smith, a retired clergyman nearly eighty years of age. Preacher Smith penned a warm tribute to the clan when he accepted his appointment. I quote from it:

> In Kings II, Chapter 24, we read that when Nebuchadnezzar took Jerusalem he carried away captive "all the princes, all the mighty men of valor, and all the craftsmen and the Smiths." We were rated by that conqueror as among the very choicest personages he could carry home. For the very next verse says, "None remained, save the poorest sort of people." In other words the Smiths were not among the white trash from the very ancient days, but among princes and nobles. . . .
>
> To add brightness to the sun in the heavens and glory to the name SMITH are both impossible. Let the world utter the name SMITH with reverence

and awe and then leave it in its naked, deathless
splendor shining on!

Among the most interesting communiqués in the files of Glenn
Smith is the one from Chard Powers Smith, poet, critic, and novel-
ist. He recommended an even more impressive consolidation of
Smiths.

"At the foundation," he wrote, "would be the general membership, all sworn to the great crusade. Next above them might be the
secret police, bearing the title of Smith Vigilant. Over them would
sit an awful conclave of high authority, the members bearing the
title, perhaps, of High Smith. And at the peak of all, his person
wrapped in clouds, his face never seen, his identity unknown,
should sit in state one who could be mentioned only in whispers,
one bearing the ultimate and classic title, THE SMITH."

Any nominations?

The Ordeal of Smith

Mr. Don Elder remembers that when he was a teen-age boy in Niles, Michigan, he had dates with a girl named Oceanwave Smith and that one day, for no apparent reason, she knocked him down.

On the third day of March in 1950, while I labored in my garden of Smiths, a boy baby was born in Michigan. He was the son of the same Glenn E. Smith whose organization, TNSDUNSPHI, is described in the preceding chapter. The new child weighed seven pounds and three ounces and was twenty-two inches long. I describe his dimensions because he is important. His first tiny bleatings against the indignity of being born were scarcely over before the father set to work on the age-old problem of finding a distinctive first name for a Smith. He had but recently been in extended correspondence with me on the general subject of Smiths and the harassments that often accompany possession of the name. He is the most Smith-conscious of all the Smiths I know, and now his job was to pick a first name for his new son that would distinguish him from the multitude of Smiths. At length he got it—he christened the child Smith. There may be others with that name; if so, I haven't come upon them. So far as I know, the state of Michigan has the only individual in the entire country whose name is Smith Smith.

He is indeed a thick-skinned Smith who has never been sensi-

tive about his surname. Among the many admirable Smiths produced in this country was one who served as Postmaster General
under McKinley and Theodore Roosevelt. He was Charles Emory
Smith, a native of Connecticut who became a newspaper publisher
in Philadelphia. He served two years as United States Minister to
Russia before becoming Postmaster General.

He was scheduled once as a speaker at a dinner where important
matters of state were to be discussed. He arrived at the dinner from
a drinking bout and he was, in a word, stiff. When the time came
for his address he was given a long and eloquent introduction, and
all eyes in the banquet hall turned to him. He was unable to get
out of his chair. After an embarrassed pause the meeting proceeded
without him.

The following day Smith's own newspaper carried a full account
of the dinner on its front page, reporting the other speeches in
detail and concluding with this sentence: "Charles Emory Smith
was called upon and his remarks will be found on the following
page." The next page of the newspaper was a vast white blank,
save for a single line in small type at the bottom, which said:
"What else could he say?"

Our chief concern with Charles Emory, however, has to do with
another public dinner where he was the principal speaker. The
toastmaster in this case chose to expatiate on the subject of Smiths,
delivering himself of all the known stale and wheezy jokes growing out of the commonness of the name. Then Charles Emory
Smith got up.

"Sometimes," he said, "I find myself wishing that I had lived in
the time of Moses, for then I might have escaped such an introduction as has just been accorded me. It is written quite clearly in the
Bible, I Samuel 13:19: 'Now there was no smith found throughout all the land of Israel.' It must have been a happy land."

Every person named Smith, in high places and in low, must
have had similar feelings at one time or another. I remember how
I first became aware of the fact that there was something un-
pleasant about being named Smith. My older sisters had arrived in
their teens and were just beginning to blossom socially, and one
day I heard one of them exclaim in tones of anguish:

"Oh, if only we had some other name besides Smith! Even *Jones* would be better!"

At this late date I could give her an argument. Assuming that the name Smith has its undesirable points, I could show that there are many other surnames that are worse. H. L. Mencken, who devotes large space to the matter of personal names in his books on the American language, spent years collecting examples of unusual surnames in the United States. I offer some of Mr. Mencken's collection as solace to any person named Smith who squirms under the label. If you were not named Smith your name might be:

Argue, Baby, Barefoot, Beanblossom, Bilious, Boop, Buggerman, Burp, Buttermilk, Cabbage, Camphor, Crysick, Death, Dingbat, Dippy, Dumbell, Fatter, Flowerdew, Girl, Goforth, Gotoff, Guitar, Hair, Hash, Hatchet, Hogshead, Ill, Itt, Ix, Jelly, Junk, Kick, Kidney, Laughinghouse, Lillywhite, Louis XVI, Loveall, Lung, Matches, Mayhem, Necessary, Oatmeal, Organ, Outhouse, Oxx, Pancake, Piano, Pickle, Pimple, Pinwheel, Ram, Ratskin, Sewer, Sex, Shortsleeve, Shovel, Sinner, Sinus, Sofa, Spinach, Stolen, Sugarwater, Swill, Tank, Tart, Teats, Tickle, Ut, Whale, Wham, and Yopp. There have been people in the United States bearing each of those names, and if the list is not long enough, let me add Dumb, Soup, Looney, Vinegar, Waffle, Petticoat, Grunt, Foulfish, Hogflesh, Hustler, Maggot, Smelt, Hiccup, Bugg, Sucksmith, Smy, Maw, Pitchfork, Gumboil, and Rump.

If you have ever suffered embarrassment simply from possession of the name Smith, consider the predicament of the immigrant girl who came to Manitoba and was required to stand when she heard her name called in school, and who had to face the inevitable tittering of her classmates when she identified herself as Helen Zahss. There are, in fact, many non-Smiths in the world who are subjected to endless ribbing because of their surnames. Think of the Peckers of New York City—dozens of them. And I once knew a man named Newton who told me he wished his name was Smith because people were always saying to him, "Mind if I call you Fig?"

As early as the beginning of the nineteenth century Sydney Smith, the great English wit, recognized the difficulties confronting a Smith afflicted with a common baptismal name. He named his daughter Saba, after a king mentioned in the Seventy-second Psalm, on the theory that anyone with the surname of Smith ought to have an uncommon given name by way of compensation. We will find more striking examples of this theory at work as we go along. For the present let us look at 5/8 Smith, a respected citizen of Pearson, Georgia. 5/8 is a person of some prominence in Pearson, being a member of the City Council, owner of a jewelry store, owner of a farm, and operator of a plant which produces concrete blocks. He was born in Dupont, Georgia, in 1912, the son of a man named Frank Smith who was fed up with being mistaken for other men named Frank Smith (there were five other Frank Smiths in Dupont alone). When his son was born Frank Smith sat down and considered the problem, thought of all the confusions and embarrassments he had suffered because of his name, and the more he thought about it, the more determined he became that his son should have a first name the like of which no other mortal on earth possessed. In the end he chose 5/8. Not Five-Eighths, spelled out, but 5/8 Smith. In the interests of accuracy it must be reported that while everyone else calls him 5/8, and while he gets his mail in that name and pays his taxes as 5/8 Smith, his wife calls him Willie. His given name has its opposites in the matter of length. A Negro child born during a flood was named William McKinley Louisiana Levee Bust Smith. And in 1901 a boy born in Oklahoma was baptized Loyal Lodge No. 296 Knights of Pythias Ponca City Oklahoma Smith. I think it improbable that there is anyone else of that name in the world today. Xenophon P. Smith is head of the Peoria Public Library system. I have seen a picture of him, and he doesn't look like anyone who would be named Xenophon P. Smith.

Exploring among legions of Smiths living and dead, there is endless fascination in the discovery of uncommon given names borne by members of the clan. Here is a note about a Tennessee lawyer, Leonidas d'Entrecasteaux Smith, who named his children Keilah and Ucal. Another note concerns Zemro Smith, who was a leading editorial writer in Indianapolis years ago. There have been several Smiths christened with a first name that seems singularly appropriate—Increase Smith. The father of a Michigan congressman was named Wanton Smith. Somewhere in the jungles of the Belgian Congo there is, or was, an old drum master, skilled in the use of that instrument as a means of communication, named Quarrelsome Smith. Scientists are aware of a man generally called Main Smith, who was J. D. Main Smith, prominent in early atomic investigation.

One Lung Smith was a character in the Chicago underworld years ago. Fox Smith was the name of a "sea poetess" in England. Ulysses Grant Smith was a top diplomat for many years, and Paul Revere Smith is prominent in New York society. Young Smith is dean of the Columbia School of Law, and then there is Nevada Smith. Nevada Smith is not a cowboy (that's Whispering) but one of the most publicized of New York's showgirls. She brought considerable honor to the clan when Earl Wilson, the Watchdug of Broadway, put her on his list of the best-busted women in America.

Erasmus Peshine Smith was an international lawyer and diplomat. He invented the word "telegram." Think of how it would be if he hadn't. My alma mater would not have been the *World-Telegram*, for the *Telegram* wouldn't have been the *Telegram* when it absorbed the *World* but perhaps would have been the *Sun*, and the *Sun* would have been something else, maybe the *Herald*, and things would have been so bollixed up generally that the *Herald Tribune* today would be known as the *Journal-American*, and the *Journal-American* the *War Cry*, and the paper we know as the *World-Telegram and Sun* might have wound up as the New York *Daily Peshine*.

Crapo Cornell Smith was graduated from the University of Michigan Law School in 1896. He practiced law in Detroit until he had become an old man and then he asked the university authorities if he might come back and live on the campus. They gave him permission, and for the last eleven years of his life he occupied a tiny room in the Student Union. He was frugal in all his habits and appeared to be doing nothing but loafing around the campus. He was a joke to the students, who always referred to him as "Old Smith" and who were, generally speaking, pretty rude to him. They didn't know that he was the grandson of a governor of Michigan and a cousin of William Crapo Durant, the automobile man. What's more important, they didn't know that his old eyes were sharp. He was quick to spot a needy student who deserved help and just as quick to see that such a student got money. His secret benefactions were not revealed until after his death in 1948, when it was also announced that he had bequeathed a million dollars to the university.

A man bearing the interesting name of Coffin Smith was a character around Exeter, New Hampshire, some years ago. Coffin was a well-to-do citizen and particular about what he ate. In his old age he had a set daily routine. Each morning he called at the homes of each of his six children in Exeter, inquired about the menu for dinner, arrived back at his own house, sat down and considered, and then chose the one he would eat with that evening.

Near Hartford, Connecticut, is a house that was once occupied by a Sandemanian (Glassite) minister named Zephaniah Smith, who had an eccentric wife named Hannah and five eccentric daughters bearing the interesting names of Hancy Zephinia, Cyrinthia Sacretia, Laurilla Aleroyla, Julia Evelina, and Abby Hadassah. These females are said to have been the first of their sex to champion the Abolitionist cause and, later, the cause of woman's suffrage. Hannah, the mother, was a great one to read and she had a big glass cage built in her yard so she could sit inside it and enjoy the sun while she read, without being distracted by the noise made by her five daughters. Of the daughters, Abby Hadassah Smith became the most celebrated. She grew up to become an even more militant foe of taxation methods than her modern Connecticut counterpart, Vivien Kellems. Abby got into a sweat because she had to pay a road tax twice, so she struck against taxes. At the age of seventy-six, after her cattle had been seized and sold to satisfy a tax judgment, she wrote a book called *Abby Smith and Her Cows*. That book was to taxation what *Uncle Tom's Cabin* was to slavery, and for quite a while people everywhere, inspired by Abby's example, were chasing tax collectors with sharp hatchets.

Thus some of the clan who have borne unusual first names. The Manhattan telephone directory is in itself a good source book for studying the onomatology of Smith. In the first place we find variations of the surname, such as Smit, Smithberger, Smithe, Smithea, Smither, Smithers, Smithken, Smithkin, Smithline, Smithson, Smithwick, Smits, Smitt, Smitti, Smyth, Smythe, and Smythwick. Then let us examine some of the given names in this single book. Among the first names of Manhattan Smiths are:

Aaron, Abel, Albertine, Albine, Alphonza, Ardeth, Arletha, Arneida, Arrietta, Arzalia, Aug, Berthea, Birdie, Booker, Bronna, Bullet, Carpathia, Cleona, Coager, Corena, Corteria, Coy, Deta, Dinwiddie, Dorcey, Dutilh, Earthalene, Eradine, Hausine, Harder, Havilah, Houston, Huldah, Israel, Kimber, Landus, Liliemay, Mendozia, Modie, Narlee, Nemia, Oskomon, Queen, Roosevelt, Royal, Telza, Temperance, Ulrichia, Versal, Vieva, Ving, Ysobel, and Zada.

No other family group is subjected to the application of such colorful nicknames as the Smiths. There is an old schoolroom story illustrating the point. It was the first day of the new term and the teacher was walking down the aisle, getting acquainted with her pupils. She came at last to a grubby little girl.

"And what is your name?" she asked.

"Snotnose Smith," said the little girl.

The teacher was adequately shocked but made an effort not to show her feelings.

"No," she said, "I mean your *real* name."

"My name is Snotnose Smith!" the girl replied defiantly.

"Please!" said the teacher. "You know very well that isn't your real name. Now, tell me, what is your name?"

"Snotnose Smith," insisted the little girl.

"Well, Miss Smith," said the teacher, thoroughly upset now, "you get right up and leave this room and go to your home. And don't come back until you have learned to tell me your real name."

The little girl got up, started for the door, then turned and, addressing herself to her small brother across the room, sang out: "Come on, Fartface, you might as well go home too."

We shall see, as we go along, that Smiths of every degree have gone through life with nicknames that are sometimes beautiful, sometimes comic, and sometimes spectacular. Russell Annabel once wrote in the *Saturday Evening Post* about an Alaskan sourdough named Starvation Smith who survived the discomfort of having a one-ton moose sit down on his chest. An eighteenth-century actor named William Smith was commonly called Gentleman Smith. A lady in Arkansas has told me about a citizen of her town called Pick Handle Smith. He acquired the name while serving as a guard in a Louisiana prison camp when, the story goes, he killed six convicts with a single sweep of a pick handle. A beeman of local fame around Philadelphia is named Euphonius Smith. His father selected that name for the usual reason—he wanted the boy to have a distinguishing mark, or label, and he thought Euphonius would serve admirably. Almost all his life Euphonius has had to put up with a shortened version of the name—everyone calls him Phony Smith. And just lately the newspapers reported the retirement of Rear Admiral Edward H. Smith after forty years of service with the Coast Guard. Because he is one of the greatest authorities on northern seas and icebergs, he is known familiarly throughout the service as Iceberg Smith.

My mother is responsible for the fact that I part my name on the side. When I got my first job on a newspaper back in Indiana and it appeared that I might soon be honored with a by-line, she gave me a little lecture touching upon the commonness of our name and the need to fancy it up a bit in the forepart. You might assume that the name H. Allen Smith has enough distinctiveness about it to make it quite satisfactory as a writing name. A great moment of my life came some years ago when a girl reporter for a college newspaper came to interview me. Right at the beginning she fixed me with a beady eye and demanded: "Now, tell me what your *real* name is." She insisted throughout the interview that "H. Allen Smith" was quite obviously a nom de plume, a thing I had invented, and she went away convinced that I was lying.

In another book I have written briefly of confusions with other Allen Smiths and one other H. Allen Smith. The latter gentleman, an employee of the Baltimore & Ohio Railroad, sought me out back in 1930 after a letter addressed simply to "H. Allen Smith, New York City," and meant for me, was delivered to him. There was the case, too, of an Allen Smith who was city editor of a newspaper in Passaic, New Jersey, who once almost got his head knocked off by a group of naked people on account of me. I had visited a nudist camp back in the hills and had written an article about the peculiar activities I had observed at the establishment while I myself was mother-naked. My published story aroused great heat in the bare breasts of the nudists, and they descended upon the first Allen Smith they could find—the Allen Smith in Passaic. He convinced them that he was not the snake, and escaped the humiliation of being cold-cocked by a band of nuts.

In more recent years I have encountered all manner of Allen Smiths and Allan Smiths and Allen H. Smiths. The name in assorted combinations is met with everywhere, and my curiosity is not aroused any more except by straightaway H. Allen Smiths. When someone sent me a pamphlet containing the information that Mrs. H. Allan Smith had been appointed a lobbyist for the Indiana League of Women Voters, I accepted the situation with equanimity. When the battleship *Missouri* got stuck in Chesapeake Bay and Rear Admiral Allan E. Smith, commander of cruisers in the Atlantic Fleet, was given the job of dislodging the big ship, I was curious in only one direction: I wondered what caliber of cussing the admiral achieved when *his* towline broke.

There is a family of J. Allan Smiths living about three miles south of me, and a young man named J. Allan Smith two miles to the east. They are not related. In books dealing with the cultural history of the United States I sometimes meet with the name of J. Allen Smith, a professor of political science who died in 1926 and whose ideas apparently were important. And a man named Allan Smith was one of the founders of the Philadelphia publishing house of Macrae Smith.

We come now to the other H. Allen Smiths. The first of these is H. Allen Smith, representing the Glendale district in the California State Assembly. He is about three years younger than myself and was born in my native state, Illinois. He attended Hollywood High School, U.C.L.A., and U.S.C., taking a degree in law and entering practice in Los Angeles. For some years he was a special agent of the Federal Bureau of Investigation. I do not know what the "H" in his name stands for, and he won't tell me. He writes me that his parents agreed on the name Allen for him but that they couldn't agree on a name to precede it, "with the result that they gave me a name that neither of them liked. Thus I was always known as H. Allen Smith and have gone through life with that name." I wrote back to H. Allen asking for that first name, but apparently he'd rather not mention it. It must be horrible.

Assemblyman Smith says that he is commonly called Al and that some of his friends call him Snuffy Smith, which appears to be the name of a character in a comic strip. During a period when he was teaching police schools for the FBI in various cities throughout the United States, many of the student officers made a point of addressing him as "H. A." Assemblyman Smith suspects that the salutation was not employed in a complimentary sense.

In addition to all his other activities, he is a television performer. For some time he has been master of ceremonies on a program called "Armchair Detective," for the reason that he is an authority on murder and such. During several months of 1949 a kinescoped version of this show was televised in New York, causing considerable confusion. I still run into people who first remark about "how different you look on television" and then express surprise to know that on the side I am a dick.

In his turn the California H. Allen Smith has had his troubles on account of me. Mail addressed to me in Hollywood usually winds up at his house in Glendale. And all during the late war he had to put up with telephone calls, many of them collect, which were intended for me. In the war years I carried on an elaborate correspondence with servicemen. My letters were calculated to make the soldier, the sailor, or the marine feel that I was his pal. There were some unhappy consequences. Many of these servicemen, the moment they hit the home shores, decided that the first thing they wanted to do (that is, the second thing) was to get drunk with me. Most of them apparently tried to get a head start before phoning me, and then they phoned the H. Allen Smith in

Glendale. He didn't say so in his letter, but I know there were times when he would have happily strangled me.

In addition to Assemblyman Smith I must make mention of H. Allen Smith, the football player. This is an H. Allen Smith for size. He stands six feet two and weighs 225 pounds. He was an All-Conference end at the University of Mississippi. In 1947 he joined the Chicago Bears as an end and played through the season of 1948.

End H. Allen Smith provoked some amusing speculation on the part of William F. Fox, Jr., dean of Indiana sports writers. Mr. Fox announced one day in his column that George Halas had signed H. Allen Smith to play end for the Bears. Mr. Fox and I are old friends, so he proceeded on the tongue-in-cheek supposition that Mr. Halas had signed *me*. He described my physical characteristics unflatteringly and at some length and suggested that while I might contribute some novel touches to the game of football, I would surely be dead within three minutes of my first appearance on the playing field. He concluded that Mr. Halas quite obviously had flipped his wig. I notified Mr. Fox that while I would be thrilled at the prospect of playing football for the Bears, I was not the H. Allen Smith who had been signed. I recommended that Mr. Halas sign me up to play the opposite end, so that he would have an H. Allen Smith operating at either wing, just for laughs. Nothing ever came of it. Mr. Halas apparently is a man of limited imagination.

There is at least one other H. Allen Smith knocking around somewhere in the advertising business. He has been with advertising agencies in Chicago and St. Louis, and the last I heard was working in Detroit, which is his home town. I have never seen the H. Allen Smith who played football—he is now end coach at Mississippi Southern College. But I have seen a picture of the Detroit H. Allen Smith, and it is my considered judgment that he's a better-looking man than either H. Allen Smith of Glendale or H. Allen Smith of Mount Kisco.

At the very time this chapter was being written the mail brought an item clipped from the *Shore Line Times* published at Guilford, Connecticut. It says: "Mrs. H. Allen Smith of Warner

Road, who was operated on in St. Raphael's Hospital, New Haven, on Friday, is coming along nicely." You see how it is? And what's this? A misdirected tax bill, meant for me and sent by error to an H. Allen Smith in the Indiana town where I once made my home. Now, where the hell did *he* come from?

I have in my files a telegram that was delivered to me one night during World War II. It was date-lined Paterson, New Jersey, a town in which, so far as I know, I have no single acquaintance. Sometimes I get it out and study it, trying to make something out of it. Thus far I am as bewildered as I was the night it came. It says:

PASSED THE WORD TO ARSINO
MICHTELDIS RADIGINDE SMITH

It could be a gag, but nothing about it has any meaning to me. I can only conclude that it must have been meant for some other H. Allen Smith, and if that be true, I strongly suspect that the son of a bitch was a spy.

Studies in the Psychology of Smith

*When Augustus John was asked, not long ago,
to name the three greatest British artists, he said:
"Well, there's Matthew Smith, and there's Smith,
M., and then—there's Smith."*

An enumerator for the Census Bureau called one day on a backwoods family living in a cabin reminiscent of Jeeter Lester's country home. The census taker questioned the lady of the house, seeking the names of each member of the family. She had three small children and she said she didn't rightly know their names. Well, what did she call them to distinguish one from the other? She replied that she called one the Lap Baby, one the Floor Baby, and one the Yard Baby.

On another day I was approaching the home of Noel Houston in one of the Confederate states when I came upon a lean Negro, cast in the mold of Stepin Fetchit, standing beside a mule that was hitched to an old wagon. I stopped to talk.

"That your mule?" I asked him.

"Yassuh."

"How old is he?"

"He about sebm years old."

"How long you had him?"

"I had 'im a long time."

"What's his name?"

"Well, suh," he replied uncertainly, "I don't know his name, but I calls him Bill."

The lady with the babies and the Negro with the mule were singular people because they apparently attach no great importance to personal names. Most human beings, believing themselves to be better than the next fellow, regard their personal names as symbols of their superiority. The pride they take in their family name, or in the things that name stands for, is almost as common to the race as defective teeth. Yet it is a difficult matter for a Smith to flaunt his surname before the public as an indication of his worth. He would cut a ridiculous figure if he mounted to the roof tops, raised his fist to the sky, and cried: "I'm a Smith!"

Manufacturers of soap know better than to put a new product on the market called simply Soap or Laundry Soap or Hand Soap. They demand names that will distinguish their particular product from all other soaps, and their advertising geniuses toss in their beds at night trying to dream up names comparable in beauty to Lux, Rinso, Ivory, Palmolive, Brillo, Lifebuoy, Duz, and Vel. A man's name is his label, and in this competitive racket called Life he cannot be condemned for seeking a label unlike other labels. A Smith christened by some common name such as John or Fred or William is clearly justified if he jiggers it around, parting it on the side or hyphenating his second name or his last name, or even installing his mother's maiden name as part of his label. I, for one, am not actually at odds with the Smith who changes his name altogether. There are quite a few who do it.

A clergyman in Atlanta, the Reverend W. B. Garrison, has spent the last dozen years studying personal names and he has concluded that an individual's name often has an important effect on the development of his character and personality. For one thing, Mr. Garrison warns parents against naming girls for historical happenings coinciding with their birth. He cites the case of a girl who was christened Manila Bay and who blamed the fact that she never married on the circumstance that she was never able to conceal her age. Mr. Garrison also mentions a man who was able to achieve eminence in spite of a ridiculous name—If Christ Had Not Died For Thee Thou Hadst Been Damned Barebone. He grew to prominence as a theologian and was known and honored as "Dr. Damned Barebone."

Theodore Pratt, the novelist, is a man burdened with a name that sometimes evokes smiles, but he takes pride in it and goes forth to battle in its behalf. He wrote to me once objecting to a line in one of my books, to wit: "I'd have kicked her pratt off." Mr. Pratt complained:

> At least you didn't put a capital on the pratt. Some time ago I appointed myself a committee of one for all people named Pratt to set straight the spelling of this expression. It comes, of course, from burlesque where a sudden, comic sitting down upon the behind is a prat fall. That, boy, is the way it is spelled, even when kicking her prat off. Mr. Webster says "prat" means posterior or buttocks, but makes no mention of pratt. The *Thesaurus of American Slang* says it is "prat fall," not "prattfall," as it is usually spelled. I have corrected *Variety* on this and Abel Green has accepted the correct usage. "Prat fall" is a swell expression which I reserve for the house I sometime want to get, but pratt for behind ain't no good. It doesn't make us Pratts feel right.

It pleasures me to report that Mr. Pratt met with success in his valiant campaign against those who abused his good name. Before he started yelling there were actually some authorities who preferred "pratt," but he argued them around and now "prat" and "prat fall" are almost universally accepted as the proper forms.

The Genealogy Room in the New York Public Library enjoys a brisk traffic during all the hours it is in operation. The customers sit at long tables with stacks of books in front of them and a sort of wild eagerness is apparent in their manner, and sometimes a wild delight dances in their eyes. If an H-bomb exploded in Bryant Park they would not notice it and they would continue tracing out the intricate pattern of their family trees until the death dust drifted in and then, perhaps, they might have just enough time to scribble their own name at the end of some remote twig of that tree before falling dead across their ancestry.

People who spend months and years and even decades exploring backward among billions of chromosomes which ultimately led to their own important selves are often subject to bitter ridicule; they are accused of the worst form of snobbery on earth—worship of family. They are bruised and berated by cynical individuals who argue that seventy-five per cent of all humans have been villainous in one way or another, meaning that three fourths of a person's ancestors would be better forgotten. On the other hand, those who indulge in eager genealogical research defend themselves sometimes by describing their digging as a game, a quest, a form of sport. It is much the same, they say, as a game of golf, or the working out of a Double-Crostic. There are spaces to be filled in, and the goal is to find the precise names that belong in those spaces. For my own part I would recommend leaving these people alone. If they were not preoccupied with their prowlings in the past, they might be out somewhere making trouble, subverting their government, suborning perjury, or committing mopery on a public highway.

In a way this book is a sort of genealogical project. One of its aims is to furnish the Smiths with some things to boast about. And it seems to me that during the digging period a million specific Smiths have come beneath my hand. I've taken them as they came and cast them aside unless something about the work they did or the art they wrought or the capers they cut distinguished them from the common run. Smiths came at me in battalions out of books, out of correspondence, out of talks with people, and out of my memory. To get at them I exposed myself to the equivalent of a liberal education, for the trail led into every boulevard and back alley of human endeavor. I found myself reading extensively in physics, chemistry, history, navigation, mythology, religion, biography, athletics, finance, railroading, exploration, the cult of flying-saucerism, carpetmaking, heraldry, etiquette, and the origin of the mule train. Two full days were spent, without success, trying to connect John Paul Jones to the Smith clan—he certainly was not a Jones. At one point I found myself involved in the story of the Donner Party, because someone had told me that a Smith was one of those who ate other members of the expedition. This proved to be a libel. No Smith ate anybody, and nobody ate a Smith. Again I was tracing out the story of the Canadian Pacific Railway, or trying to puzzle out just what it is that T. S. Eliot is driving at.

The spoor of Smith is discernible in almost every avenue of history. The range of the Smiths covers every octave and every note of the social scale. The peerage of Great Britain has never lacked for Smiths. The Earls of Derby, for example, are said to be Smiths in elegant disguise, the first of the line having been Robert de Ferrers, meaning Robert de Smith.

Among the notable British Smiths was the first Earl of

Birkenhead, originally Frederick Edwin Smith, who served as Solicitor General, Attorney General, Secretary of State for India, and Lord Chancellor. Matching him in eminence was William Frederick Danvers Smith, Viscount Hambleden, who was First Lord of the Admiralty and Secretary for War.

Mr. A. D. Peters of London informs me that it is much easier for an individual to change his name in England than it is in America, that the matter is up to the individual himself and not to the courts. It would seem probable, therefore, that many more Smiths have disappeared from view in Britain than elsewhere. Yet even the lists of the most distinguished Britishers are loaded with Smiths.

There was Donald Alexander Smith, son of a Scottish merchant, who came over to America as a junior clerk with the Hudson's Bay Company and became one of the greatest men in Canada's history. In 1897 he was raised to the peerage and became Baron of Strathcona and Mount Royal. This Smith was the driving force behind construction of the Canadian transcontinental railroad.

Lieutenant General Sir Arthur Francis Smith, K.C.B., K.B.E., C.B., D.S.O., M.C., long of the Coldstream Guards, was one of Britain's foremost heroes of World War I. Sir Bracewell Smith was Lord Mayor of London in 1946 and 1947. Sir Alexander Rowland Smith gained fame as an executive of the British Ford Motor Company while Evan Cadogan Eric Smith was chairman of the Rolls-Royce Company. And Sir Ben Smith, prominent in the Labor government, began his career as driver of one of London's first taxicabs.

Also in England we have the interesting case of Mr. Psmith, a dashing young character invented by Mr. P. G. Wodehouse. In the novel *Leave It to Psmith* we find him engaged in colloquy with a young woman as follows:

> "The name is Psmith. P-smith."
>
> "Peasmith, sir?"
>
> "No, no. P-s-m-i-t-h. I should explain to you that I started life without the initial letter, and my father always clung ruggedly to the plain Smith. But it seemed to me that there were so many Smiths in

the world that a little variety might well be introduced. Smythe I look on as a cowardly evasion,
nor do I approve of the too prevalent custom of
tacking another name on in front by means of a
hyphen. So I decided to adopt the Psmith. The p, I
should add for your guidance, is silent, as in
phthisis, psychic, and ptarmigan. You follow me?"

The most famous American example of a Smith switching to
another name is that of Gladys, who became Mary Pickford, and
the second most famous is the case of Walker Smith, who became
one of the greatest of modern boxing champions under the name
of Sugar Ray Robinson. There have been, of course, many others.

A bit later we shall have a look at Smith College, but right now
let's consider another celebrated girls' school, Wellesley, which
was founded in 1870—one year before the establishment of Smith.
Save for a man's dissatisfaction with his own surname, Wellesley
could have properly been named Smith College, and that would
have left Smith College scrabbling around for another label. The
founder of Wellesley was born Henry Welles Smith in New
Hampshire. He became a lawyer in Boston and, unhappy over
the commonness of his name, went to court and became Henry
Fowle Durant. Later on he was an evangelist, preaching in
Massachusetts and New Hampshire, and ultimately he founded
Wellesley. Too bad that he didn't retain his original name and
give it to his college. Smith College has proved conclusively that
Smith College is a good name for a college.

Some years ago there was an important firm of contracting engineers called Sooysmith & Company whose president was Charles
Sooysmith. His grandfather, Sooy Smith, lived in Ohio and had a
son whom he named William Sooy Smith. William attended the
United States Military Academy and was in the Army for
a while, resigning to become a civil engineer, building harbors,
bridges, lighthouses, and the like. He named his son Charles
Sooy Smith, and Charles in turn became an engineer, associated
with his father. They are credited by some authorities with making
the modern skyscraper possible, having devised methods for constructing foundations that would support heavy buildings in

Chicago and elsewhere. When Charles Sooy Smith grew to man-hood he squirmed under the onus of being a plain Smith and shoved his middle name in close and made it Sooysmith. Person-ally I can't see that he improved things a great deal; Sooy is a cry used in calling hogs.

There have been writers and artists who scorned the use of their true name when it was Smith and there have been others who assumed the name Smith for professional purposes. Ernest Bramah Smith was a writer of popular mystery fiction in England for forty years and always wrote under the name of Ernest Bramah. In our own country Claude Smith, a cartoonist, signs a simple "Claude" to all his work. On the other hand we have the example of Stephen Crane, who chose "Johnston Smith" as his nom de plume when he published his novel *Maggie: A Girl of the Streets*.

One of the nation's important Smiths in recent years was John Lawrence Smith, head of a big chemical- and drug-producing com-pany in Brooklyn—a firm whose laboratories have contributed in large measure toward the advancement of medical knowledge. Ironically this Smith's celebrity rested not so much on his achieve-ments in chemistry (he was himself a brilliant laboratory man) but rather on the fact that he was part owner of the Brooklyn Dodgers, or Bums. He was born in Germany and grew up with the name Schmitz. In 1918, when we were at war with Germany, he was one of the many who went to court and had the Germanic spelling changed to plain Smith. He died in the summer of 1950.

In San Francisco there was once a newspaper photographer, a man of considerable skill at his profession and one who took great pride in the excellence of his work. He was a Smith and his first name was one of the common variety and he cringed when-ever he saw it as a credit line beneath his published photographs. The day came when he decided to change it, and he used imagi-nation—he went to court and became, legally, Another Smith, and that was the name he carried thereafter and used as a credit line.

Interlude at sea:

Having accumulated a small mountain of material to go into this book, I was sitting on a frosty hill in North Westchester staring at that accumulation and wondering how I would ever go about assembling it into a readable manuscript. Then suddenly and swiftly, by a seeming miracle, I was transported southward and onto the deck of a luxurious yacht cruising off the north coast of Cuba. The company on board was all-male, and a group of us sat talking on the afterdeck while wild and ferocious barracuda slashed at the single line we were trailing. Topic Smith would not dislodge itself from my mind, and I steered the talk into the field of nomenclature, hopeful of getting even more theories and anecdotes.

"A man's name," I said, "is a mere label—nothing else—and has no more meaning or significance than a label on a can."

"I disagree with you," said a big handsome man sitting opposite me, "and I can prove you're wrong." I wasn't sure about his identity—we had boarded the yacht within the hour. He spoke with a rich tobacco-shed accent and when he talked even the Ambassador, who owned the boat, paid attention. Now he reached for his jacket and got out a wallet and fingered around in it until he had found a clipping. He handed it to me without comment.

It was a column by George Dixon, the bright and sassy Washington writer for King Features Syndicate. Mr. Dixon's little essay was about an assistant attorney general of the United States named Theron Lamar Caudle. He wrote that for years he had been fascinated by that name and had sometimes wondered how a man ever got to be called Theron Lamar Caudle. As I read the clipping I realized that the big man across from me was none other than Mr. Caudle in the flesh.

Mr. Dixon reported that by chance he had learned something about the name, having cross-examined Mrs. Theron Lamar Caudle on the subject at a Washington party. Mrs. Caudle had furnished him with the derivation of her husband's three names.

"His whole name," she said, "represents a complete sentence. It is old Anglo-Saxon. Theron means 'go seek.' Lamar means 'the sea.' Caudle is a 'hot toddy.' Translated literally, the name means: 'Go seek a hot toddy by the sea.'"

I finished the clipping and handed it back without comment.

"Now," said Mr. Theron Lamar Caudle, "don't you see where

my own name has significance? Look out yonder"—he waved his hand toward the horizon—"and what do we have? The sea. I have come down to the sea from Washington. And if you please, suh, what I'm holding in my hand is not a glass of Doctuh Peppah."

"All right," I said. "Your name has meaning and your presence here is a fulfillment of that meaning. But if the rule obtained in every case, I might be expected to rise out of this chair right now and belt you one with a large hammer. My name happens to be Smith."

A priest sitting near me, a small jovial-looking man who had not been talking much up to now, spoke quickly. "And I might come right behind him and smite you with another hammer," he said, "because *my* name is Smith."

It turned out that he was Father Francis P. Smith, then president of Duquesne University. With his assistance it was easy to keep the talk going on the subject of Smiths. I undertook to poll the company with the aim of finding out how many of them had relatives who are Smiths or, barring that, close acquaintances named Smith. Aboard the yacht as elsewhere the rule held: almost everyone either has a Smith knocking around somewhere in his family or a close friend bearing that name.

We came to a rugged citizen who was stripped down to a pair of flowered shorts, a certain Arthur Morton Godfrey.

"Yes," said Mr. Godfrey, "it happens that there is a strong line of Smiths in my own family background. I get depressed about it sometimes." He looked squarely at me. "I get depressed," he went on, "over the thought that one of these days I might find out that I'm actually related to you. If I do find it out, I intend to forsake the world and retire into a Trappist monastery."

This resounding declaration met with vigorous comment, some of it quite spicy, and Father Smith spoke again: "I hate to think what might happen to a poor defenseless Trappist monastery after *you* retired into it. And remember one thing: you won't be able to take that confounded ukulele with you."

Mr. Godfrey roared with laughter, which he does well.

Eventually I got around to the point of telling about this book

and how important a book it would be in the over-all history of literature. It was indeed a heartening thing to hear the expressions of enthusiasm for my project, ranging from a hollow "Huzzah!" to rapid vibration of the tongue between the lips. It was not a false enthusiasm; it was genuine, for every man on board asked me to send him a free copy, autographed.

There have been others who were helpful.

One afternoon I arrived at a television studio where a young woman named Dorothy Doan was to help publicize a book about baseball in which I had an interest. On stage I found Miss Doan sitting with a redheaded man whose presence was a surprise to me. "Mr. Smith," she said to me, "have you met Mr. Smith?" (Laughter.) We shook hands and I mumbled something about having admired Mr. Smith from afar. "This is really an event," said Miss Doan, "having two Smiths on the show and both of them experts on baseball." Actually I was more than a little thrilled because, quite obviously, this was the celebrated Red Smith of the *Herald Tribune,* and I felt deeply flattered that he should take the time to come over and appear on the same television program with me. We had some time to waste, so we sat down and talked about baseball. This Red Smith, I decided, talks the same way he writes, sardonically and eloquently. And he certainly knew baseball history. It must have been fifteen minutes later that I discovered that this wasn't Red Smith at all. This was Robert Smith, author of several novels and an excellent history of baseball. The remarkable thing about the mix-up was the fact that he never once suspected that I had him confused with another guy.

Since that day Robert Smith and I have become better acquainted. He runs the Magazine Institute, a correspondence school for beginning writers, and among his published works is the recent novel, *One Winter in Boston,* which intelligent readers, as well as the New York book critics, saluted as a first-rate literary work. Beyond that he is a man who revels in the anonymity of the name Smith. He stubbornly refuses to use his middle name, which is Miller, or even his middle initial, and he gravitates to other people named Smith. I once found him in a Manhattan restaurant deep in conversation with an actor named Cyril Smith, who has since died. Bob told me later that Cyril Smith's chief claim to fame was his participation, years ago, in certain recordings made by Rudy Vallee, "including that notorious bit of vulgarity, 'The Old Sow Song,' which consists of loud vulgar noises such as grunts, burps, and wind-breaking, largely contributed by our Cyril and all set to music." On the strength of this and other recordings, Bob said, Cyril Smith had described himself as the most imitated actor in America.

"I suppose," said Bob, "that he figured that every person who grunted or burped or broke wind was imitating him."

Robert Smith contends that he profits from the use of that simple designation. There are several other Bob Smiths of importance, including the affable radio and television performer who gave Howdy Doody to the world. Says Robert the author:

"Whenever I want to talk with some big wheel in show business and the girl asks who's calling, I say 'Bob Smith,' and you can immediately hear people unplugging wires and disconnecting long-distance calls in order to put me through. If your name is Bob Smith, you can get away with anything. When you are accused of some petty crime you can always lay it to a namesake; I kept out library books so long that the other Bob Smith in my town finally tore up his card rather than pay the fines.

"When I was in college and first got enough dollar bills together to wet my finger when I counted them, I put them in the bank under the name of R. Miller Smith, so none of the people who pretended to be me could get at them. Well, the money lasted so quick that the name never had a chance to stick, though I did go along for a few years signing my first stories Robert Miller Smith.

"Then I got a job with the Newspaper Institute, criticizing and encouraging writers by mail, and the people in charge had me sign my letter 'Kenneth MacNichol' and 'John C. Klein,' and I first tasted the pleasures of being a nameless ghost. People used to come into the office and talk to me about what a wonderful old man Mr. Klein was, how sympathetic and intelligent and all—they wouldn't have said it to my face if they had known I was Mr. Klein. And other correspondents would weep to me that Mr. MacNichol was never available when they came in to see him though they had come to love him through his wonderful inspiring letters. Then they'd go home and write to Mr. MacNichol or Mr. Klein and say that the uncouth jerk named Smith or something was so dumb he ought to be canned.

"Somehow, out of all this, I got to enjoy being a nobody so thoroughly that when I set up in business for myself I cut all the lace off my name, and when something appeared in print or was otherwise blamed on Robert Smith, nobody would ever think it was me, even when it was."

Early in 1949 I was talking on the telephone with a writer friend, Joe Alex Morris. We discussed some personal matters and then I said:

"What are you up to these days?"

"I'm collaborating on a book."

"With whom?" I asked.

"Man named Ira Smith," said Mr. Morris.

"You serious?"

"Certainly, I'm serious."

"My God," I said, "that's exactly what *I'm* doing!"

"What do you mean?"

"I mean," I said, "that *I'm* collaborating on a book with a man named Ira Smith."

It was true. Mr. Morris was working on the memoirs of Ira R. T. Smith, who for fifty-one years had been in charge of mail at the White House. And at the same time I was working on a book of baseball anecdotes with Ira L. Smith, a Washington journalist. My Ira Smith is, among many other things, an artist at the business of research, and his contribution to this book has been a major one.

Ira wouldn't seem to be an especially common name, yet Ira L. Smith has had his share of confusions. He is forever getting clippings sent by his friends: Ira Smith found drunk while driving a car in Georgia; Ira Smith, an upstate New York cabdriver, kidnaped, tied to a tree, robbed, and then murdered; Ira L. Smith, a retired Virginia lumberman, dying at the age of ninety-one. In Ira's collection is a classified ad which says:

> FOOL your friends. Pretend you are in San Francisco. 3 postcards sent 25 cents (20—$1). You write message, address, return. I remail in San Francisco. Letters mailed 15 cents. Your friends will think you're traveling. Ira Smith, 153 Liberty St., San Francisco, Calif.

My Ira Smith also has an old business card which identifies him as "I. Lepouce Smith." He was once under consideration for a good job with the American Mining Congress in Washington and he ran into trouble because his name was Smith. One of the big executives of the organization also was a Smith and, when he heard that another Smith was about to be hired, put in a strong objection, saying he didn't want any more Smiths around the place messing up phone calls and mail and all that. When Ira L. Smith heard of this development he went straight to the other Smith with a proposition. "I have a middle name," he said, "the likes of which no other Smith has ever borne, and if I get this job I'll promise to use that name in all correspondence and phone calls." The executive wanted to know the middle name and Ira told him, whereupon he said: "Anybody who would permit himself to be called I. Lepouce Smith in order to get a job must want that job pretty badly. You're hired."

Ira, incidentally, has an interesting theory about his first and second names. Lepouce was his Belgian mother's maiden name and means "the thumb" (Ira suggests that it would be a wonderful name for an umpire). The Ira came from Ira D. Sankey, the evangelistic singer, and the name means "watchful" in the ancient Hebraic. The owner of these two names suspects that when he was an infant he spent his time sitting around staring at his thumb and that his parents therefore named him Watch-the-Thumb Smith.

The search for interesting people named Smith was publicized by way of several radio broadcasts and fetched a volume of mail. Let us consider at this point a couple of prime examples sent in by correspondents. A friend of mine in Detroit heard my appeal and passed along the story of a Canadian Smith who, in his own fashion and because of a single incident in his life, deserves consideration alongside the Baron of Strathcona and Mount Royal. I quote the letter:

> I just don't seem to know any good stories about the Smiths. Once I lived in a little Canadian town where the town drunk was a character named Side Arm Smith. Can't remember why he was called

that. Rather late in his life Side Arm developed a
painful condition—a tough, meaty cord running
along the underside of a certain portion of his
anatomy. This thing gave Side Arm considerable
pain and discomfort and one day in a sober moment
he called upon the town doctor, an old gent with
a forthright approach to every problem. Doc examined the thing briefly and then had Side Arm lay
it out on the table. At this point the doctor spoke
suddenly to Side Arm: "Whose team is that passin'
out there?" As Side Arm turned to look out the
window, the Doc seized a medical book and gave
that thing a mighty wallop. Side Arm let out a yell,
dove for the Doc, missed him, went right through
the window and didn't stop running till he reached
the railroad junction three miles outside town.
Within an hour he had calmed himself down and
was back in town celebrating with a bottle, singing
the praises of the old doctor, because that wallop
with the book had done the trick. I'd like to get you
a good Smith story but so far haven't been able to
think of one, and if I do I'll send it along.

Side Arm Smith apparently was a man who didn't work, yet
it is in the nature of their work that certain Smiths shine. I
remember a few years back reading of a young man named Smith
who was employed by one of New York City's garment manufacturers. This Smith was good at sweating, and his job was to
sweat. His employer was a manufacturer of ladies' dresses and
was searching for materials or combinations of materials which
would be most resistant to perspiration as a destructive agent. This
particular Smith, whose first name has slipped my mind, was the
company's sweat-tester. His job was to put on a dress and go into a
room where the temperature was sweltering and just sit there and
sweat into the dress. As I recall, he told the newspaper interviewer
that it was nice work and not too tiring.

I have another letter from the Midwest, describing the dilemma
of a man named Smith employed in a meat-packing plant. His
story was sent in by one of his relatives, who cites this Smith as an

example of a man who not only suffers the discomfort of having the most common of all names, but who has a job which he finds embarrassing to describe. He works in the hog department of the packing plant. The hogs are suspended, tail down, from an overhead trolley, a sort of disassembly line. Early in the processing most of the bristles are removed by hand and then the hog is moved up to a deep vat which contains some kind of liquid resin (known to Dizzy Dean as rawzum). The carcass is lowered into this vat, then pulled out, and moves on up the line. The resinous solution dries quickly, and when it is scraped off it takes with it all the remaining bristles. Now, what is the job of our Mr. Smith? He stands at the near side of the vat with a box of wooden plugs. As each hog arrives he deftly inserts one of the plugs into the pig —stoppering him so that none of the rawzum can get inside and ruin his chops and flitches. That's all there is to it. All day long Mr. Smith stands there shoving in the plugs. His embarrassment, of course, stems from the fact that people sometimes ask him the precise nature of his work. For a long time he practiced evasion, but in recent years, my correspondent says, he has found that if he gives a frank and straightforward answer people do not believe him and think that he is making a joke.

Look Homeward, Smith

In the time of World War I an American of
some political importance was widely known as
"Mr. Smith of Smithville." He was Frank O.
Smith, a native of Smithville, Maryland.

Not long ago a survey was made of American college seniors, the
purpose of which was to find out what kind of people we are
turning out in our major educational plants and whither they
were going. Among many other things, the students were asked
what they did in their spare time and, as I recall, at least half of
them gave the same response: writing a novel. Scattered over the
land are thousands of housewives who don't know an asterisk
from a stone quarry but who are hammering away at short stories
and novels and even poetry. Semi-literate comedians are writing
novels, and strippers, and sheepherders, and wholesale hardware
dealers, and Kathleen Winsor, and even the late Franklin D.
Roosevelt had a try at it.

A majority of these neophyte litterateurs, according to the testi-
mony of English instructors as well as publishers of books and
magazines, choose their own lives as the subject matter for their
first novels. The result is usually quite horrible in the case of
college students, for the reason that their own lives haven't been
endured yet. They need to be stood up, pointed in the direction
of a fresh idea, and given a shove. So I have a suggestion to make.
Let one of them who would follow in the footsteps of Sinclair

Lewis or Sherwood Anderson or Thomas Wolfe proceed forthwith to the geographical center of the United States, live there for a year or two, and then write his novel.

The geographical center is located by means of an interesting bit of scientific procedure. A string is attached somewhere near the middle of the United States and then the whole country is lifted into the air. The point where the string is hooked on is shifted about until the suspended nation achieves a balance and hangs level. The scientists didn't actually lift the country off its foundations, for the reason that they could not have achieved an accurate calculation by doing it. The disproportionate weight of the various regions would make for an irregularity—Rockefeller Center in the East, for example, wouldn't quite offset the drag of all those mountains in the West. So the scientists simply took a cut-out map of the United States, attached their string to that, found the point where the whole thing balanced nicely, and thus located the geographical center. The precise spot at which our nation achieves perfect balance is near Smith Center in Smith County, close to the northern border of Kansas.

Here is a town (and a county) called by the most common of all American names and set in the exact center of the one nation indivisible with liberty and justice for all. Where could you find a more appropriate spot for the locale of a truly American novel? Where but in Smith Center would you be most likely to meet the American spirit head-on? Let the eager and aspiring young novelist hasten, then, to the umbilicus of America. I would not attempt to suggest a plot for his story, but I can pass along a brief sketch of the community which advertises itself with the slogan: "In the heart of the United States where Life is Real."

Smith Center is a town of approximately two thousand God-fearing citizens. The town and the county were named for a certain Major James Smith who was killed in a Civil War battle near Kansas City in 1864. The county comprises nine hundred square miles of gently sloping prairies where, it is stoutly contended, the buffalo once roamed and the deer and the antelope played. Today those prairies are the fat of the land. Smith County brags of its wheat, its corn, its hogs, its cattle, its horses, and its chickens. A

poultry census taken some years ago revealed that there are about fifty chickens for every human in Smith County.

Smith Center is a neat town laid out in the traditionally formal squares, proud of everything it possesses, including the new teardrop globes on its street lights. Its Chamber of Commerce boasts of its City Building, its churches, its trees, its buffalo-grass golf course, its airport, its two banks, its volunteer fire department, its big high school band with eight adroit baton twirlers, and its "vast public library with a full-time librarian."

The principal highway from Kansas City to Denver, U.S. 36, passes through the town, and tourist traffic is heavy. On this highway, about eight miles due east of Smith County, a sign marks the turnoff which leads to the geographical center of the United States. Thousands of tourists make the turn, drive two and a half miles north, and stop at the monument which sets on the core of the country. It stands beside the road at the edge of an immense wheat field and it resembles one of those barbecue ovens usually found in the back yards of Hollywood screen writers, being constructed of native stone into which has been set a bronze plaque identifying the site. A flagpole surmounts the stone structure, and there is a weatherproof box containing a ledger in which the tourists inscribe their names. It is a delightful place for having your snapshot taken and for thinking about America.

Fatty Arbuckle was born in Smith Center, but for some reason the citizens seldom mention him. They prefer to talk of Dr. Brewster Higley and "Smith County's Own Song." Dr. Higley, they say, wrote "Home on the Range" while he was occupying a homestead cabin near Smith Center in 1873. Seldom is heard a discouraging word about the revered Dr. Higley, and the song is played and trilled and bellowed in every quarter of Smith Center. Sigmund Spaeth has investigated the history of "Home on the Range" and has concluded that nobody knows for sure who actually wrote it. He weighs the claim for Dr. Higley and admits that it might be true that the eccentric doctor wrote the words or, rather, an early version of the text, while the music may have been provided by a man named Dan Kelly who lived in the village of Gaylord, south of Smith Center. On the other hand there have been people in Arizona who claimed authorship of the song, and a preacher in Oregon, and a prospector in Colorado, and there have been lawsuits involving as much as half a million dollars over it. The people of Smith Center, however, do not recognize that any dispute exists. "Home on the Range" was written by one of their own as a tribute to their countryside, and twenty-three skiddoo to anyone who says different. Their present-day athletic field, night-lighted for baseball, has been christened Higley Field.

In describing how Smith Center brags I have not meant to be derogatory. Bragging is as much a part of community living as water rates; the filthiest down-at-the-heels hamlet may still boast that it once produced a congressman or that it has the most ferocious rats in a hundred square miles. The biggest brag of the Smith Center people, however, I've reserved for the last.

Standing in the town's pretty park is the Old Dutch Mill. It was erected originally many years ago on the prairie fifteen miles northwest of town by a Hollander named Swartz. In 1942 it was dismantled and set up again in the park—a beautiful weather-beaten old structure about thirty feet high. The townspeople are proud of it and urge tourists to go look at it and write their names in the ledger, and they speak of the "Old World charm" it imparts to their prairie community. They love the Old World charm when it is reflected by a gristmill, but they don't want people contributing any of the same.

"Smith County," said the Chamber of Commerce, "is populated by an aggressive citizenship, practically 100 per cent native-born. Its people are fundamentally sound from cultural and economic standpoints."

And one of the town's leading citizens elaborates on this municipal virtue in a letter to me:

"The most outstanding thing besides the grand air and sunshine is that the population is *strictly* American as we do not have a Hebrew, Colored Man, Italian, Spaniard, Mexican or anything at all, only friendly white Americans."

There you are, kid—a setting for the Great American Novel. Hop to it. Hitch-hike out U.S. 36 to the Belly Button of the United States and get busy absorbing the flavor and atmosphere and traditions of this splendid community. Just be careful about one thing: don't take sides on anything.

Far to the south of Smith Center I had occasion one day to leave the main highway, plunge into the steaming jungle, and spend a couple of days in the lovely old Louisiana town of Natchitoches. This is the home of Mr. James Aswell, who wrote a novel called *The Midsummer Fires* a few years ago. The book was considered obscene by some people, and a Natchitoches clergyman, amid a burst of publicity, burned it in the public square. The story of the book-burning went out on the press association wires and was published all over the country. Over on the Atlantic coast lived an elderly lady who was related to Mr. Aswell, and she got the news of the burning secondhand. A neighbor had seen the story in the paper and had telephoned her excitedly about it. The old lady promptly went into hysterics and put in a long-distance call to Natchitoches, for she had misunderstood the message—she thought that *Mr. Aswell* had been burned in the public square.

The man who ate the first oyster had nothing on the man who first looked at the word Natchitoches, screwed up his courage, licked his lips, and had a whirl at trying to pronounce it. I have no official record of the event, but it's certain he didn't get it right. The proper way to say it is Nack-a-tosh. It's easy enough to memorize that pronunciation in a dark room; the difficulty comes when you look at the word Natchitoches and then try to pronounce it correctly. When I arrived to visit Mr. Aswell I spoke the name the way it looked to me on the road map, and he corrected me but said I shouldn't worry about the error—the most erudite professors fail to recognize Nack-a-tosh in Natchitoches the first time they come up against it.

"In fact," said Mr. Aswell, "during the war, when we had a lot of soldiers stationed around here, they gave up completely and all of them, including the officers, called the town Smith."

There is an extremely remote significance to that story. Louisiana happens to be one of the few states having no town actually named Smith. Elsewhere our family name has been given to towns and counties and mountains and rivers and capes and waterfalls and bays and arroyos. In addition to the one in Kansas there are counties named Smith in Mississippi, Tennessee, and Texas, and there's a Smyth County in Virginia. There are two towns called Smith in Indiana—one near Jeffersonville and one near Vincennes—and there are other Smiths in Delaware, Florida, North Carolina, Nevada, Pennsylvania, and South Dakota. There are Smithboros, Smithburgs, a Smithsburg, and in Ireland a Smithborough. The gazetteers show towns named Smithdale, Smithfield (thirteen of them), Smithflat, Smithmill, Smith Mills, Smithonia (in Georgia), Smith River, Smiths Basin, Smith Creek, Smiths Falls, Smiths Ferry, Smithshire, Smithson, Smithtown, Smith Valley, Smithville (a dozen), Smithville Flats, and a Smithwick in South Dakota. The town of Smiths is a few miles east of Pansy Park in Massachusetts.

The celebrated Smithfield hams owe their name to Arthur Smith, a farmer who once owned the land on which the town of Smithfield, Virginia, was built. Arthur himself knew nothing about them. If, in his lifetime, someone had approached him and asked if he had a Smithfield ham kicking around the premises, he'd likely have responded with a blank look and perhaps the announcement, "Ah bin smokin' Luggy Straikes fer nigh onto thutty yeahs." It is the law of the state of Virginia today that no ham can be called a Smithfield ham unless it has been cured within the corporate boundaries of the town of Smithfield. My wife and I once drove a hundred miles out of our way to buy a Smithfield ham in Smithfield. In the town we stopped at a garage to ask about procedure and a young man, native of the place, shocked us by saying: "To tell you the truth, us folks here in town, we don't care much for them Smithfield hams. Don't eat 'em. We go out to the farms and get country-cured hams." I hope that his identity is never discovered by the civic leaders and the ham doctors of Smithfield—they'd surely flog him to death with the hickory-cured haunch of a peanut-fed pig. I must add, however, that we went ahead and bought a genuine Smithfield ham and took it home and enjoyed it immensely.

At least a half dozen islands named Smith are scattered over the Western Hemisphere. Two of these are in the Chesapeake Bay area and were named for Captain John Smith. During one of his explorations in 1608 Captain John touched at a tiny island near Cape Charles. Later, when he learned that it had been given his name, he complained bitterly and called it a piddling tribute. "I could spit across it," he said.

Smith exists as a place name in South Africa because of the nineteenth-century adventures of a great British soldier, Sir Henry George Wakelyn Smith. He was a real dashing sort of fellow, and in spite of the honors and titles that were piled on him, he always preferred to be known as plain Harry Smith. (My father is the same way.) He entered the British Army in 1805, saw active service in South America, then fought through the Peninsular War. He married a Spanish girl named Juanita Something, and she was at his side through most of his campaigns. Harry was present with the British when they burned the United States capitol in Washington and he was a brigade major at Waterloo. He smote the Boers and the Kaffirs in South Africa and the Gwaliors and Sikhs in India. Juanita was still with him when he returned to South Africa as governor of Cape Colony, and the famous town of Ladysmith was named for her. His own name was given to a town in the Orange Free State—Harrismith.

The city of Fort Smith, Arkansas, was named for General Thomas A. Smith, who ordered a stockade built on the site back in 1817 during the Indian troubles. And the community of Smith-town on Long Island was named for a celebrated character known as Bull Smith. His proper name was Richard and he came to the colonies early in the seventeenth century. He married a Sarah Folger and they had nine children, and these nine spawned gloriously for the Smiths, producing innumerable Obediahs, Deborahs, Tabithas, Temperances, Charitys, Gamaliels, Seviahs, Rhuhamahs, Hezekiahs, and Ebenezers. Within a few generations this section of Long Island was so rife with Smiths that they were divided into subtribes like the Iroquois Indians. One group called

themselves the Bull Smiths after the patriarch; another branch con-
sisted of the Rock Smiths, after the Reverend Mordecai "Rock"
Smith for whom the town of Rockville Centre was named, and a
third division was made up of the Wait Smiths, from Wait Still
on the Lord Smith. Quite a few of these subdivided Smiths on
Long Island were christened with those long sentences lifted out
of the Bible, as was the custom among certain families in the days
of the witch-burnings and the scarlet letter. It must have been a
lot more fun choosing a name for a baby in those times than it
is today. Few parents nowadays strive for any great originality in
naming their own get the way they strive for distance and originality in naming their pedigreed dogs. (I must mention, in passing,
a little runny-nosed girl who came past my house one day and
stopped to talk. In answer to my question she said her first name
was Tecla. It wasn't until after she had gone that I realized that
this was the modern way to name a child Pearl.) Those old-timers
who used biblical passages for names surely enjoyed the business
of making a choice. Let us, in dramaturgical form, see if we can
visualize the way it worked.

NAMING THE BABY

(The Scene: Interior of a rude dwelling, ancestral
home of the Schwartz family. Warming his back
before the fire is the happy father, My-Cup-Runneth-Over Schwartz. Sitting near him on an up-
turned lard bucket is Grandma—Use-A-Little-
Wine-For-Thy-Stomach's-Sake Brokenshire, thrice
a widow. As the curtain rises she is sound asleep.
Across the room, spooning Jamaica molasses into
her day-old infant, is the joyful mother, Sufficient-
Unto-The-Day-Is-The-Evil-Thereof Schwartz.)

FATHER: Well, Sufficient-Unto-The-Day-Is-The-
           Evil-Thereof, my dear, how do you feel?
MOTHER: Tuckered.
FATHER: There you go! I left you lay in bed all
           day yesterday. Now, git on with that
           churnin'.

MOTHER: I got to feed little—little—what air his name, My-Cup-Runneth-Over?

FATHER: We didn't name him yet. I was jist a-figgerin' we orta name him suthin', now we got him.

MOTHER: Don't look at *me*—it was your doin's!

FATHER: God damn you, I'll belt you one with this candle mold if you don't quit that naggin'. Nag, nag, nag—that's all I git outa you! You got any notions about a name fer him?

MOTHER: Well, I kinda favor Joe.

FATHER: In the name of the Great Jehovah and the Continental Congress! (*He turns to the old woman.*) Hey, Use-A-Little-Wine-For-Thy-Stomach's-Sake!   Wake up!

GRANDMA: Whup. Wurp. Woomp.

FATHER: What do you think we orta name the baby?

GRANDMA: What baby?

FATHER: The one your dopey daughter Sufficient-Unto-The-Day-Is-The-Evil-Thereof had yesterday.

GRANDMA: Oh, that one! Well, now, I did give it some thought, come to think of it. How about O-Death-Where-Is-Thy-Sting-Question-Mark Schwartz? That's nice.

FATHER: Don't like it. Got no swing to it. This modern world we live in, you gotta have a name's got rhythm in it. I'd like to have him baptized They-Sewed-Fig-Leaves-Together-And-Made-Them-selves-Aprons Schwartz.

MOTHER: Never! That's a girl's name.

FATHER: Okay, you're so damn smart, why don't *you* have an idea? And I don't mean any of that crazy Joe stuff neither!

MOTHER: I want he should have a name that will

FATHER: inspire him to great things so maybe someday he'll have his own cow.

FATHER: Good God, woman! O Lord, presarve me from this grasping, greedy female!

MOTHER: I'd like to name him Go-To-The-Ant-Thou-Sluggard-Consider-Her-Ways-And-Be-Wise Schwartz. I think that sounds real distinguished-like. He might even grow up to be called for jury duty someday.

FATHER: Well, I be consarned! Never thought of that! Sufficient-Unto-The-Day-Is-The-Evil-Thereof, you got a head on you. Leave me have another look at that sweet little varmint. There you are, Go-To-The-Ant-Thou-Sluggard-Consider-Her-Ways-And-Be-Wise, gitchee, gitchee, gitchee!

MOTHER: Oh, you like the name?

FATHER: Shore! And listen, Sufficient-Unto-The-Day-Is-The-Evil-Thereof, darling—let's have us some more of these little tykes. It's so dern much fun namin' them!

GRANDMA: You do and by God I go back to Ipswich!

(CURTAIN)

Lack of space, lack of time, lack of energy, and lack of information make it impossible for me to examine each of the forty-eight states for Smiths. We have had a hand in the settlement and development of every state in the Union, even Texas. Let's have a quick look at Texas and some of the Smiths who have figured in its history.

In the first place, Texas became the Lone-Star State because of a Smith. The man who made this large contribution was Henry Smith of Brazoria, first and only provisional governor of Texas before independence. Henry, incidentally, was a candidate for president of the Republic of Texas, running against Sam Houston, and Houston later made him his Secretary of the Treasury. In those early times the leaders were so preoccupied with other matters that the need for a state seal was overlooked. Then one day a situation arose requiring such a seal, and Henry Smith, being resourceful, simply ripped a big brass button off his overcoat, pressed it into the wax, and that impression became the emblem of Texas—a five-pointed star and a wreath of oak leaves—and a couple of years later the lone star was affixed to the official flag of Texas. The importance of Henry Smith's act becomes apparent when we go back to *The Button Book,* which was mentioned earlier. By chance the buttons on his overcoat that day had the single star and wreath. There are hundreds of other designs on old buttons. There is one featuring a beetle, and another with a big corkscrew on it, and several more picturing umbrellas. We find bicycles, wild boars, kittens, frogs, donkeys, possums, rabbits, rats, squirrels, zebras, fairies. Here's one with a fiddle and beneath it "D D," the whole signifying "Fiddle Dee Dee." And here's one with the head of Mrs. Siddons. Think of Texas as the Lone-Fairy State, or the Fiddle Dee Dee State, or the Lone Mrs. Siddons State. It was a good thing that Henry Smith was standing there when the cry went up for a state seal. Someone else in the room might have been wearing buttons with the figure of a character identified as "Mom's Little Sailorman."

One of Sam Houston's most trusted collaborators in Texas was Ashbel Smith. He was a young man from Connecticut, fairly well educated, considering the fact that he went to Yale, and his purpose in going to Texas was to forget a girl. He forgot her. He became surgeon general of the Army of the Republic of Texas, then Texas Minister to England and France, and after that Secretary of State.

The most famous Smith in the early history of Texas was Old Deef. He was born in New York in 1787, the son of Chillab Smith, and Chillab gave him the name Erastus. As a boy he was taken to Mississippi Territory, living for a while at Natchez, where he was known as Rastus Smith. He went to Texas in 1817 and didn't like it, but when he got back to Mississippi he didn't like that either, so he returned to Texas and never left it again.

He settled in San Antonio, where he married a Mexican woman by whom he had several children, including a son named Trinidad Smith. As Deaf Smith he became one of the most skillful frontier-style scouts in American history—quite an accomplishment for a man who couldn't hear a mule bray if the mule was in bed with him. The Mexicans never believed that he was deaf, and there is a legend that one day when he was engaged in a parley with them, under a flag of truce, a Mexican soldier crept up and fired off a gun alongside his ear. He didn't bat an eye. His skill was explained, of course, by the fact that his other senses were extraordinarily keen. He could see a Mexican three miles away, and smell him at a distance of six miles. His feats are commemorated on the map of Texas. Deaf Smith County is on the panhandle plains bordering New Mexico, a region of cattle ranches. The county is sparsely settled, having a total population of about seven thousand. The county seat is Hereford and in its turn is famous as The Town Without a Toothache—the low rate of dental decay is attributed to fluorine and iodides in the soil.

Texas also has a plain Smith County in the eastern part of the state, named for James Smith, who was a pioneer and one of the early governors. There is a town named Smith, and others named Smithfield, Smithland, Smith Oaks, Smith Point, Smiths Bluff, and Smithville.

And Dollilee Smith of Cleburne was once poet laureate of all Texas. I have no samples of her work, but I venture to say it rhymed real good.

The name Smith has been spread round the world much more than it would have been otherwise because of Smith College in Massachusetts. It is probably the most famous institution in the world wearing our family brand. There are twenty-six thousand living alumnae in the forty-eight states and in forty-four foreign countries. And there are ninety-eight Smith Clubs in the United States, Hawaii, England, France, Japan, and China.

Sophia Smith, founder of this institution for the education of young women, came from one of the oldest families of Smiths in the country. Both Sophia and Mary Lyon, founder of Mount Holyoke College, were descendants of Lieutenant Samuel Smith, who came over from England in 1634. Samuel helped get the town of Wethersfield started in Connecticut, then settled at Hadley, Massachusetts. Sophia's father and two of her uncles fought in the American Revolution, and one of her uncles was Oliver Smith, a character who lived at Hatfield, a few miles from Northampton. This Oliver Smith was a wealthy man. A historical writer of some prominence has lovingly described him in a letter to me as follows:

"Oliver was the stingiest man who ever lived. When he was born his paw died of a fit. Oliver was a rich man but he wore the same suit for thirty years. He quit his church because the damn-fool spendthrifts up and bought a stove. He refused to pay taxes all his life and he was so cautious about the disposition of his money that his will was a masterpiece of confusion and defied the best legal minds for years."

A more tolerant view of Oliver is furnished by Richard C. Garvey, author of a booklet called *Oliver Smith, Esquire.* Mr. Garvey contends that Oliver was not a penurious, narrow-minded man destitute of public spirit, but rather "a gentleman of charity, tolerance, and Christian ideals." Mr. Garvey reports that Oliver's will provided funds for the transportation of freed slaves back to Africa and that another bequest provided for the care of indigent women and children.

I'm not altogether clear on the matter, but my impression is that Oliver's money eventually went into the founding of Smith College. His nephew, Austin Smith, wound up with a lot of money and Austin was the brother of the spinster Sophia, and Sophia acquired the bulk of *her* wealth on the death of Austin. They were funny people about money, these Massachusetts Smiths. Austin charged Sophia a nickel every time he hitched up her horses for her and, in turn, Sophia made Austin pay for every meal he took at her house. "Austin," Sophia might say, "come over for supper tonight. We got Yankee pot roast. Thirty-five cents. With bread and butter, forty cents." "Wait a minute, Sofe," says Austin. "Don't forget I hitched up your team t'uther day when you went to macket." (Note the New England dialect touches in there.)

It was not Sophia's idea to found a college for women. When she had become an old woman, loaded with gelt, she consulted her pastor, the Reverend John Morton Greene, asking his advice on the disposition of her wealth. He suggested that she use a part of it to found a college exclusively for females and he framed the bequest which provided a fund of about four hundred thousand dollars for that purpose.

Smith College opened in 1875 with fourteen students. Today there are something over twenty-two hundred. The campus spreads across 214 acres and includes forty-four dormitories and thirty-three academic buildings. A recent check showed eighteen girls named Smith attending Smith, and one of these was a Sophia Smith. Four Smiths are currently members of the faculty. Smith College has always been Smith-conscious. There are two student singing groups called the Smithereens and the Smiffenpoofs. A couple of years ago when an epidemic of coughing hit the campus, the student government communicated with the Smith Brothers Cough Drop Company and the company shipped in more than two thousand boxes of its product.

During the last few years a campaign to raise seven million dollars for the college has been in progress. The campaign managers mailed out pamphlets to thousands of people named Smith, asking for their contributions, saying:

> Smith College has added great lustre to the already illustrious name of Smith. Her daughters carry her traditions all over the world, by their example, by their words and deeds, and because they are engaged in the world's work, at peaceful occupations and in peaceful homes.
>
> Smith College is as forthright and American as her name, and we want you who share her name to be as proud of her as we are. We offer you a chance to do your part so that Smith College shall stand as a living memorial of what is best in American life and Smith families everywhere may claim a share. Will you join the ladies?

No figures are available, but I understand that not many Smiths did join the ladies. The response from Smiths was quite feeble, even though the pamphlet suggested that a dollar would be welcome.

Many interesting traditions are associated with Smith College. There are so many bicycles on the campus that the student government maintains squads of "grass cops" to enforce traffic and parking regulations and issue tickets to offenders. Almost everything at Smith is done on the floor—coffee on the floor, bridge on the floor, canasta on the floor, study on the floor, writing love letters on the floor; a Smith dormitory could get along famously without a stick of furniture in the house. The girls of Smith are much like the girls everywhere. They invite one another to drop dead in German, they have "step sings," and on a day in spring they have a big hoop-rolling contest which is run off in two sections—one for the unmarried girls and one for the married. The winner

among the maidens is awarded a bridal bouquet and will be the first senior to bag a husband; the winner in the married division is given a rattle, for she will be the first to have a baby.

No account of Smith College, however brief, could be written without mention of William Allan Neilson, who served as its president from 1917 to 1939 and whose name is all but synonymous with Smith. President Neilson was celebrated as a wit, and I cannot forgo the opportunity here to recount a few of his exploits.

When he came to Smith smoking was prohibited among the students. He spoke to them about it. "Smoking," he said, "is a dirty, expensive, and unhygienic habit—to which I am devoted." And when the ban was finally lifted he told them: "Smoke if you must, but smoke like gentlemen."

A small scandal developed one day when a couple of his students invited two Yale men to go swimming with them in the

Northampton reservoir. President Neilson delivered his scolding publicly in chapel but tempered it in his last sentence when he said: "I prefer my drinking water unflavored by either Smith or Yale."

A freshman returning from a date found herself locked out of her dormitory one dark night at an hour when all students were supposed to be in bed. She succeeded in opening a window on the lower floor and was hoisting herself up, struggling to get through it, when a hand was placed on her posterior and she was boosted on through. She turned in time to see President Neilson, who smiled, tipped his hat, and walked away.

Another time Dr. Neilson went to an undergraduate play and later to a party given for the cast. During the evening he paused to congratulate one of the students who had played the part of a loose woman. "You acted very well," said President Neilson. "That *was* acting, wasn't it?"

Once when the seniors went to serenade him, his new collie pup began to bark furiously. "My dog thinks you are sheep," he told the girls, "but I think you are lambs."

And when a delegation of townspeople came to complain that the girls were not pulling down their shades when they disrobed, President Neilson told them: "Pull down your own shades."

It may seem silly that just because a person is named Smith he should have affectionate feelings toward a college named Smith. However, if an atom bomb falls on us and has the effect of scrambling the sexes and I come out of it a girl, I intend to head straight for Northampton and enroll as a freshman; and further than that, I'll have nothing whatever to do with nasty old boys.

William Smith College at Geneva, New York, is "co-ordinated" with Hobart College, and the two are known as the Colleges of the Seneca. Hobart is for boys and William Smith for girls. The William Smith involved here was a wealthy Geneva nurseryman, and at least one book describes him as having been a bachelor who had no use for women. This statement doesn't jibe with the fact that he contributed half a million dollars to establish a college for them, unless he had a notion that education would blight their lives. His name is splashed liberally around the campus, as is proper, there being a Smith Hall, a Smith Observatory, a William Smith Gymnasium, and a William Smith Green.

Johnson C. Smith University in North Carolina is a school for Negroes with an enrollment of about eight hundred. And we must not overlook Smith Academy in St. Louis, long out of existence but quite famous in its day. Anyone who undertakes an examination of all the biographical sketches in Who's Who in America will find a surprising number of successful men listing themselves as former pupils at Smith Academy. The school, at Nineteenth Street and Washington Avenue, prepared boys for Washington University and was known as the Academy of Washington University until James and Persis Smith came along with their hands full of money in 1879, providing the institution with new quarters and giving it the name of Smith.

Smith Academy attracts our interest for several reasons, not the least of which is the fact that it turned T. S. Eliot loose on the world. Mr. Eliot was born in St. Louis and was literary almost from his cradle days. When he was six or seven years old he wrote a two-page biography of George Washington which concluded with the following line:

And then he died, of corse.

There were hidden spiritual meanings in Eliot even in those days.

The Importance of Being Smith

Concurrent with the 1950 British elections, a hot political campaign was waged in a school at Menston, England. The "Communist" candidate was nine-year-old Dale Smith, whose platform demanded: (1) each child to receive a five-shilling-per-week pension; (2) free ice cream for all children, and (3) hang all teachers. He was elected.

As in botany and zoology, the Family Smith can be broken into subdivisions, one of which consists of the Almost Smiths. This genus also is subject to division into various species and subspecies, including Quondam Smiths, Parvenu Smiths, and Counterfeit Smiths.

When we approach the subject of Smiths in government we find ourselves dealing frequently with Almost Smiths. The term is not used in reference to the late Alfred E. Smith, who almost became President, for he was an Unalloyed Smith. Generally speaking, an Almost Smith is a person whose mother's maiden name was Smith. One of the most distinguished of these was President John Quincy Adams. I cite a few others:

Tom Mix's mother was Elizabeth Smith. The Firestones of Akron are Almost Smiths—Harvey Firestone married Idabelle Smith, who reigns today as matriarch of the clan. She, of course, is a Quondam Smith. Other prominent people whose mothers were named Smith include Sherwood Anderson, the writer; George Bellows, the artist; Charles Warren Fairbanks, vice-president under T. Roosevelt; H. J. Heinz, the pickle king, and Freeman (Amos) Gosden, of the radio.

A Counterfeit Smith is a non-Smith who has assumed the sacred name usually in an attempt to cover up criminal operations. And a Parvenu Smith is a non-Smith who has acquired the name usually through marriage. In the Webster definition of *parvenu*, if we substitute the name Smith for wealth, we get the following: "A person who has risen, as by the acquisition of the name Smith, above the station in which he was born; usually, in a bad sense, such a person when unaccustomed to his new station; one who makes great pretensions because of having acquired the name of Smith; an upstart." Senator Margaret Chase Smith of Maine is a Parvenu Smith, but only in a good sense, for she has brought fresh glory and honor to the name.

The phrase Almost Smith was coined by an old friend of mine, Ted Bonnet (pronounced Bonn-ay). Long before he wrote his novel *The Mudlark,* Mr. Bonnet, a resident of Hollywood, where he was once *agent provocateur* for Cecil B. DeMille, sat down at his typewriter and composed a short dissertation on Almost Smiths. His inspiration was a brief passage in one of my books concerning my own family. Mr. Bonnet wrote:

> Each of us is the son of a woman named Smith. You had an Aunt Nellie and so did I. Your grandfather owned a brickyard and so did mine. Your grandmother was Irish, and mine was too. And neither of us is English. In a motion picture this would clear up everything and when they found the birthmark on my brain it would clinch the case at the reading of your last will and testament.
>
> Actually, there is more to this than meets the eye. All is not Smith that glisters. By your own confession you are not a genuine, full Smith. The name used to be Schmitt. That makes you only H(alf) Allen Smith. By an odd quirk, I too am only half Smith. Your great-grandfather was a Schmitt in Switzer-

land. By a curious coincidence so was my wife's great-grandfather. And your great-grandmother married an Allen from Memphis. Strangely enough, my sister-in-law married an Allen from Indianapolis. Do you begin to see?

My mother's grandfather was a genuine Irish Smith from the town of Mallow, County Cork. He brought his wife and thirteen children to Philadelphia. My grandfather was but a child at the time. He grew up and married a Devine and took her to San Francisco. That's all I know. But what happened to his twelve brothers and sisters? I am haunted by the thought that Philadelphia and surrounding territory must be crawling with Smiths, Half-Smiths, Quad-Smiths, and Octa-Smiths who are my long lost relatives.

This brings into focus a whole new field for research. Everybody is always talking about the Smiths but nobody ever mentions the Almost Smiths. They are the stepchildren of the clan, the absorbed ones, the lost tribe. They are everywhere and they are all incognito. Scratch a Throttlebottom, a Moriarity, a McHaggis, or a Tschorunonovnikoff; a senator, a poet, a bartender, or a cornet soloist and bingo—you find a Smith!

Any extensive investigation of Almost Smiths is impossible at the moment. For confusion's sake, regardez voo John Ford, the famous movie director, whose name formerly was Sean O'Feeney and who married Mary McBryde Smith. Or switching it around, take the case of Fanny Hayes, daughter of President Rutherford B. Hayes; Fanny married a naval officer named Harry Eaton Smith. And a peculiar sort of Almost Smith was Smith Thompson, a justice of the United States Supreme Court from 1823 to 1843. Almost an Almost Smith is Ethel Merman, who was married in 1940 to William B. Smith, a Hollywood agent. When the news of the marriage leaked out and a reporter cornered Miss Merman for a statement, she roared: "Kid, love is wonderful!" It wasn't wonderful very long.

Two Quondam Smiths have occupied the White House. Zachary Taylor's wife was the former Margaret Mackall Smith of Maryland. Taylor was a rather dumb, or average, President and died in office sixteen months after his inauguration. His Smith-born wife was certainly one of the most colorful females ever to occupy the White House, where she sat around smoking a corncob pipe. In her husband's soldiering days she had lived with him in tents and stockades, and it wouldn't surprise me to learn that she spit in the skillet to see if it was hot enough to fry the beefsteak. Their daughter Sarah, an Almost Smith, was the first wife of Jefferson Davis—a marriage which Zack didn't approve, disowning Sarah because of it.

Abigail Smith, the parson's daughter who married young John Adams, was a Smith of considerable merit and certainly one of the greatest female Smiths we have had in this country. Her mother was a Quincy and her father, the Reverend William Smith, ran the church at Weymouth, southeast of Boston. John Adams, the lawyer who was to be called the Atlas of the American Revolution, married "Nabby" Smith when she was twenty.

Janet Whitney's biography of Abigail Adams, published in 1949, makes "Nabby" out to have been little short of co-President of the United States, consulted by her husband at every turn and possessed of extraordinary political acumen. On the other hand, Cleveland Amory, writing in *The Proper Bostonians,* declares that Abigail was no political asset to John, but that she was "the biggest social asset an Adams ever had and is generally rated the most illustrious of all the Adams wives."

This woman who was married to a President and the mother of another President was the first mistress of the White House in Washington and is best remembered and admired for her act of hanging out her washing in the East Room of the Executive Mansion. During many of the years when her husband was away from home on government affairs she ran the Adams farm at Braintree; she knew at first hand how to swing a scythe, prune a tree, and extract milk from a cow.

The important thing about her, however, is that she mothered a dynasty. Dixon Wecter, in his book *The Saga of American*

Society, states without reservation that "the most distinguished family in American history, though of minor social activity, is that of the Adamses of Massachusetts." Mr. Wecter means the Adamses who are descended from Abigail. Among them have been the Charles Francis Adams who was Minister to Great Britain in the time of the Civil War; the Henry Adams whose "Education" produced an American classic, and the Charles Francis Adams who was Secretary of the Navy in the Hoover cabinet.

And while John Adams was regarded by many as a pompous old poop, the fact seems to be that he was unswervingly patriotic and unquestionably honest—the first shaper of American foreign policy, the first Ambassador to Great Britain, the first Vice-President of his country, and its second President. His son John Quincy Adams, called the ablest Adams of them all, served as Ambassador to Russia, Ambassador to Great Britain, Secretary of State, and then President of the United States. His passion for public service is demonstrated in the fact that when his term in the White House was over he returned to Washington as a plain congressman, continuing for seventeen years as representative of his Massachusetts district.

John Quincy Adams was an Almost Smith by reason of ordinary relationship to a Quondam Smith. In the later years of his life his trail crossed that of a more complex Almost Smith. This was James Smithson, whose money was used to establish the Smithsonian Institution in Washington. Smithson was the natural son of Sir Hugh Smithson, one of the leading peers of England. (Why do we say such a person is a "natural" son? My own folks happened to have been married. Does that make me an unnatural son?) James Smithson, whose mother was a widow woman named Macie, grew up to become a prominent scientist. He always resented the fact that he had been deprived of his father's titles and position in society through the circumstances of his birth, and he said that by George he'd make his own name remembered long after the name of Sir Hugh was forgotten. When he made his will he set up a fund of about half a million dollars which eventually would go to establish the Smithsonian Institution at Washington "for the increase and diffusion of knowledge among men." In time the money was brought over from England and the politicians began scheming ways of getting their claws on it. John Quincy Adams, then a mere congressman, appointed himself as a sort of watchdog over the Smithson gold and he was largely instrumental in putting through the legislation which made the Smithsonian Institution a government project.

Abigail Adams was not the only Smith to figure in the Adams dynasty. She was the mother of five children. Her daughter Abigail married Colonel William Stephens Smith, a ne'er-do-well New Yorker who held minor government posts and had a talent for boggling nearly every job he put his hand to. He was, from all I can gather, a bum of the first magnitude, but his folks all loved him. Another of Abigail's children, Charles Adams, married Sarah Smith, who was sister to Colonel William Smith. Charles was the cross that Abigail had to bear. He drank.

Abigail Adams was the first Smith to get into the White House; in fact, she was the first anybody to get into it. The first and only Smith to come anywhere near to the presidency was, of course, the late Alfred Emanuel.[1] When the man in the brown derby was barnstorming the country in 1928 I can remember that he was a great and shining hero to me as he was, I'm sure, to many other Smiths. Today I find it difficult to attempt an evaluation of him. There are still people who revere his memory and speak of him as a great man; there are many others who grasp their nostrils when his name is spoken. It is all a matter of personal politics, where things are black or white but never gray.

Al Smith was easily the most famous of all modern American Smiths. The rags-to-riches theme ran through his life story and certainly was part of his great appeal. He actually rose from the sidewalks of New York. He was born in 1873 in the shadow of Brooklyn Bridge. His father was an impecunious truckman who died when Al was about thirteen. The boy quit school when he was in the eighth grade, tried his hand at trucking, and wound

[1]A man named Green Clay Smith, a Kentuckian who became territorial governor of Montana in the 1860s, was the presidential candidate of the National Prohibition party in 1876. If memory serves, he lost.

HAPPY
WARRIOR
SMITH

up as a clerk in the Fulton Fish Market, where he spent seven long odorous years. He was a lively young fellow with a talent for elocution and clog dancing and for a time he daydreamed of a career on the stage.

When he was around twenty-two the Tammany leader of his district got him a job as an investigator for the commissioner of jurors. Eight years later Al was a member of the State Assembly in Albany and in another ten years he had risen to become Speaker of the Assembly. The record shows that he always obeyed the orders that came up from Tammany and he was opposed by reform elements because of this subservience to the machine. In 1915 Tammany rewarded him for faithful service (staying in line) by making him sheriff of New York County—a juicy political plum because of the fee system, which, incidentally, was discontinued after Al's term. The year 1917 found him president of the Board of Aldermen, and he resigned from that body in 1918 to run for governor. He wasn't conceded a chance against Charles S. Whitman, but he squeaked through. Two years later, running for re-election, he was beaten by Nathan L. Miller, so he quit politics and went into business. His father had been a failure in the trucking trade, and so had he, but now he became head of the United States Trucking Corporation. In 1922 he was drafted to run for governor again and this time he beat Miller. In 1924 he defeated Theodore Roosevelt and in 1926 won over Ogden L. Mills.

Let's look at the record. As governor he fought for adequate housing, better factory laws, proper care of the insane, child welfare, state parks, and many other progressive programs. He reorganized the state government in the interest of greater efficiency. He was a first-rate governor, a man of the people who was for the people.

Al was the first Roman Catholic ever to receive serious consideration for a presidential nomination. His candidacy was responsible for that famous 1924 deadlock in the Democratic National Convention at Madison Square Garden, when the issue was clearly rum and Romanism and where the bitter snarl between Smith and McAdoo brought, in the end, the nomination of John W. Davis. Four years later in Houston, Al Smith was handed the nomination on the first ballot after his name had been placed before the convention by Franklin D. Roosevelt. When the votes were counted in November of 1928, Al Smith had 15,430,718; Herbert Hoover had 21,943,328.

Political historians are agreed on one thing: Al didn't give up. He had his sights set on the White House and 1932 was to be The Year. But the convention chose Roosevelt. Meanwhile the boy from the Lower East Side had become a rich man—president of the new Empire State Building, tallest man-made structure in the world. Parenthetically let it be noted that when a bomber crashed into the Empire State tower in 1945, killing thirteen persons in one of the most spectacular tragedies in New York City history, the pilot was Lieutenant Colonel William Franklin Smith, Jr.

Al went along with F.D.R. in 1932 and even campaigned for

him, but by 1936 he could no longer stomach the Squire of Hyde Park, so he "took a walk" and spoke for the Republican candidate, Landon. From then on, to the time of his death in 1944, he was a bitter foe of Roosevelt.

He was still a hero to a multitude of people. More than 200,000 filed past his bier in St. Patrick's Cathedral, and 40,000 attended his funeral. But he was not a hero to many others. In the years following his defeat in the presidential race, two such disparate characters as Heywood Broun and James J. Walker had their say about him. Broun wrote that Al had been living too long in that ivory tower on Fifth Avenue.

"From his office window," said Broun, "Al can nod to any passing plane, but the noises of the street, the words of the people, and even their cries came faintly to his casement."

Jimmy Walker's feeling was somewhat the same. Walker had been a protégé of Al's in his early days at Albany, but later the governor had cooled toward the brash young man from Manhattan. Jimmy always called him "Algie," and Smith complained that the nickname wounded his dignity. He also resented the fact that Jimmy didn't always hop when Al spoke. After Al's defeat in 1928 Jimmy said it wasn't altogether a matter of religion—that there were other reasons why the people rejected him.

"He exchanged the old blue serge suit for a white tie and tails," said Walker, "the brown derby for a top hat. He took off the square-toe brogans with which he had climbed from the sidewalks of New York to dizzy heights, and put on a pair of pumps."

The ancestry of Al Smith was often discussed in the time of his political campaigns. The truth of the matter is, almost nothing is known about it. Henry F. Pringle, in his biography of Al, published in 1927, said that both of his parents were native New Yorkers and then wrote of Al's father:

> Smith, the truckman, is now a vague figure. He died while comparatively young, and not a great deal about him is remembered. His wife, it is known, was Irish-American. But the genesis of the blood that flowed in his own veins is not known. It is now

recalled by the family that he had dark hair and eyes, as well as a dark complexion. They think it possible that far back there may have been Italian forebears. It is asserted with emphasis by the Smiths, however, that he was not partly German. There is still in existence a certificate showing membership in a volunteer fire company. Dated 1857, it is made out in the name of Alfred E. Smith. In this way is refuted a canard published by the *Gaelic-American* last year, which set forth that the father of the Governor of the State of New York was really a Teuton named Schmidt who had later called himself Smith. This cruel charge caused terrific excitement among the Irish members of Tammany Hall. Al, himself, thought it rather funny.

Canard? Cruel charge? Rather funny? What the hell goes on here? I've got German blood in me, and if Tammany Hall doesn't like it, they can kiss my foot until it's red, red, red.

If we employ the method of reasoning used by people who have studied logic, we can arrive at a conclusion about Presidents and Smiths. Given the fact that one American in every one hundred is a Smith, then if a President had one hundred personal friends, ergo quid nunc propter hoc and Q.E.D., one of those friends was a Smith. If he had two hundred personal enemies, he was a sure thing to have two Smiths on his spit list. Under this type of reasoning, however, we don't get their names. It is necessary to prowl around in the history books to find specific Smiths whose careers impinged on the careers of our Presidents. And these Smiths have been beyond counting.

George Washington could number at least seventy-five Smiths among the officers of his Army during the Revolution. Thomas Jefferson had traffic with several Smiths, both politically and socially. They included the brothers Samuel and Robert Smith of Maryland, both quite celebrated characters in their day. Sam was a hero of the Revolution—his exploits were described not long ago in a historical novel by Neil H. Swanson. Jefferson offered him the post of Secretary of the Navy, but Sam had to turn it down—his wife didn't like the mud in the streets of Washington and put her foot down in the mud in the streets of Baltimore and said she wasn't budging. So the cabinet post went to Robert, who was a wealthy Baltimore lawyer and shipowner. Robert was quite a fellow in his own right—a tall and handsome man of commanding presence with a flair for high social didoes. He served as Secretary of the Navy, as Attorney General, and when Madison came in he was made Secretary of State. Historians say he was a capable cabinet officer, although he was frequently and bitterly maligned by Albert Gallatin, the Secretary of the Treasury. Gallatin had yearned for the appointment as Secretary of State, so when it went to Smith, Gallatin called him a low character, a simpering pantywaist, an unprincipled serpent, and several other terms of endearment common to the lexicon of upper-grade politics.

During this same period there was another important Smith in Washington—Margaret Bayard Smith, whose husband was editor of the Jeffersonian newspaper, the *National Intelligencer*. Margaret was a favorite Washington hostess, and her salon rivaled that of Dolly Madison. She entertained all the top people at her big house on New Jersey Avenue and at her country place on the grounds of the present Catholic University. She was an intelligent woman with an instinct for protocol and political talk and she is remembered for the book she wrote called *First Forty Years of Washington Society*, a work that has been of great value to all historians of the period.

Four Smiths have been members of presidential cabinets, including Robert. Caleb B. Smith was Secretary of the Interior under Lincoln—a reward, presumably, for having seconded the nomination of Abe. Hoke Smith of Atlanta was Secretary of the Interior under Cleveland, and Charles E. Smith, once Postmaster General, has already been met with in this book.

Outside of Caleb there seem to have been few Smiths associated with Lincoln. One, however, will long be remembered for having inspired a remarkable document. This was Franklin W. Smith of Boston, who had a contract to furnish war supplies to the Navy Department. He was court-martialed on a charge of having diverted certain moneys to his own pocket, and convicted of the charge. In

due course the papers arrived on the desk of President Lincoln.
He studied them briefly, then wrote out his judgment:

> Whereas, Franklin W. Smith had transactions
> with the United States Navy Department to a mil-
> lion and a quarter dollars, and had the chance to
> steal a quarter of a million; and, whereas, he was
> charged with stealing only ten thousand dollars, and
> from the final revision of the testimony it is only
> claimed that he stole one hundred dollars, I don't
> believe he stole anything at all. Therefore, the rec-
> ords of the court-martial, together with the finding
> and sentence, are disapproved, declared null and
> void, and the defendant is fully discharged.
>
> A. LINCOLN

Among the many stories Lincoln enjoyed telling was one concerning a famous marriage certificate given to a certain John Smith
back in Illinois by a justice of the peace who hadn't yet received
his authorization of office. The certificate read:

> State of Illinois,
> Peoria County ss
>
> To all the world Greeting. Know ye that John
> Smith and Peggy Myres is hereby certified to go to-
> gether and do as old folks does, anywhere inside
> coperas precinct, and when my commission comes
> I am to marry em good and date em back to kivver
> accidents.

We come now to a tragicomic character named Smith who was
closely associated with one of our Presidents. Jesse Smith of Ohio,
to be sure. Of all the wretched Smiths in our history, this one
ranks pretty close to the top, or bottom. Jesse was an obscure and
fatheaded young man in Washington Court House, Ohio, when
destiny somehow brought him to the attention of a Columbus
lawyer, Harry M. Daugherty. The lawyer took a liking to this
dopey boy and even set him up in business in a small department
store. Soon Jesse was Daugherty's shadow, serving as his secretary,

valet, nurse, bartender, errand boy, and buffer; the relationship was somewhat like that of hound-dog and master. Jesse was not a pretty man. He has been described as a large, loose, pulpy, sputtering, horse-lipped country sport who was crude, naïve, eager to be friendly, and a passionate devotee of the funny papers.

Warren G. Harding was elected President in 1920, and the Ohio Gang moved into Washington. Daugherty, a key figure in the gang's operations, became Attorney General, and at his side was our Jesse. The country sport had suddenly become a figure of incredible importance and he was starry-eyed about it. Jesse has had his apologists, though none has ever denied his crimes; they say that he got into the business of shakedown and bribery by slow gradations—beginning with the passing of little gifts, such as a case of whisky or a tip on the stock market. Before long Jesse was a frequent visitor to the Little Green House on K Street where deals were made and knapsacks stuffed with money changed hands. Jesse used to stand on the curb at Fifteenth and H streets, two blocks from Harding in the White House and a block from Daugherty in the Department of Justice—he'd stand there and preen himself and simper and pick his teeth and occasionally he'd burst into happy song, warbling, "Good God How the Money Rolls in!" In time the enormity of his misdeeds turned him into a frightened weasel. He got so he was afraid of the dark, afraid of people on the street, and then one day he was found shot to death in his Washington hotel room, a gun lying at his side. The death was entered on the records as a suicide, but even today when the old sordid story is hashed over there is still talk that Jesse was murdered—that he had become the weak link in the chain and was growing weaker, and those above him saw the possibility of his breaking and howling out the whole nasty tale.

Harding had his Jesse and Roosevelt had his Harold, and these two Smiths stand poles apart. Harold Dewey Smith, Director of the Budget during the most eventful years of our national history, gives us a glow of pride to replace the blush of shame that comes when we think of Jesse. The public knew almost nothing about Harold Smith, even during the war years when he was called the most important man in the Roosevelt administration and "the man who runs the government." He grew up on a Kansas wheat farm, got a degree in electrical engineering at the University of Kansas, and became a teacher of government at the University of Michigan. Roosevelt reached out and grabbed him after he had become budget director for the state of Michigan. In the years that followed few others were as close to F.D.R. as was this undistinguished-looking Smith who lived quietly with his family across the river in Alexandria. He wore a small mustache and rimless glasses and usually smoked a pipe and he always insisted that he was in no way a politician; that he had absolutely no talent for the connivance and the false front that is a part of political life. When he was asked to define his political affiliations he grinned and replied: "I am what you might call an independent Republican with Socialist leanings who frequently votes Democratic."

He resigned as Director of the Budget in 1946 to become vice-president of the International Bank for Reconstruction and Development, and he died early in 1947. Summing up his career in 1943, *Time* said:

"In a sense, he is any and every Mr. Smith of the U.S.A. In his high government post he is a solid, reassuring symbol of the average American's patience, common sense, and optimism."

Forty years ago in one of this nation's smaller towns there lived a slip of a girl in her early teens, the daughter of a local barber. There were six children in the family and they lived in a frame house which their grandfather built with his own hands, and next door to the house was the one-chair barbershop operated by the father. Our teen-age girl had an almost depressingly normal sort of upbringing. At home she learned to cook expertly and to sew so well that for a long time she made all her own dresses. She learned the intricate science of shopping economically, and how to use a saw and hammer, and how to oil a clock, and a million other things. When she was still quite young she got a job clerking in the five-and-ten, and after that she became a telephone operator. Meanwhile in high school, where she was among the brighter students, she played basketball on the team that won the state championship. She couldn't go to college after high school, but worked for the local weekly newspaper and later got a job as a bookkeeper and office manager.

Now, where would you suppose a girl like that might end up?

Well, she isn't sitting on her front porch with her lap full of unshelled peas, yelling at the kids to get down out of that tree before they break a leg. She is today being talked about, more than any other woman, as possibly the first person of her sex ever to become President of the United States. We salute her in this catalogue of Smith because she has carried the name into high places and may carry it even higher. She is, of course, Senator Margaret Chase Smith of Maine.

She is a Smith only by marriage, but she belongs to us just the same; if she should ever become President she will be President Smith, not President Chase. She considers this presidential talk to be ridiculous. One evening Bob Trout asked her, "How would you feel if you woke up one morning and found yourself in the White House?" Senator Smith's quick response was: "I'd thank Mrs. Truman for a pleasant visit and then go on home."

She is the first and only woman ever to be elected to the United States Senate strictly on her own, and the story of that election is a sort of political epic. In 1930 she was married to Clyde H. Smith, a man who was prominent in Maine politics, and six years later she went with him to Washington after he was elected to Congress. When he died in 1940 the voters chose her to fill out his term. As it turned out, this was not merely the usual sentimental gesture, for she went to work with zest and intelligence, and the people of her district back in Maine re-elected her three times.

In 1948 Margaret Chase Smith entered the race for United States senator and knowing political experts smiled, even smirked a little, because she didn't have a chance. The race was considered to be strictly between two other candidates—Governor Horace Hildreth and ex-Governor Sumner Sewall. Both of these men were wealthy, had their own political machines, and possessed records which ranked them among the biggest vote getters in Maine history. Margaret Chase Smith had nothing but a small automobile, a smile, a way with people, and a lot of energy. She campaigned back and forth across the state during January and February, driving through raging blizzards and never missing an appointment. One morning in February she slipped and fell, breaking her arm. At a Bangor hospital the arm was put in a cast, and by noon she was in Rockland, sixty miles away, filling a speaking date at a luncheon. Right down to the last day people said she was making a fool of herself trying to buck those two veteran campaigners, and then they counted the votes.

The outcome of the election brought from the Boston *Post* the enthusiastic shout that Mrs. Smith was the biggest New England political story since Calvin Coolidge. She got 63,000 votes while her nearest competition, Governor Hildreth, polled a mere 30,000. Today her vigorous activities in and out of the Senate chamber have brought her a universal respect—even the Democrats love her and admire her. And back in Maine they say: "That Margaret Smith is as straight as a yard of pump water."

Meeting her recently during a television program, I joshed her about being a Parvenu Smith. Later I learned that she had just come from a dinner where she had been given some sort of achievement award. Several of the speakers had referred to her as "Senator Chase." When it came her time, she got up and said: "Let's get one thing clear—my name is Smith."

The Eighty-first Congress has two senators and four representatives named Smith. The other senator, also a Republican, is H. Alexander Smith of New Jersey. His most important recent activities have been as a member of the Foreign Relations Committee.[1]

A Smith holds the record for the longest continuous service in the United States Senate—the late Ellison DuRant "Cotton Ed" Smith of South Carolina. John Gunther described Cotton Ed as "probably the worst senator who ever lived, no mean honor." He

[1]In the summer of 1950, North Carolina voters added a third Smith to the Senate in the person of Willis Smith, former president of the American Bar Association.

spent thirty-five years in the most exclusive gentleman's club on earth, but he was no gentleman. He was born during the Civil War and all his life he was a country feller. He was agin the twentieth century, and one of his most erudite public statements was: "We are right in the smack-dab middle of a jackass age." He was just plain downright anti-Negro and fer lynchin'. In 1944, running for his seventh term in the Senate, he was rejected by the voters of South Carolina, possibly because he was now eighty years old, and four months later he was dead. Along toward the close of his life he appeared as a speaker on a nationwide radio program. His political opponents always had fun with his middle name, making two words out of it, exclaiming: "How he Du Rant!" He was ranting along through this radio broadcast and multitudes of listeners were enjoying his performance, when he stopped in the middle of a sentence. The unseen audience heard a rustling of papers, and then a growl from old Cotton Ed: "Ah knowed th' son of a bitch would git these pages all mixed up."

The Smiths have not always been people of sound judgment. A Smith of my acquaintance, a news executive who was inclined to be pontifical in his opinions, sat in his office one day in 1936 looking at the first issue of *Life* magazine. He turned the pages briskly, glancing at each one and then going on to the next. When he had finished he sat back, screwed up his forehead, rubbed his nose vigorously, and then delivered his judgment: "I'll give it three months."

Out of political history comes the story of James Smith, Democratic boss of New Jersey back in 1910. In that year reform was in the air and our James decided to play it clever. He looked around and spotted a liberal professor down at Princeton, man name of Wilson, and gave him the nomination for governor of New Jersey. Smith figured Wilson to be a man not too far removed from imbecility, being a professor and all. He'd use this Princeton visionary to keep the party in power, and things would go on just as they had before. What he got when Wilson was elected governor was more than he had anticipated—Woodrow simply busted him all over the Jersey bogs.

Al Smith was the most famous Smith in the annals of Tammany Hall, but there was another, Silver Dollar Smith, who achieved a certain eminence. He was a Tammany district leader around 1900. He kept a saloon on Essex Street, and the concrete floor had one thousand silver dollars embedded in it, with a fifty-dollar gold piece in the center. There was a chandelier trimmed with five hundred silver dollars, and the big coins were used as decoration elsewhere in the place. Three days after Silver Dollar opened this establishment he was able to report that he had taken in more than four thousand dollars from men who flocked in to "see how this damn idiot wastes his money." On the side Silver Dollar had a prosperous business bailing out prostitutes at twenty-five dollars per prostitute. He was not a genuine Smith; the historians say his true name was either Solomon, Goldschmidt, or Finkelstein.

In more recent times we have, in politics, the incomparable Gerald L. K. Smith, a by-product of the Huey Long circus in Louisiana, who began as a preacher and became, in the considered judgment of H. L. Mencken, the greatest rabble-rouser of history, greater even than Mr. Mencken's earlier favorite among the "boob-bumpers"—William Jennings Bryan. Gerald's business is bigotry, and it pays him well; in 1949 he got about $150,000 out of his followers, most of whom are members of his Christian Nationalist Crusade, dedicated to the preservation of America as a white Christian nation. Gerald claims he has a following of more than three million, but he is full of deletion.

Huey Long had another Smith in his stable, the remarkable Dr. James Monroe Smith, president of Louisiana State University. The doctor was a great hand at financial manipulation and speculated extensively in wheat. Whenever his broker called, wanting more money, Dr. Smith simply printed up a fresh batch of LSU bonds. He finally fled the country but was bagged in Canada and sent to prison.

Among the present-day influential Smiths in Congress is "Judge" Howard Worth Smith of Alexandria, a key man in the Byrd political machine and one of the bitterest enemies of the labor unions. Purcell L. Smith, employed by the National Association of Electric Companies at $65,000 a year, is known in Washington as

"King of the Lobbyists." And Earl C. Smith, out of Pike County, Illinois, has often been described as the most powerful farm lobbyist operating in the nation's capital.

This syllabus of political Smiths would not be complete without a few words concerning Ida B. Wise Smith, who served as president of the Women's Christian Temperance Union for eight years. She didn't believe in moderation—she was for total abstinence. In 1942, when she was seventy years old, she wrote the so-called Sheppard Bill prohibiting prostitution in army camp areas and forbidding the sale of all liquors in these precincts. Ida got her start in Iowa, where she was first a schoolteacher, then an ordained minister of the Church of Christ. She was once designated the "most distinguished woman in Iowa." We, the Smiths, don't have to take her if we don't want to. Her maiden name was Speakman, she married a man named Wise, and later she married a Malcolm Smith. Malcolm is the one I'd like to know about. Must have had an interesting life. We don't have to take Ida, but we're stuck with Edith Smith of Wisconsin, who was assistant to Frances E. Willard in Social Purity Work.

On a different plane in the war against liquor we find Moe Smith, who, with his partner Izzy Einstein, delighted a nation during the years of prohibition. Moe and Izzy had been cronies on New York's East Side. Izzy was a minor clerk in a post office, stood five feet five, weighed 225, and was bald. When he heard that the government was going to pay as much as twenty-five hundred dollars a year for prohibition agents, he joined up. After a few weeks he began to miss his old pal Moe, who ran a small cigar store. Moe was a couple of inches taller than Izzy and weighed ten pounds more. They had been celebrated before as neighborhood cutups, and now Izzy got Moe to join him as a booze raider. Before long these two were occupying the front pages almost constantly. They went in for fantastic disguises and they were so comical that few people, even among their victims, ever got really sore at them. On a cold night, for example, Moe would lead a shivering, chattering Izzy into a resort and yell, "Give this man a drink quick—he's been bit by frost!" It usually worked. And after they got famous, Izzy sometimes had success by simply walking to a bar and saying with a smirk, "I'm Izzy Einstein. How about a snort?" The bartender's response was usually, "Yeh, and I'm Buffalo Bill, and here's yer drink." In about five years Moe and Izzy confiscated over five million bottles of liquor and made more than four thousand arrests.

Valiant Is the Word for Smith

Donald Ellsworth Smith was the first person in history to get a degree in dude ranching. He took a special course at the University of Wyoming and won his sheepskin in 1938.

"Ubiquitous and sempiternal" are the Smiths, according to one of the mass-market genealogical services, which is trying to say that we are everywhere and will last forever. This particular pamphlet with its grand rhetoric has more than a faint odor of tea-leaf reading, declaring as it does that a person named Smith is likely to have a brisk imagination, to be a lover of liberty, possessed of practical business ability, quick wit, and capacity for leadership.

That sort of group psychoanalysis, silly as it is, can be more edifying to a Smith than the research projects of the scholarly genealogists. Let us examine *The American Genealogist* for April 1949, an issue devoted to Smiths. There are seventy-nine pages of tight type in it, and nowhere a single lively incident. It deals with the lines of descent from such dull-sounding forefathers as John Smith of Mespat, Richard Smith of Lyme, and the Miscellaneous Smiths of Guilford, Connecticut. For purposes of illustration, let us consider Daniel Smith of Milford and see what he contributed to the world by genealogical reckoning. Daniel married Sarah Johnson and they had issue as follows: Elizabeth, married Daniel Tuttle; Sarah, married Isaac Nettleton; Susanna, married John Prindle; Patience, married Simeon Sperry; Thankful, married

Daniel Smith; Hezekiah, married Esther Beecher. (Notice that Thankful Smith married a man named Daniel Smith, which was Thankful's father's name. The genealogist in this case apparently didn't even notice it, or else didn't give a damn. I think it ought to be investigated.) Now, going back to Hezekiah, who married the Beecher woman, he in turn begat Truman Smith, who married Huldah Alling, bp. I don't know what that bp. means. Baptist, perhaps, or big party after the wedding. Then Esther Smith married Isaac Hemingway, and—but that's enough of it. The whole booklet is about as exciting as a stock inventory of a carpet-tack factory. Occasionally there is mention of a will or a transfer of property, but such matters are set down solely for the purpose of establishing the relationship of one Smith to another.

The finished chart is a history of sorts, but there's no life in it. You get the names of sires and dams and all the foalings and the dates of births and marriages and deaths, and that's all. There is no mention of the one who got cidered up and goosed the preacher, the one who squandered his patrimony at the cribbage board, the one who slaughtered his wife, or built a bridge, or horsewhipped an editor, or wrote a poem, or treed a possum, or played the zither.

In the realm of formal genealogy there seems to be no recognition of achievement other than begetting. The business of begetting is a wondrous enough sort of thing, but anybody can do it— even an idiot hog—and I've never been able to understand why a man, immediately his wife has a baby, goes around with a smirk on his face, with his chest puffed out like a Mongoloid pigeon, as if he had just built another Boulder Dam, or discovered a cure for the common cold, or got selected by the Literary Guild. What did he do that was so much? What did he do that a Japanese beetle couldn't do better?

The thing we all want to know about a man is what he has done that sets him apart from the common run of men. The Eldon (Mo.) *Advertiser* reports that a Westminster College student named William Smith found a six-foot blacksnake that had swallowed a jar of mentholatum. That boy is a far more interesting individual than Truman Smith who married Huldah Alling bp. So far as human achievement goes it wasn't much, yet I venture the opinion that William Smith was the first person on earth ever to find a snake that had swallowed a jar of mentholatum.

The clan of fire and forge has had its share of adventurous and picaresque characters. In exploration, in combat, in aviation, in all the pursuits of man where courage and boldness are required, there have been Smiths. Most famous of these, of course, was Captain John Smith of Lincolnshire and Virginia; there have been many others, from Paul (Apollos) Smith, the celebrated huntsman and guide of the Adirondacks, to W. A. "Shotgun" Smith, who in 1867 faced a band of aggravated Apaches in Arizona and fought so ferociously that he killed everyone in sight. There was Tom Smith, the no-gun marshal of Abilene before Wild Bill Hickok took over. Tom was a former New York City policeman who had a theory that if he didn't pack a gun nobody would use a gun on him. He enforced the law with his fists and maintained order in tough Abilene for about a year. Then one day he went out to arrest a murderer and met armed resistance. In the fight Tom Smith was killed, but he wasn't shot. Possibly in deference to Tom's no-gun policy he was knocked in the head with an ax.

At Bent's Fort in Colorado a staff of Indian fighters was usually in residence, and among them was Blackfoot Smith, who got his name from one of his exploits. He was captured by five Blackfoot warriors on the Missouri River at a time when, for some reason, he happened to be carrying a jug of laudanum. He made out that this tincture was a new kind of whisky and got the Indians to join him in an apéritif. Each warrior tipped the jug, and within a few minutes all five were unconscious. Smith quietly killed them, scalped them, glanced up and saw two others arriving, killed those two, scalped them, and went on home.

In the early history of the Southwest there lived a wandering breed of trappers and Indian fighters called the Mountain Men. They are just now beginning to achieve their rightful place in American history, largely through the writings of such men as Bernard De Voto and Robert Glass Cleland. One of these was Peg-leg Smith, sometimes called the Bald Hornet. This Smith was famous for several things, including the fact that he amputated his own leg, using a hunting knife and a keyhole saw, and then sat down and whittled a replacement out of the limb of an oak tree. On the side he was a rustler of mules and might be described as still holding the world's championship in that event; he once stole three thousand head of mules in a single operation.

The most imposing figure among all the Mountain Men was Jedediah Strong Smith. The Rocky Mountain historian David Lavender describes him as "probably the greatest explorer the United States has ever known." And Professor Cleland, in his recent *This Reckless Breed of Men,* says that Jedediah "deserves a place in national tradition equal in every respect to that accorded Meriwether Lewis, William Clark, Daniel Boone, Kit Carson, or any other American explorer."

He was born in upstate New York and left home when he was thirteen to work as a clerk on a Great Lakes freighter. Becoming interested in the fur trade which was even now making John Jacob Astor the richest man in America, Jed Smith made his way to St. Louis, arriving there just in time to see an ad in the newspapers asking for stout young men to join an expedition up the Missouri River, object beavers. Thus Jedediah threw in with William H. Ashley, leading fur trader of the West, and disappeared into the mountains with a party of trappers. He was gone for three years, and during that time, having decided that fur was the thing, he applied himself to a careful study of all the angles. When he emerged from the wilderness he was the embodiment of the Mountain Man. He was over six feet tall, clean-shaven, and wore fringed buckskin. He knew all there was to know about woodcraft and weather and the habits of fur-bearing animals. He knew how to placate an Indian, or deceive him, or kill him if necessary. He could build a boat and dress a wound and break a horse and move a mule. More than that, he had developed a natural talent for leadership. He was a devout Christian, and in the years of his rovings read the Bible to massive boulders and sang Wesleyan hymns to the quaking aspens.

During that three-year expedition up the Missouri, Jedediah was actually scalped by a grizzly bear. He was riding along at the head of his men when the bear came out of a thicket, rushed him, knocked him off his horse, pounced upon him, broke several of his ribs, bit off one of his ears, and then tried to bite his whole head off. The bear opened his mouth as wide as he could and got hold of the top of Jed's head and laid the scalp back as neat as a Paiute could do it. Right then I'd have quit and gone home. But Jed called one of his men, told him where to find the needle and thread, and directed the sewing back on of his ear and the replacement of his scalp. Moreover, he didn't use a single swear word in speaking of the grizzly.

Jedediah's employer, Ashley, got rich in a hurry and went off to Congress, selling out his fur business to Jed, William Sublette, and David Jackson. These three crossed the mountains with their company of trappers and set up camp in the Bear River country north of Great Salt Lake. While their men piled up pelts, the leaders sat down to consider the future. They were camped in country as wildly primitive as Westchester County, New York, surrounded by murderous savages with forked tongues and by grizzly bears that would bite a man's scalp off. To the west and the south of them lay an immense unexplored land. Jed Smith allowed as how he'd like to penetrate this country, locate new trapping grounds, then push on to California and figure out some way to ship furs by water. In August of 1826 Smith started at the head of a party of eighteen men. After three months of plodding progress through mountains and deserts and much intense suffering from heat and hunger and thirst, they came to Mission San Gabriel in the vicinity of Los Angeles; and you may be certain that the eyes of the padres popped when this ragged and bleary-eyed band came abruptly out of the East. Their arrival on the California coast is described by the best historians as an important milestone in the story of America—the culmination of the long push westward, the Conquest of a Continent.

California was then under Mexican rule, so Jed Smith went on down to San Diego to see the provincial governor, who thought about arresting Jed for trespassing, but rather than risk trouble with those rambunctious upstarts back in Washington, he compromised by telling the Mountain Man to take his crowd and go on back home by the way he came. Jed wanted to go north to Oregon, but the Mexican governor wouldn't permit it. Nevertheless, he did go north, into the San Joaquin Valley, where he left most of his men while he and two companions set out to conquer the wide Sierra Nevada Mountains, which lay between them and the Bear River camp. They nearly killed themselves doing it, but they made it across the mountains and then all they had in front of them was the Great Salt Desert, which no white man had ever negotiated. It was a nightmare adventure, crossing that desert, but they managed it and finally came crawling in to the camp on Bear River. Possibly they didn't know it at the time, but these three men had completed one of the greatest exploits in the whole history of western exploration.

Jedediah rested for ten days, then decided to try it again—he had to go back to relieve the men he had left in the San Joaquin Valley and he wanted to locate some more good beaver country. He assembled another small party and headed into the Southwest. On the first trip most of his trouble had been with bears, but on the second the Indians turned against him. Down on the Colorado River the Mojaves pretended friendliness until the white men had relaxed their guard, and a massacre followed. Half of his men were slaughtered, but Jed got the remainder across the river and they straggled on westward. This time he steered clear of the Mexican authorities, made a right-hand turn, and went on up to the San Joaquin Valley. At San Jose he ran afoul of the governor once again and was a prisoner for a while; when he got matters straightened out he took all his men and started north, blazing the trail from California into Oregon, and then the Indians caught up with him again. While he and three others were away from camp, the redskins rose up and massacred everyone else in his party.

Jed and his three companions made it to Fort Vancouver and finally, without escort and without even a guide, set out on still another fantastic journey—back to the Bear River by a devious northern route. By the time he had rejoined his partners, Jed had just about reached the decision that he had done enough exploring. He had money now and it was time for him to retire and take it easy. So he went back to Missouri and was looking around for a quiet spot when someone approached him with a story about a wagon train that was leaving for Santa Fe and needed a leader.

He simply couldn't resist it. He was thirty-three years old and adventure was strong in his blood. He took his place at the head of the wagon train. On the dry plains between the Arkansas and Cimarron rivers the expedition ran out of water and conditions grew quite desperate. Jedediah rode on ahead and reached the Cimarron and found a little water in it. He was crouched down getting a drink for himself when all hell broke loose. The Comanches had him surrounded. He killed at least two of them before an Indian lance pierced his back, and that was the end of one of the greatest of all Americans ever to bear the name of Smith.

In 1943, when Edison Marshall published his novel based on the life of Captain John Smith, he chose a felicitous title for the book—*Great Smith*. Any way you look at him Captain John was great. He was a great soldier, a great colonizer, a great diplomatist, and a great lover. Yet almost every authority I have consulted puts special emphasis on his talent for exaggeration, and some of them call him the greatest liar the world has ever known.

Granted that the captain, sitting around the taverns in the closing years of his life, chose to exaggerate certain aspects of his own career. Show me a man who sits around taverns in the closing years of his life who doesn't. As for his writings, I think it improbable that he went out of his way to violate beauty (which is truth). People who, like myself, write non-fiction works dealing largely with their own personal adventures simply don't stoop to exaggeration. That takes care of that.

Captain John was born in Lincolnshire in 1579, and from the moment he first began to feel a swelling in the neighborhood of his *biceps brachii* he was off on the trail of adventure and romance. When he was sixteen he went out to fight against the Spanish and after that he decided to take on the Turks. He was captured by the Turks and sold as a slave and turned over to a Turkish princess named Charatsa Tragabigzanda, who lived in a palace at Constantinople. This Tragabigzanda in the beginning called our John by such names as "giaour dog" and "Christian swineflesh" and said she was going to have him blinded and gelded and his ears stopped

up with molten lead, and then she got a closer look at him. Right away she went away somewhere and switched costumes and came back with her belly button showing and a loud twinkle in her eye. Poor John Smith! He couldn't help it! He had to do it! There wasn't any getting out of it. Oh, what a cruel thing is human slavery! Tragabigzanda was beautiful and sensuous and built good. For several months . . . Well, it's a wonder that John Smith ever in his life recovered strength enough to go settle Virginia. The strangest part of the whole story, as John himself told it, was how he managed to get away from her. She caught him in the hay with one of her maids and condemned him to hard labor, with his hands. After further hardships he finally got back to Christendom and he was properly sorrowful and contrite about the whole thing, but, as he explained, what can a man do to protect himself when he's a mere slave? And this is the Smith they call liar!

He was twenty-six when he returned to England and at once he plunged into the colonization projects of the London Company. He was chosen a member of the Council of Virginia and set sail with the company which was to found Jamestown.[1] He was not the nominal leader of the expedition, but as it turned out he was the strong man, the driving force, the one individual whose hard-headed sense saved the little colony from annihilation time and again. He explored and mapped the coast, led trading expeditions to get corn from the Indians, and insisted upon a program that might have interesting results if it were tried out today: any man who doesn't do his share of the work doesn't eat.

The classic story of John Smith and Pocahontas has long been disputed, usually by that type of skeptic who says of other men: "He *talks* a good piece." This Indian girl, daughter of the mighty chief Powhatan, was only twelve or thirteen at the time she interceded and saved the life of Smith. The Indians of Virginia had a scandalous code of etiquette. Whenever a party of white men arrived at an Indian settlement, they were compelled by savage tradition to pick out Indian wives and go into the woods and make love to them. If they didn't do it, the Indian husbands would be insulted, and an insulted Indian is an Indian who is likely to remove your follicles in one lump. Distasteful as it must have been to them, the Englishmen obeyed the rules—all except Captain John Smith. He was too honorable for that sort of thing. He simply refused to violate married women. He took Pocahontas.

The captain was wounded in a powder explosion and had to

[1]Two men named Smith were key figures in the colonization of Virginia. Sir Thomas Smith, first head of the East Indies Company and one of the most influential men in England, furnished the chief moral and financial support which made the Virginia adventure possible. He wore ruffles around his neck.

return to England, and that was the end of him so far as Virginia was concerned. When he recovered his health, however, he engaged in new expeditions across the Atlantic. He gave the northeast shores of our country the name of New England and mapped the coast from Penobscot to Cape Cod. He also gave the name Plymouth to the mainland opposite Cape Cod, and there's a legend that the town of Gloucester was first called Tragabigzanda, after the insatiable Turkess.

We come now to the Pilgrim Fathers. It seems to be a fact that there was not a single Smith among the 102 passengers aboard the *Mayflower* and, saints presarve us, the captain's name was Jones. However, if those Puritans hadn't been so miserly, they'd have had a Smith as their leader. In England they had talked over their plans with Captain John because he knew more about New England than anyone else. He had written his book, *A Description of New England,* in 1618, and it contained accurate maps of the region. He had even been honored with the title of Admiral of New England. He was eager to go along as guide and adviser, but the Pilgrims turned him down, saying that it would be cheaper to buy a copy of his book than to hire him. This they did, and it got them there, but they had a wretched time of it. Captain John himself said later: "Their humorous ignorances caused them for more than a year to endure a wonderful deal of misery . . . thinking to find things better than I advised them."

In prowling around for a fresh approach to the character of Captain John, I learned that Clements Ripley, the distinguished author of Charleston, South Carolina, had lately been doing some research into the Smith story. Mr. Ripley has given me some of his own conclusions, which follow:

> As to Marshall's novel, *Great Smith,* it's a lively and entertaining book, and I think it follows the main facts of Smith's life so far as anybody can follow them. Smith was a monumental and engaging liar, but when you come to break down his tall stories there is usually a basis of truth in them. He was a roistering, tough, bawdy young man with force and brains. I think that there is no doubt of

CAPT. JOHN

his having been the slave and boy friend of the
Lady Tragabigzanda.

I estimate him as the last of the Elizabethans
and the first of the Americans. He came into command just as the rowdy, swaggering days of Elizabeth were giving place to the slick diplomacy of
James. He didn't fit the James picture. He had a
romantic dream of empire, coupled with a steel-like
practicality. He was gentry by his own say-so and
he could lick anybody who disputed him. He invented a coat of arms because he needed it to deal
with the insufferable crowd he was cursed with in
Virginia. He made friends with the Indians, not because he gave a damn about Indians, but because
Powhatan had about eight thousand good fighters
all set to wipe out the 147 ineffectives who made
up the Jamestown colony. He saved the colony
from massacre and starvation, so naturally the other
colonists hated his guts. He took the trouble to learn
the Indian language, so naturally he was accused
of treason and came close to being hanged. Actually he was a very smart boy who could handle

Powhatan and keep him bluffed out of destroying the English—which Powhatan could have done with ease. What Smith couldn't handle was the brass back home, and the incredible and fantastic brass that was sent out annually to show this man who knew his job just how he should do it.

Smith's own motivation was twofold. Virginia could supply pine, iron, tar, oak timber, all the stuff that England's sea power needed and had otherwise to import from potential enemies on the Continent. And Virginia could make a lot of money and position for Smith himself. Yet he bulks a lot bigger in the fumbling efforts to colonize America than he usually gets credit for.

As for the Pocahontas story, there is not much to substantiate it except a narrative Smith wrote years later when he was trying to pry money for a new venture out of a flock of reluctant duchesses. Probably someone told him there ought to be some love interest in his manuscript. However, the story makes good sense and I think it happened. My wife and I started to write a story about Pocahontas, but Smith keeps intruding himself, and he is so much more interesting than most of the others involved that we have had to let him take over and have his own way. He generally did anyway.

Pocahontas, by the way, judging from her portrait, could have been quite a dish. As for Smith, it is hard to realize, looking at his picture with all those deceptive whiskers, that he was stealing a continent at an age when the present-day bright boys are still in Harvard Law. He knew what the score was right from the beginning. I like him. I suggest that what this country needs today is a good fifteen-cent highball, a lot of dead politicians, and more John Smiths.

I never see one of those lean, tough Charleston tom-cats, walking a wet roof at the top of his lungs with his tail boldly in the air, without thinking of that great man, Captain John Smith.

From one of the more formalized accounts of his career we learn that this Smith of Lincolnshire, who lived three and a half centuries ago, had to contend with quipsters who made small-caliber jokes on the commonness of his name, belike: "Smith? Smith? Meseemeth to have heard ye name eftsoons, but what diddest thou with thy whiskers, Trade?" It is gratifying to know that those who uttered such gibes usually woke up in a pool of their own blood a block and a half from the scene of the crime. Captain John Smith was ever proud of his name.

In the pantheon of American folk heroes, amid the busts of the Bunyans and Crocketts and Boones and Finks, there just had to be a Smith. Thus far comparatively little has been written about him and he isn't mentioned in some of the fat books which purport to cover the major folk legends of the land. His name was Windwagon Smith and he was, to speak conservatively, a doozy. Stanley Vestal of Oklahoma wrote about him a dozen years ago; Wilbur L. Schramm did a later sketch of him for the *Atlantic Monthly,* and the most recent account of his exploits appears in Professor Walter Blair's book, *Tall Tale America* (1944). It requires a special sort of talent to write American folklore, and I don't think I have it; I'll try it just this one time:

Tom Smith was a Yankee sailor in the days of the clipper ships. Becalmed once in the South Seas, he picked up a book about the Western plains. He read of the wagon trains and the slow and painful work of getting them across the prairies. He recognized the trouble at once—the motive power was at fault, the oxen and the mules were inadequate. When he got back to Massachusetts, Smith sat down and gave the matter some thought. He *almost* invented the gasoline engine, but not quite. He got to thinking of the prairie in terms of the open sea; a prairie, he reasoned, is actually nothing more than a dry ocean and should be treated as such. He went to work and built himself a prairie schooner in his back yard, up there in Massachusetts, while his seafaring neighbors stood around and scoffed, using their index fingers to make circular motions in the neighborhood of their sideburns. In the manner of all great (and crazy) men, Smith ignored the derision of the mob, saying only, "I dad, they laughed at Clumbus too!"

His wagon conformed to the general specifications of a standard prairie schooner, but there were differences. Above the canvas top he built a deck, and projecting from the center of the deck was a tall mast. There was no rigging at the prow for hitching oxen or mules; the craft was to be steered with a tiller which moved the rear wheels, and there was a rope ladder for mounting to the deck. When he got all this completed Smith fashioned his sail, installed his binnacle, packed his sextant and telescope, thumbed his nose at his neighbors, and went zipping out of Massachusetts.

The town of Westport in Missouri was the jumping-off place for the wagon trains, and the citizens were more than mildly astonished one day when the windwagon came sailing down the main street, her skipper standing proudly on the bridge and bellowing: "Avast there, mulelubbers, sheer off!" Ignoring the livery stable, Windwagon Smith docked in front of a tavern, dropped his anchor, gathered in his sail, came down the rope ladder, and swaggered into the bar, where he confused everyone present by ordering hot rum, unbuttered. The townspeople crowded around him, inspecting his sou'wester, his gold earrings, and the naked women tattooed on his arms. They were slow to realize that he had come out to revolutionize Western transportation.

The businessmen of Westport were skeptical (they had but recently voted down parking meters) and wouldn't have a thing to do with the windwagon until its skipper had given them another demonstration, cruising over to Council Grove and back, then maneuvering his craft briskly up and down Westport's main street. It was an impressive exhibition, even to the mules of the town. One of these, possessed of a woman's intuition, is said to have watched the performance for a while and then quietly committed suicide by eating rhubarb tops.

Having convinced the town that he could reduce the travel time over the Santa Fe trail by at least six weeks, Windwagon Smith announced the formation of the Westport & Santa Fe Dry Ocean Navigating Company, Inc. Leading citizens bought stock in the company, and work was started on a super-windwagon, double the size of the biggest prairie schooner.

When it was finished, preparations were made for the launching, and Windwagon invited the principal stockholders to participate in the shakedown cruise. So these favored individuals put on claw-hammer coats, and some speeches were made (the Secretary of the Navy had been invited but couldn't come), and a band played "Red Sails in the Sunset," which hadn't been written yet. Big Nose Kate, a winsome lady who ran a tent of ill repute on the edge of town, broke a bottle of rotgut across the brow of the wooden Indian which served as figurehead; the skipper uttered the traditional cry of "All ashore that's goin' ashore," and cast off. The super-windwagon moved out onto the prairie, riding faultlessly. Satisfied that she was landworthy, Smith now crowded on full sail and she began to fly across the rolling plains. In no time at all the leading citizens of Westport began to turn assorted shades of green, and soon some of them were hanging over the rails, feeding the prairie dogs. The skipper turned back, uttering mighty profanities, cursing the Missouri landlubbers, and they in turn spoke feelingly of him as a fiend out of hell. The windwagon got back into town and the passengers staggered ashore, heading as one man for the little saloon kept by old Mother Sill. Windwagon Smith, however, purpled the welkin with shouts of contempt for the yellow-bellied landlubbers, turned his mighty vessel around, and rolled out of town. He had a favoring wind and disappeared over the western horizon quickly, and nobody ever heard of him again. Yet he left his mark in Missouri—from that day to this a native of the state is known as a Puke.

Nowhere among the roster of famous pirates do we find a first-rate bloodthirsty buccaneer named Smith. Unquestionably there were Smiths among the crews of the great pirate ships, though none ever rose to leadership. Every phase of seagoing activity, from the designing and building of ships to the sailing of them, has had its share of our clansmen. They have created beautiful ships, as in the case of Archibald Cary Smith, famous naval architect; and they have wrecked beautiful ships, as in the case of Captain E. J. Smith, who as admiral of the White Star fleet was on the bridge of the *Titanic* when she went down. (An inquiry headed by United States Senator William Alden Smith blamed Captain Smith, who went down with his ship, for going too fast.)

The great sea epic which began with the mutiny on H.M.S. *Bounty* in 1789 is familiar to most literate Americans by virtue of the *Bounty* trilogy written by Nordhoff and Hall, and to many illiterate Americans by virtue of the motion picture that was made from the book. The two chief characters in the drama were Captain Bligh and Fletcher Christian, but there were also two Smiths involved, and one of them ranks high on the dramatis personae. The *Bounty* had a company of forty-five officers and men. In the mutiny John Smith, a cook and personal servant to Bligh, remained loyal to the captain and went in the ship's launch with him. Among those who stayed behind with Christian after taking an active hand in the mutiny was a seaman named Alexander Smith. Christian took the *Bounty* to Tahiti, where all but eight of his men left him. He was joined, however, by eighteen Polynesians, twelve of them women, and the ship went wandering off to Pitcairn Island. The story of the settlement of this uninhabited island and the slow growth of the community there is told in the final volume of the trilogy. The last of the mutineers to survive was Alexander Smith. He was an old man when the American sealing ship *Topaz* called at Pitcairn twenty years after the mutiny. Up to that moment the world had no knowledge of what happened to the mutineers; the assumption was that they had all perished. Yet here was old Alexander Smith, heavy with years and contrition, and it was his story of the mutiny itself and the subsequent flight to Pitcairn that finally rounded out the picture. If anyone rises to say that his real name was not Smith, but Adams, well—it may have been. But let no pip-squeak Jones make the allegation, else I'll have to remind him that his hero, John Paul Jones, was no more a Jones than I am, his true name having been simply John Paul.

I like to think that someone named Smith had an important hand in the events of that December day back in 1903 when the Wrights did it at Kill Devil Hill. Of all those in the little group that witnessed the first flight, the one I'd enjoy identifying as a Smith was the coastguardman who got the news out to the rest of the world. He ran all the way back to town, rushed into the telegraph office, and cried out certainly one of the most historic announcements of all time: "They have flew!"

Since that day among the dunes the profession of flying has been our chief producer of heroes. And almost from the beginning the Smiths have had a hand in it. Back in the time of the earliest barnstormers there was a daredevil named Art Smith who used to tether his plane to a tree in a pasture until the engine was going good, and who went around the country proving to multitudes of skeptics that it wasn't all just newspaper talk. Many other Smiths were flying in the period when a pilot almost invariably wore a Norfolk jacket, a waxed mustache, and a cap with the bill turned to the rear; and when the planes were made from bamboo, weak spit, and piano wire.

In the early 1920s, when the air-mail service was just beginning, the Smiths all but ran the show. In 1920 a writer named John Goldstrom arranged to fly with a sack of mail from Long Island to San Francisco—the first time mail was carried by plane from one coast to the other. At the Long Island airport Goldstrom was handed the mail sack by Paul W. Smith, who was superintendent of air mail for New York. The pilot on the first leg, New York to

Cleveland, was Wesley L. Smith. At Cleveland a flier named Williams took over for the hop to Chicago, where Walter J. Smith succeeded him at the controls. Walter flew Goldstrom to Iowa City, then Harry H. Rowe took over, but at Cheyenne the fourth Smith involved in the adventure entered the picture—Harry G. Smith was at the controls for the hazardous flight across the Rockies.

Another famous air-mail pilot was Dean Smith, who subsequently became one of Admiral Byrd's pilots in the Antarctic. In his air-mail days Dean Smith wrote a classic report on a forced landing. It said:

"Dead-sticked . . . flying low . . . only place available . . . on cow . . . killed cow . . . wrecked plane . . . scared hell out of me . . . Smith."

It was in the 1920s, too, that a teen-age girl from Long Island, Eleanor Smith, attracted national attention for her flying skill and broke the endurance record for women flying solo, staying aloft something over twenty-six hours.

In early transoceanic flying, at a time when the blue yonder was really wild, three Australians and an American army officer were the most important air-borne Smiths. One of these was Captain Charles Kingsford-Smith, a genuine Smith in spite of that hyphen, who flew from the United States to Australia in 1928. More spectacular was the feat of Sir Ross Macpherson Smith and his brother, Sir Keith Smith, who made the first flight from England to Australia in 1919 and won a prize of about $50,000 for doing it.

Hero of the first round-the-world flight, undertaken in 1924 by the Army Air Corps, was Lieutenant Lowell H. Smith. He was already widely known for having proved that an airplane can be refueled while in flight. When the world-circling adventure started at Seattle, Smith was second in command to Major Frederick L. Martin and was at the controls of *The Chicago,* one of the four Douglas cruisers to start. Major Martin's plane cracked up in Alaska, and the three others went on with Smith now in command of the whole operation. Only two of the ships got back to the United States, and only one—*The Chicago*—with Lowell Smith at the controls, made it back to the starting point.

Today, as suggested in the opening lines of this book, aviation has more than its proper share of Smiths. The personnel lists of the big commercial aviation companies sparkle with the name. It is possible, for example, to get aboard a Capital Airlines plane and find it being piloted by Captain Harry Smith, who has been flying for more than thirty years, and to find sitting beside him, as co-pilot, his son Harry, Jr. Go to the executive offices of the American Airlines in New York and call on President Cyrus R. Smith, the Texas-born business genius who ran the Air Transport Command during World War II. You might find "C. R." in conference with his vice-president in charge of public relations, Rex Smith, who was once an editor of newspapers and of *Newsweek*. And with these two could be C. L. Smith, account executive for the agency which handles American Airlines advertising. In the entire American Airlines organization there are 106 individuals answering to the name of Smith, ranging from Obediah and Ira Smith, who are in the Tulsa shops, and Waldemar Smith, who is inspector of line maintenance in Chicago, to Bessie Smith, chief switchboard operator in Washington, and William B. "Red" Smith, superintendent of flight manning in New York.

Inasmuch as our highly polished civilization continues to treat bloody war as a glorious adventure, we must now consider the role the Smiths have played in the clash of arms. There is no record of it, but surely at one time or another, probably in one of the two World Wars, a bullet fired by a Smith found its mark in another Smith; more likely still, a bomb turned loose by a Smith (or a Schmidt) killed whole families of other Smiths (or Schmitts). The name crops up in almost any military engagement we examine. A Captain Smith died fighting close beside Custer at the Little Big Horn. The contingent of redcoats sent out from Boston to destroy military stores at Concord, only to meet the resistance of the Minutemen at Lexington, were under command of Lieutenant Colonel Francis Smith. And a sort of Smith, Sir Hugh Percy, had to come to the rescue. This British earl was the son of the first Sir Hugh Percy—originally Hugh Smithson—the same man who done wrong by the widow woman, with the consequence that we now have the Smithsonian Institution. For all the idle speculation that has surrounded the identity of our Unknown Soldier, the best bet of any is that his name was Smith.

The records show that there were 75,656 Smiths in the armed forces of the United States during World War II. This figure does not include the author, a heroic air-raid warden ordering lesser citizens to step lively along the streets of Jackson Heights. Nor does it include the war correspondents who were scattered over the globe. John Lardner tells me of three Smiths who were correspondents on Guam along toward the end of the war. They were called Wonderful Smith, Horrible Smith, and Pack Rat Smith. Wonderful Smith was not the Wonderful Smith who performs on the Red Skelton radio show, nor was he called Wonderful because he was wonderful. He acquired the name because his inevitable reaction to everything he saw or heard was "Wonderful!" If someone told him Spam was on the menu for dinner, he said "Wonderful!" If he heard that Colonel So-and-so had fallen into a latrine, he said "Wonderful!" If the word flashed round that a Jap attacking force was due in twenty minutes, he said "Wonderful!" On the other hand, Horrible Smith was called Horrible because those who worked with him considered him to be horrible. And Pack Rat Smith, an immense reporter out of the Midwest, had a passion for collecting all manner of souvenirs. He once flung himself into the midst of a fierce battle in order to grab a boulder the size of a basketball to place on his mantel back home.

I have heard, too, that in the Pacific theater there was a first lieutenant known affectionately to his men as Chicken S. Smith.

The Number-One Smith on our side, beyond question, was General Walter Bedell Smith, who was Eisenhower's chief of staff. This tough but agreeable Hoosier had the job of co-ordinating the European invasion plans and served so capably that Eisenhower called him the best chief of staff in the world, and Montgomery freely confessed that he'd like to steal him. He was the man, too, who signed the surrender papers as representative of the Supreme Allied Command, and we all know, of course, of his postwar service as American Ambassador to Soviet Russia. If all these things were not enough in the way of honors, let it be known that he is

perhaps the only Smith ever to have a giraffe named for him—the beast's name is Bedella and lives in the Washington zoo.

General Smith has long been known as "Beetle." Winston Churchill referred to him as "Bulldog" Smith. I asked the general if he had ever suffered any embarrassment from the fact of his being called Smith.

"When I was a small boy," he said, "I was inclined to be sensitive about the wide distribution of the name. Then I started to school and the other boys immediately gave me a nickname, Fishface, and then everything was all right—I had acquired distinction. After a while, however, that new name grew intolerable and I came to appreciate the beautiful simplicity of Smith."

As for the Smiths of Soviet Russia, the general has this to say:

"The Russian Smiths (Kuznetzov) are a much smaller clan than here, but they have made the name respected in the Soviet Union. The head of the Soviet trade union organization is a Kuznetzov, and an abler and smoother article I have yet to see."

Another great and fascinating figure in World War II was General Holland McTyeire Smith, commander of the United States Marines in the Pacific, sometimes called the father of modern amphibious warfare, and known far and wide as "Howlin' Mad" Smith.

He started out in Alabama to be a lawyer and actually practiced law in Montgomery for two years before he decided torts were not lively enough for his taste. He deserted the bar and entered the Marines and was a captain during World War I. As a preliminary to the later conflict, he organized the amphibious training operations which were to lead to major invasion successes during the actual fighting. He became known as a fierce and truculent man under some circumstances, but he could also be good-natured and jovial. His quarrel with another Smith, the Army's Major General Ralph Smith, was one of the zestful sidelights of the Pacific campaign. Ralph Smith was one of his division commanders and differed with "Howlin' Mad" on how a battle should be fought. The Marine Smith believed in plunging in and kicking the living bejazus out of them right quick, no matter what the cost; the Army Smith favored a more cautious approach which he believed would save many lives on our side. This quarrel reached a climax at the Battle of Saipan when "Howlin' Mad" canned Ralph, and for a while the big brass of the Army and the Marines forgot about the Japs and went at each other in the Pentagon. "Howlin' Mad" himself retired in 1946 with the rank of four-star general.

During the war I had a letter from two soldiers who were stationed at a camp in Florida.

"There is a guy here," they wrote, "a first sergeant who calls himself William Smith, eternally a sonofabitch beyond belief. This lying bastard enrages us constantly by claiming that he is your brother. It may not seem important to you, but you ought to do something about it, stop this insufferable jerk from claiming relationship with you."

There wasn't much I could do. He was my brother Bill—an old hand at soldiering and good at the game.[2]

There is a fairly long list of important Smiths in the Civil War between the States for Southern Independence. Among these was

[2]Some extraordinarily tough army men have borne the name of Smith, notably "Hell Roarin' Jake" in the Spanish-American War and a fabulous character known as "Hardboiled" Smith in World War I.

Andrew Jackson Smith, a native of Bucks County, Pennsylvania, where today the fecund earth grows sonnets and novels and one-act plays, not to mention a fine yield of chiaroscuro. Andrew was a West Point man and achieved early prominence as one of the leaders assigned to guide the famous Mormon Battalion on its long march to California. He became a brigadier general in the Civil War, fought through the Vicksburg campaigns, and is credited with playing a major role in the victory at Nashville. It is claimed for him that he defeated Nathan Bedford Forrest—a feat which Southerners today will tell you couldn't be done. After the war General Smith served as postmaster at St. Louis.

On the Confederate side the most eminent of all the Smiths was General Edmund Kirby-Smith. His name is revered in the South for the reason that he was the last Confederate general to give up. He was born a plain unhyphenated Smith in St. Augustine and was graduated from West Point. He was decorated for gallantry in the Mexican War and then fought the Indians in Texas. When Florida seceded he entered the Confederate service as a lieutenant colonel and advanced to brigadier general. Though severely wounded at Bull Run, he came back fighting and licked the Yanks at Richmond, Kentucky, after which he was given command of the department comprising the Confederate states lying west of the Mississippi.

Recently I heard from Tracy Hollingsworth, an old-time foreign correspondent, who furnished me with a postscript to the story of Edmund Kirby-Smith. Here is Mr. Hollingsworth's tale:

> Back in 1909 I was in Mexico for the old New York *Herald*. One day I was in a boat off Campeche when a storm came up and I was forced to land on the beach. I was surprised to find a pier jutting out into the Gulf, so I went inland until I found a native who said I was on the property of Señor Smeeth. The name did not register as Smith, and I followed the guide to the hacienda where I was received with great courtesy. Supper was served and all the conversation was in Spanish. Señor Smeeth did not look like an American and neither did I.

After dinner, however, I noticed an old copy of the Nashville *Banner* lying on a table, and I made some remark about it in English, and got an immediate response from Señor Smeeth. He turned out to be E. Kirby Smith, son of the Confederate general. He said that after the Civil War his father had been so bitter over the defeat that he had left the States, taking his two sons with him to Vera Cruz. Señor Smeeth, one of the sons, had married a Mexican girl in Vera Cruz and then settled on this five-thousand-acre property at Campeche. He owned several small ships and sold coconuts and sugar in New Orleans. Years later when I returned to Mexico I inquired about him and was told that after the Mexican revolution he had moved to Cuba where he owned a large sugar plantation.

It is a good story, illustrating as it does how a Smith is likely to pop out of the cactus in unexpected places. However, I don't vouch for the authenticity of it. The records show that General Kirby-Smith, after the war, became president of the Atlantic and Pacific Telegraph Company, president of the Western Military Academy, Chancellor of the University of Nashville, and professor of mathematics at the University of the South. If he did forsake the country and go to Mexico, he didn't stay long.

In the intersectional quarreling that preceded the Civil War a Richmond shoe dealer named James A. Smith achieved a degree of national prominence. Smith packed a Negro named Henry Brown into a wooden box only three feet long and two feet wide, labeled the crate "Shoes—This Side Up—Handle with Care," and put it on a train. In the box with Henry Brown were "a large gimlet, a bladder of water, and a few biscuits." The crate reached Philadelphia, the lid was pried off, and out stepped Henry Brown, a bundle of cricks, quickly to become famous as Box Brown. Back in Richmond, James A. Smith was so pleased with his achievement that he decided to try it again, got caught, and was sent to prison.

And a companion piece to go with the story of Box Brown is provided by Sarah Olsen. Mrs. Olsen is a native of the town of Ninety Six, South Carolina, and remembers hearing the old folks tell of the time Carpetbagger Smith came to Ninety Six after the war. He was a loud and overbearing Yankee, from all accounts, and one of the first things he did was to announce publicly that he was a Republican and that he was going to run for office as a Republican. Of course a Republican was as rare a creature in Ninety Six as a red-arsed baboon, and the folks were willing to tolerate him as a sort of curiosity, but Carpetbagger Smith got out of hand. He began trying to run the town, talking big in public places, and so one day the citizens grabbed him, crammed him into a wooden crate, nailed on the lid, and threw the crate onto the next train that came through. Tacked on the crate were two signs. One said, "Livestock." The other: "Anywhere in the Damn North."

The Proper Smiths

*Lord Byron spent a month at Malta in 1809,
making love to a lady named Mrs. Spencer
Smith. She appears as "the fair Florence" in*
Childe Harold's Pilgrimage. *Quite an honor.*

Rigid adherence to traditional forms of etiquette is required of
those who would fly in the upper echelons of society. The true
aristocrat will suffer death before he'll violate the traditions of his
class. Some of this cosmic foolishness, bordering on superstition,
drifts down into the lower divisions of the race, often with unhappy consequences. If the thought contained in the foregoing
lines isn't clear, which it isn't, let me illustrate.

I have a long and interesting letter from a lady describing certain members of the Smith branch of her family in Little Egypt
(southern Illinois). Inasmuch as I have publicly confessed to
Egyptian nativity, my correspondent suggested that her Smith relatives might be relatives of mine. It could be. These Smiths had
no drawing room, but they had their social traditions and those
traditions were dear to them. They lived beside a crick, and there
were fourteen children in the family. There was also a feud with a
neighboring clan, the Bents. The Smiths said the Bents were white
trash, and the Bents said the Smiths were so low that hogs
wouldn't stay on their place, and there was considerable shooting
and knifing back and forth in the classical American tradition.

Among the Smith girls was Effie, described by her relative (my correspondent) as "a young lady of exceptional character who could outdrink and outcuss any human being I ever knew." Came the time when Effie fell in love with one of the Bent boys, and after a brief and secret courtship in the woods, an elopement was plotted. On the appointed afternoon Effie was to creep out of the Smith house and meet her lover near the edge of the woods, where he would be waiting with a mule. Then off they would go into wild and distant lands—the adjoining county—to live in happiness ever after. As the hour for her departing approached, Effie began to worry about violating a social tradition. In those parts when a girl married it was traditional for her family to give her a feather bed, and the gift had come to have special meaning—it would insure lasting happiness to the newlyweds. So Effie sat in an upstairs room fretting about a feather bed until at last she heard the whistle from the woods. She stood up and started to leave the room, then stopped and said: "By God, I ain't a-goin' without my feather bed!" Quickly she seized the one that belonged to her mother, hurried to a window, and threw it out. It landed on a chicken, and the chicken screeched as if an H-bomb had hit it. The screech so alarmed the romantic young man in the woods that he yanked out a revolver and fired a wild shot at the barn, and within a few seconds shotguns were roaring and the whole plot was laid bare and Effie Smith was Effie Smith the rest of her life because she had rebelled against violating a social tradition.

From the crick in Egypt let us move swiftly to Park Avenue and the latest issue of the New York *Social Register*. This catalogue of Acceptable People is put together with occult characters and cryptograms, and it is almost necessary to spend a year at Miss Spence's School in order to get at its meaning. After wrestling with it a couple of hours, alternately bellowing swear words and crying out in anguish over the fate of the world, I arrived at the conclusion that there are 306 individuals named Smith listed in its main section, and 124 Smith girls who married acceptable people with other names, and one Smith girl who married a Smith. Among the society Smiths I find Senator H. Alexander Smith of New Jersey, and Mr. and Mrs. Paul Revere Smith of Staten Island. There is an Allen T. Smith, 2nd, and B. Hunt Bancroft Smith, and Abel, and

Philo, and St. Clair; also Mrs. King Smith, Mrs. Snell Smith, Mr. and Mrs. W. Schuyler Smith, and Mr. and Mrs. Harry Clapp Smith. The book lists Warren P. Smith as governor of the Society of Mayflower Descendants in the State of New York, and Miss Alla H. C. Smith as president of the Daughters of the Cincinnati.

Proportionately there appear to be more Smiths in society today than there were in the so-called Great Days. When Ward Mc-Allister compiled his list of the Four Hundred in 1892, there was but a single member of our clan on it—J. Clinch Smith, a lawyer. No Smith whatever appears among "The Four Hundred for 1950" which was rigged up by Igor Cassini (Cholly Knickerbocker) for *Cosmopolitan*. In 1941 James McKinley Bryant put out a book called *Café Society Register,* and fifteen Smiths were given the nod, including Kate, Kent, Stanley, and C. Aubrey.

Those Smiths who are acceptable in society are comparatively well behaved. No Smith, to my knowledge, has ever stood on his head at the opera, or flapped a wizened thigh onto the dinner table, or thumbed her nose straight into the lens of a newspaper camera. The only major social contretemps on the part of a Smith which I have been able to find concerns Adjutant General Ben M. Smith of Alabama. In 1941 he was aboard a yacht in Mobile Bay when he was formally presented to Evie Roberts, wife of "Chip" Roberts. General Smith bowed sweepingly, took one graceful backward step, and prat-fell into the harbor.

Oblique recognition of the fact that the Smiths are socially eligible is to be found in the writings of Mrs. Emily Post. Her famous book of etiquette includes a section devoted to the proper wording of invitations, with examples. We find in this section that Mr. and Mrs. John Huntington Smith request the pleasure of Miss Pauline Town's company at breakfast on the first of November at half after twelve, 43 Park Avenue. Later in the text these same John Huntington Smiths are found pitching a larger party, and Mrs. Post takes up the problem of responding to their invitation. Mr. and Mrs. Robert Gilding, Jr., accept with pleasure, but Mr. and Mrs. Richard Brown regret that they are unable to attend. Soon after that Mr. and Mrs. John Huntington Smith send out a bulletin, calling off the party "owing to the sudden illness of their daughter." (My own opinion is that the Smith daughter didn't get sick at all. The party was called off because Mrs. John Huntington Smith was bedded with an attack of the vapors, brought on by the refusal of the Richard Browns to come.)

In *Vogue's Book of Etiquette,* the work of Millicent Fenwick, the Smiths get scarcely any recognition at all. There are Bentons and Beechers and a Dr. van Kleburg and Thayers and old Arnold Stover and Mr. and Mrs. William Gwathmey Crosby (they flang a dance at the Plaza). The only Smith I found in the Fenwick book was not a member of society at all, but the Honorable William Addison Smith of the United States Senate. Alice Harwood Cartwright is pictured writing a letter to Senator Smith about "the proposed legislation for continuing the Office of Temporary Controls."

There is one place in the United States where the Smiths are top-hole aristocrats. The descendants of Landgrave Thomas Smith, a colonial governor who acquired class by marrying a rich widow, live in and around Charleston, South Carolina, and have been described as the most aristocratic Smiths on earth. There are Smiths in South Carolina who would make the Proper Bostonians look like week-enders on Tobacco Road. A Carolina newspaperman once told me a story about an incident in the lives of a Charleston family of highest pedigree, and in the story he called them Smiths. At that time I assumed he was using the name for purposes of hypothetical illustration; I didn't know that there were Smiths of flaming virtue and impeccable escutcheon anywhere in the United States of America.

These Smiths of Charleston were above reproach, at least in the eye of the public, and it was their chief aim in life to continue in that condition. But there was one member of the clan—let us call him Gregory—who drank more than he should and had been caught cheating at cards, and who had even been suspected of sleeping with females of questionable ancestry. He was hounded and nagged by his kinfolks until his noodle fogged up. One morning he went quietly into the bathroom and, using a straight razor, slashed both his wrists and then his throat.

When his people found him they decided, after some debate,

that the democratic thing to do would be to summon the coroner. That dignitary arrived and went into the bathroom, closing the door after him, and made a brief inspection of perhaps the goriest mess he had ever looked upon. Then he walked into the adjoining room, where the Smiths were standing, ranged against the wall, grim and silent. Their eyes were all fixed on the coroner challengingly. Their eyes were *telling him*. And he knew exactly what was expected of him.

"Well," said the head of the clan at last.

The coroner cleared his throat. "A perfectly simple case," he announced. "Gregory died a natural death, of heart failure."

And so it appeared in the press—to the satisfaction of all concerned.

The Rhetts of South Carolina constitute one of the oldest families of the region, dating back to colonial times, and it should be mentioned here that some of them are actually Smiths. Among the early governors of North Carolina was General Benjamin Smith, who was, incidentally, the first benefactor of the University of North Carolina. He had a brother named James, and they got into a long-term quarrel which ended with James getting so all-fired fed up that he renounced the name of Smith, took his grandmother's surname, Rhett, and moved to South Carolina, settling in the Beaufort area. His descendants are, of course, known as Rhetts today, but they are Smiths.

While we are still in South Carolina, let us take notice of a lady who is one of the state's foremost citizens—Alice Ravenel Huger Smith, a Charleston aristocrat who is nationally prominent as a water-color artist.

Since fox hunting is generally associated with the gentry, we may also mention Harry Worcester Smith, a native of Massachusetts and a famous master of foxhounds. Polite history says Harry was the key figure in the "golden era" of Virginia fox hunting. In England, Thomas Smith was master of Hambledon hounds. He was the author of *The Life of a Fox, Written by Himself,* meaning the fox wrote it, and he was reputed to know foxes better than dogs know them. He is not to be confused with Thomas Assheton

Smith, master of the Quorn pack, who was acclaimed as the foremost fox hunter of his day.

In 1870 at Mobile, Alabama, there lived a plump and proper young lady named Alva Smith, daughter of a well-to-do cotton planter. Alva was sent to France for her education and soon after her return, in 1874, when she was twenty-one, she married William Kissam Vanderbilt of New York, grandson of the old Commodore and heir to half of an estate estimated at $200,000,000. Thus she became the Smith family's greatest contribution to American society, to be known in time as "the indefatigable duchess of the Gilded Age."

Following her marriage Alva said: "I was the first girl of my set to marry a Vanderbilt." What she meant was that she had dropped below her social station in choosing a husband. In that era of elegance the Vanderbilts were regarded as a vulgar, parvenu tribe, and when Alva established herself in New York she found she was not quite acceptable because Mrs. William Astor wanted no part of her. The Astor clan, wealthy beyond belief, ruled the social roost. Their money came from old John Jacob Astor, who took his profits from the fur trade, invested in mortgages on New York business property, foreclosed on them, and became the Landlord of New York. And Mrs. William Astor was the Queen.

Alva Smith Vanderbilt was a spunky lass. Nuts, quoth she, to Mrs. Astor. And she drew her battle lines, determined that she would conquer New York society; and not only conquer it, but rule it. She hired a famous architect, Richard M. Hunt, and had him design and build a three-million-dollar house at Fifth Avenue and Fifty-second Street, and she filled this house with Renaissance furniture, priceless tapestries, medieval armor, and all that sort of thing. She didn't know it, but Architect Hunt was a man with sly whims, and the mansion he built for her was a replica of the house of Jacques Coeur, the greatest social upstart of the Middle Ages. When she got her house all finished, Alva sat down and contrived a Vanderbilt coat of arms, featuring a cluster of acorns. Someone asked her why she chose this particular nut and she replied: "Because, my dear, great oaks from little acorns grow."

Now the Smith girl was ready to open the battle. She announced that on March 26, 1883, she would have a housewarming —the most magnificent fancy-dress ball in the history of America. She was shooting the works with a party that would cost upward of a quarter million dollars.

Everybody in town started talking about it, and Miss Caroline Astor, daughter of the Queen, assuming that she would be invited, began making her plans. She and several of her friends would attend as the "Star Quadrille," performing a little pageant in which each girl would wear one of those new-fangled electric lights on her forehead, denoting vacuity.

Of course Alva Smith Vanderbilt heard of Miss Caroline's eager planning and she let it ride for a while, then dropped the word that, regrettable as it might seem, she would be unable to invite Miss Caroline because no Astor had ever called on her. Now there was hell to pay in the baronial halls of the Astor tribe. Scenes of anguish and hysteria, shouting and pouting, and perhaps even the shattering of an occasional vozz. At last Mrs. William Astor grat her teeth, clumb into her surrey, rode to the Vanderbilt house, left her card in the foyer, and drove home, a beaten biscuit if there ever was one. That was enough—the mere dropping of a calling card on a table signified abject surrender—and Alva was in! The Smith girl from Alabama had beaten the enemy to its knees, and the party itself was a thing to talk about for years to come. Alva appeared as a Venetian princess surrounded by housebroken white doves. And even General Ulysses S. Grant attended and, as usual, got tiddled and burnt himself putting the wrong end of his cigar into his mouth.

Alva now invaded Newport and built another magnificent mansion, this one costing, with furnishings, something over nine million dollars. As Mrs. W. K. Vanderbilt she had three children, William K., Harold Sterling, and Consuelo. In 1895 she divorced Vanderbilt and a year later became Mrs. Oliver Hazard Perry Belmont. And as Mrs. O. H. P. Belmont she continued for many years to be one of the most potent forces in New York and Newport society. She was never one to be intimidated by other great ladies. Once she encountered the celebrated Mrs. Stuyvesant

(Mame) Fish in the Newport Casino. Mrs. Fish was in a
state.

"I have just heard," she stormed, "what you said about me at
Tessie Oelrich's last night. You can't deny it because she told me
herself. You told everybody that I look like a frog."

Alva didn't bat an eye. "A *toad*, my dear, a *toad*," she corrected.

Social eminence and wealth were not enough for our Alva—now
she wanted to get a title in the family. Her connivance in forcing
the marriage of her daughter Consuelo to the Duke of Marlbor-

ough has been argued about for years. Consuelo resisted with all her might because she was in love with an American, but Alva wanted nobility in the family and she was going to get it. At one point in the proceedings she called the recalcitrant Consuelo on the carpet and uttered a horrifying threat: if Consuelo didn't agree at once to marry the duke she, Alva, would shoot this American boy friend dead, and be hanged for it, and thus bring hideous disgrace on the family, and it would be Consuelo's fault. In the face of such a thunderous threat Consuelo surrendered and married her duke, and the duke himself got two and a half million dollars' worth of railroad stock for agreeing to the alliance. The marriage, which was later annulled in Rome, was said to have cost the Vanderbilt family ten million dollars. Consuelo afterward became Mrs. Jacques Balsan and is not to be confused with another Consuelo Vanderbilt, who married Earl E. T. Smith. This latter Consuelo is known today as Mrs. Vanderbilt Smith. I hope that I have these details straight. The difficulty of untangling the Vanderbilts has been ably demonstrated by Frank Sullivan in his essay, *The Vanderbilt Convention*, a classic of genealogical probing. Mr. Sullivan concludes:

"Now, there was a time when the Smiths outnumbered the Vanderbilts by two to one, but that era is passing. The Vanderbilts are beginning to absorb the Smiths, although as yet no Vanderbilt has overtly married a Jones. Still, you never can tell. The descendants of the doughty old Commodore are an impulsive and passionate race and if one of them ever chanced upon an unusually comely Jones there is no telling what might ensue."

Descending the social scale somewhat until we arrive among the criminal classes, we find on the evidence of the Federal Bureau of Investigation that the Smiths maintain their position of leadership here as elsewhere. But they lead in numbers only—not in quality of achievement. It is a rare thing to find our name on lists of the most spectacular American scoundrels, from Benedict Arnold down to Al Capone. In 1950 the FBI made up a list of the ten "most wanted criminals" in the United States. It is an interesting roster from the standpoint of nomenclature. The names on it are

Holden, King, Nesbit, Mitchell, Pinson, Downs, Jackson, Wright, Shelton, and Guralnick.

The FBI estimates the number of persons in the United States with arrest records at 7,500,000. Arrested persons giving the name Smith total 204,900. But the important fact here is that more than half of all those giving the name Smith when they were arrested were downright liars. Officials of the FBI devote close attention to criminal aliases, and they say that the bias of arrested persons in favor of Smith as an alias amounts to serious discrimination against our good name. Of the 204,900 "Smiths" who have been arrested, 108,597, or 53 per cent, were using the name to cover up their true identities.

It must be noted, too, that the proportion of Smiths in the general population—slightly more than one per cent—is almost exactly the same in the criminal classes. Among the items turned up in the FBI files was a sort of case history of a high-class bordello. The manager of the establishment was meticulous in her bookkeeping, and the FBI has a record of all her customers over a period of several years. The books show that slightly more than one per cent of those customers were named Smith. In my own opinion this figure is not trustworthy. A man named Smith who checks in at a cat house quite probably gives the name of Brown, while Brown in turn identifies himself as Mr. Smith.

The use of Smith as an alias has always been habitual procedure among wrongdoers. That ugly monarch, Louis Philippe, when he fled before the French revolution of 1848, carried papers identifying himself as "William Smith" in order to effect his escape to England. David Herold, in flight with John Wilkes Booth after the assassination of Lincoln, got across the Potomac bridge and into Virginia by using the name Smith. Harry K. Thaw, upon his arrival at a police station after shooting Stanford White, identified himself as John Smith, eighteen, of Washington. It seems to me that the thing should have gone out of fashion long ago—that police suspicion would automatically deepen the moment a prisoner identified himself as Smith.

The FBI people say that the Smiths of law-breaking caliber are mere journeymen criminals and that there is no really major-league monster among them. With the possible exception of a gentleman named Jefferson Randolph Smith, whose exploits shall be considered in a few moments, we have given the nation no first-rate outlaws to stand beside Jesse James and Gerald Chapman and Pretty Boy Floyd.

We have never had a Smith who could compare with England's famous George Joseph Smith. He was a shabby little man who ran an antique shop in Bristol. He wasn't much to look at, but the official record describes him as a man of immense amatory capabilities and capacities. When ladies came into his store to inspect his antiques, it was his custom to invite them into a back room where he showed them (to use Thorne Smith's phrase) his old and rare. Around 1908 he fell irrevocably in love with one of these back-room customers, a Miss Pegler, and married her. This Pegler person was an evil character, given to frenzied outbursts and mad ravings, vilifying the man who was doing the most for her, making intolerable demands, and behaving generally like a bitch in a barrel of sawdust. Moreover, she had expensive tastes, and she took to nagging her Mr. Smith unmercifully because they didn't have enough money. For love of her he launched his career in crime. He began taking trips to London and putting himself in the way of widows and spinsters and staying with them awhile, even marrying them, until he could get his claws on their savings. Between 1908 and 1912 he swindled about thirty different women, using assumed names to marry ten of them. Back in Bristol, the former Miss Pegler was still not satisfied and continued her cosmic belly-aching. So in 1912 George Joseph Smith traveled to Weymouth and there met one Bessie Mundy, a lady with a fortune of about ten thousand dollars. He married Bessie and took her to live at a boardinghouse. Almost at once he began spreading the word around that his bride was subject to epileptic fits. When Bessie was found drowned in the bathtub, a coroner's jury quickly decided that she had been seized by one of her fits, and her sorrowing husband took the ten thousand and hurried home to Miss Pegler.

The following year George Joseph hit the trail again and this time chose a spinster named Alice Burnham for his wife. He pursued the same course with Alice as he had with Bessie, and when she was found dead in the tub, it was a clear case of accidental drowning during an epileptic fit. A clear case, that is, to everyone but a London doctor who happened to read newspaper accounts of both cases and who had a hunch they might be related in some way. The doctor's name was Conan Doyle. He wrote to Scotland Yard recommending that an investigation be started, but Scotland Yard was busy with other matters and paid no heed to the creator of Sherlock Holmes. Another year passed, and Conan Doyle picked up his morning paper and read where a spinster named Margaret Lofty had married a certain John Lloyd and the day after the wedding had been found dead in her bathtub. Doyle slapped on his hat and went around to the London house where this latest death had occurred. He made his own investigation and compelled Scotland Yard to listen to him, and in the end they seized the little antique dealer, George Joseph Smith, put him on trial, and then took him out and lengthened his neck. All well and good, yet I feel somehow that Smith was not altogether culpable—that a Pegler should have been hanged too.

Back in Revolutionary times there was a family known as the Horseblock Smiths living in upstate New York, and they turned out a pretty fair felon in the person of Claudius Horseblock Smith. He was leader of an outlaw band and was sometimes called the Cowboy of the Ramapos. The term "cowboy" had no heroic connotations in those days but was applied to marauding bands of Tory roughnecks. During the Revolution, Horseblock Smith ravaged the Hudson Valley, raiding farms, harassing Washington's troops, torturing and murdering and stealing. He was finally captured by a man named Titus and was convicted of high crimes at Goshen, New York. When he arrived on the gallows he asked for a moment's delay, then sat down on the platform and took off his shoes.

"I just want to prove," Horseblock explained, "that my mother was a liar—she was always sayin' that I'd die with my boots on."

Jefferson Randolph Smith was probably our clan's most distinguished rascal operating in America. As Soapy Smith he has been celebrated in song and story, not to mention poetry. Alva Johnston has recently described him (in his biography of Wilson Mizner) as "the greatest American professor of sharp practice, gentle larceny, and all-around crime." As a boy Jeff Smith traveled with a circus and then in the 1880s, when he was in his twenties, turned up in Denver with the skin game that gave him his sobriquet.

He would set up his tripes-and-keister on a street corner in the neighborhood of the Union Station and go to work selling "lucky soap." His customers paid a dollar for the privilege of selecting a bar of soap from his basket, having seen him, with their own eyes, wrap ten- or twenty-dollar bills in with several of the bars. Usually his confederates got the soap with the money, but Smith was not so greedy that he wouldn't, on occasion, let a genuine customer get hold of a ten-dollar bill. Maybe once a year he'd let it happen. He made such a good thing out of this little game that in time he was able to open a gambling house on Larimer Street. After a while, however, the Denver police got so powerful that they were able to order him out of town, and he transferred his activities to the mining camps in the mountains.

In the 1890s, when the rush to the Yukon started, Soapy Smith was in the vanguard, still relying on his lucky-soap pitch as a basic living but never backing away from any sort of work so long as it was crooked. He settled in Skagway and before long he was recognized as "King" of that wild and roistering community. He ran the principal saloon, called Jeff's Place, and he conducted a sort of training school for neophyte swindlers and holdup men. He was not at all averse to killing and personally did away with an unspecified number of individuals whose style he didn't like. He ran the town, and it was a rare bird who came in from the States with a piece of money in his pocket who ever got past Soapy. He rooked them when they came in and he rooked them again when they came out of the hills with their gold. At the height of his reign there was a holdup every hour of the day in Skagway. If he couldn't get it that way, he'd lure them into a poker game, and nobody ever left one of Soapy's poker games with anything more negotiable than the hair on his chest. Finally the respectable citizens of the town, just as in the Western movies, got together and formed a Committee of One Hundred and announced that Soapy and his gang had to leave. Soapy in turn formed a Committee of Three Hundred and ordered the respectable element out of town. The dispute ended in a shootin' war, and a bullet ended the bright career of the most accomplished Smith who ever chose crime for his life's work.

A Child's Garden of Smiths

> A Smithfield bargain *is a business deal in which the purchaser is taken in. The phrase is sometimes used to describe a marriage for money, wherein the party putting up the money would have been better off investing in a bucket of hog livers.*

A sportive etymologist might spend a pleasant hour or so chasing *Smith* and its derivatives through the reference books. The trail would lead him into science and medicine, into the world of sports, and though a professional word-wrangler probably wouldn't venture that far—into the realm of business.

He would have to deal with the verb *smit*, which means to tarnish, to stain, to disgrace or bring into disgrace. (I ruint this girl and smit my whole family.) The same word can mean a stroke, a blow, a jingling or crashing sound. (Then I heard this smit and jumped like a ghost had just goost me.)

The word *smither* in Britain means a smith who trues blades, but the common expression *smithereens* is not related to it, meaning fragments, and is of Irish origin. (So I heaved this H-bomb at 'em and smashed 'em into smithereens.)

In Scotland the word *smithydander* means a cinder; now you'll know what to do if a Scotsman ever comes up to you and asks you to remove the blawdy smithydander from his eye. And in America a person can be called a *Dick Smith* for *Dick Smithing* it. The original Dick Smith was probably a professional ballplayer who had no inclination to mix socially with other ballplayers. He was a loner. More recently a *Dick Smith* is a person who drinks alone, a custom which some people consider to be evil. I'm told that a *Smith* means something in the game of cricket, but so do *sticky wicket* and *popping crease* and *googly*, so let's not bother about it. In England, also, there is a clumsy expression, "What an O. Smith!" It is the same as saying, "What a grim jest!" It comes from the cavernous laugh of a certain O. Smith, an actor of villainous roles around 1840.

We find a *smithite* as well as a *smithsonite* in chemistry. Smithite is a silver sulphantimonite occurring in small red monoclinic crystals and was named for G. F. H. Smith, an English scientist. Smithsonite is a mineral species consisting of zinc carbonate and forming an important ore of zinc. It is rhombohedral in crystallization and isomorphous with calcite and chalybite, as who isn't these days? A bright yellow variety containing cadmium (S. Parkes?) has been found in Arkansas and is known locally as turkey-fat ore. In Britain smithsonite is usually called calamine, though this would be sorry news to the man who gave his name to it—James Smithson. The very thing that he did was to distinguish the stuff from calamine. He is the same James Smithson who put up the money for the Smithsonian Institution.

Smith's longspur is a bird, named for Gideon B. Smith, and sometimes called the painted longspur. How does one go about getting a bird named for one? In this case, Gideon B. Smith was simply a friend of Audubon. For all I know, Gideon may have despised birds.

Coming to medicine, the Smiths have made the following contributions:

Smith's Dislocation of the Foot: Dislocation upward and backward of all the metatarsal bones, together with the internal cuneiform. (Must mean the toes turn up horribly; sounds awful.)

Smith's Fracture: A transverse fracture about 5 cm. above the lower extremity of the radius.

Smith's Reaction for Bile Pigments: Pour tincture of iodine

carefully on the liquid to be tested. A green ring divides the liquids. (Don't go to Dick Smithing it with this stuff.)

Smith's Cramp: Muscular spasm of a blacksmith's arm and hand. (The patient doesn't *have* to be a blacksmith; you could get it from milking a stubborn moose.)

Any list of distinguished Smiths is certain to contain the names of those who are famous in the medical world. Sir T. Smith was the first man to make accurate observations of infantile scurvy, or scurvy rickets, or Barlow's disease, in England in 1876. A Scottish physician named William Smith was co-founder with Dr. Andrew T. Still of the American School of Osteopathy at Kirksville, Missouri, in 1892. Nathan Smith, a physician in Massachusetts, was founder of the Yale Medical School, and his grandson, Alan Penniman Smith, a surgeon in Baltimore, was instrumental in convincing Johns Hopkins that he ought to establish the Johns Hopkins Hospital.

Theobald Smith, famous as director of animal pathology for the Rockefeller Institute, solved the problem of Texas fever in cattle after long and patient research. Texas fever in people remains to be cured. And Dr. Margaret Cammack Smith, a nutrition specialist in Arizona, lists among her discoveries the cause of mottled enamel in human teeth, and the baking qualities of Arizona soft wheat. Recently come into prominence on the American medical scene is Dr. Austin Smith, who succeeded Dr. Morris Fishbein as editor of *The Journal of the American Medical Association*.

On a spring day in 1950 Max Lerner started off his daily essay in the New York *Post* with this paragraph:

> If any painter ever crowds the history of our time
> into a single canvas, as the Renaissance painters
> used to do when they put saints and grandees and
> warriors into a vast group scene, there will have to
> be a place reserved for a man called Smith.

Mr. Lerner was saluting Dr. James J. Smith, director of research on alcoholism at the New York University-Bellevue Medical Center. Dr. Smith had but recently issued a report on certain investigations he had conducted among two thousand chronic alcoholics. He had determined, he said, that alcoholism is in large part a physical rather than a mental problem; a matter of chemistry or metabolism rather than of psychic maladjustment. This would seem to be a revolutionary theory inasmuch as the problem up to now has been considered a job for the psychiatrist instead of the medical man. The whole business is concerned with the nasty little pituitary gland and its failure, among alcoholics, to furnish proper stimulation to the adrenals and sex glands, and this condition can be rectified, says Dr. Smith, by the pumping in of certain hormones. Under such treatment the alcoholic of today can become the normal drinker of tomorrow. If this be true, it is of immense importance to thousands of alcoholics, and Mr. Lerner's evaluation of Dr. Smith is conservative, at least from their viewpoint. I never knew an alcoholic who didn't curse his condition and yearn for the ability to drink without getting slobbering drunk. Until Dr. Smith came along they had been told that they would never, so long as they lived, be able to guzzle sensibly.

Dr. Smith's conclusions are of particular interest here because a question arises: If his theory pans out, what happens to the far-flung organization called Alcoholics Anonymous? It looks to me as if it would go the way of the Whig party and the whooping crane. There would be a touch of irony in it if the researches of a Smith served to kill off this group which had its origin with a man named Smith—a surgeon in Ohio. He was in the midst of a fearful brannigan when he stumbled into a New York broker, a man who was himself between sprees. The broker nursed the surgeon back to soberness, then they sat down and discussed the horror of their mutual affliction, and out of that talk came Alcoholics Anonymous. In a few short years it has acquired a membership of nearly a hundred thousand problem drinkers—and now? It's my guess that at least ninety thousand of them are ready to yell: "Where the hell are those hormones, Doc?"

The author of this book confesses here and now that he has very likely overlooked, through his invincible ignorance, some of the most important Smiths of scientific investigation. The attainments of Mr. L. B. Smith, for example, are probably of much greater importance than the founding of osteopathy.

I came upon a mention of Mr. L. B. Smith in an old copy of the *Scientific American*. A man named Montgomery had written to the magazine raising the devil about the implied complacency of later mathematicians to accept as correct and adequate Shanks's early-nineteenth-century approximation of pi to 707 decimal places by Machin's formula. With considerable conviction the letter went on to say:

> In 1854 the calculation to 500 decimal places was verified, and in 1945 Mr. D. F. Ferguson, of the Royal Naval College and the University of Manchester, by use of Loney's formula verified Shanks's approximation to 527 places, but found the rest of Shanks's result incorrect. Then Dr. J. W. Wrench, Jr., and Mr. L. B. Smith, by Machin's formula, substantiated Ferguson's finding of Shanks's errors. Suffice it to say that at present Ferguson, Smith, and Wrench are in agreement on the value of pi through their computations to 808 places and that the checked ENIAC determination, based on Machin's formula, confirms their work and extends the value to 2,035 certain figures, and 2,037 probable.

What do you make out of that? How long do you think Ferguson, Smith, and Wrench are going to remain in agreement? I have my own theories, of course, but I'd rather keep them to myself. The one thing that is not clear to me is the whereabouts and the attitude of this man Shanks. We see Ferguson, Wrench, and Smith all going out of their way to discredit him, drilling and chipping away at his approximation of pi, which surely must have been close to his heart. Why haven't Loney and Machin come forward to defend old Shanks? I'd do it myself, but I have an appointment with the dentist.

Ira L. Smith, the indefatigable researcher, grew mildly fatigable at last in connection with some digging I asked him to do in

Washington. He called at the United States Patent Office to find out if people named Smith have done much in the way of inventing things.

"I'm willing to take oath," he reported back to me after a few days had passed, "that the Smiths of this country have done nothing since 1776 but have children and take out patents. Approximately four thousand patents have been issued to Smiths *since 1930*. Each of these inventions is represented in the master file by a sheet of thin paper. The sheets run about a hundred to the inch, and I figured there were about forty inches in the Smith section. That's in addition to the thousands upon thousands not yet herded into the consolidated file—meaning the hordes of Smiths who patented inventions between about 1800 and 1930. It would take a lifetime to go through them, and I have no lifetime handy."

From talks with A. W. Kaiser, chief of administrative services in the Patent Office, Ira did establish an important point—no really earth-shaking invention has ever come from a Smith. There have been many important ones, but nothing that will go into the schoolbooks with the cotton gin, the reaper, the electric light, and the Meyer Reversible Jiffy Bow Tie.

What we have at hand, then, is a mere sampling of inventive Smiths out of the Patent Office files. The first of the breed to get a patent was Robert Smith of Pennsylvania, who devised a mold board for a plow in 1880. Next came Moses Smith of Massachusetts with a machine for watering cattle. Number Three was Simon Smith of New Haven, inventor of "an improvement in gallows, or suspenders for breeches, pantaloons, or trowsers." Other Smith inventions include:

A patent for a smut machine was issued to Hiram Smith of New York.

Standfast Smith of Suffolk, Massachusetts, devised a method for extracting salt from sea water in 1806.

Elisha Smith of New York—a gout nostrum.

Christopher H. Smith of New York—"revolving glasses for spectacles." (The purpose of this invention is not clear—it could have been to drive people crazy.)

Newman W. Smith—a new way to have babies, in his own words: "A seat which, from its peculiar form and structure, closely resembles that part of the human form between the knees and the breech. And I further claim varying the angle which the seat makes with the back, by moving the middle posts forward and backward, to afford relief to a patient in travail by means of changing her position and furnishing supports for her feet and limbs, and objects for her hands to grip."

Charles Smith of Buffalo—a hair restorer made from burdock root, Peruvian wound balsam, lemon juice, castor oil, alcohol, oil of roses, and rain water.

William G. Smith of Pennsylvania—a self-cleaning spittoon.

Henry S. and Hiram F. Smith of New Hampshire—a beverage made by fermenting the following mixture: "American sarsaparilla, life of man, prince's pine, water, sugar, oil of checkerberry, oil of sassafras, and molasses." (Goes good with William G. Smith's self-cleaning spittoon.)

George P. Smith of Connecticut—walking stilts.

William R. Smith of New Hampshire—"an apparatus for cooling or warming the vagina or rectum."

Frank E. Smith of Toledo—an "office tickler."

William Smith of Minnesota—"a leg spreader for horses."

Ernest B. Smith of Massachusetts—a trolley-wire cleaner.

Jay H. Smith of Rochester—"sticky flypaper."

Henry Smith of New York—an undertaker's stool.

The Patent Office files, being loaded with Smiths, offer additional evidence that Smiths are likely to have unusual first names. Among them are Uzziel, Orison, Jabez, Prince, Abia, Job, Millage, Anselmo, Comly, Eliphalet, Datus, Jehial, Oleny, Scepter, and Yorick. The shortest given name in the lists is that of Ai Smith. I strongly suspect that this man's name was misread somewhere along the line, that actually he was A-1, or A Number One Smith. If so, he had his counterpart in West Virginia, where for many years the publisher of the *Daily Oil Review* was Okay Smith.

Possibly the most-talked-about invention ever to come from the mind of a Smith was the costume for females called bloomers.

Time after time I have heard or read that bloomers were invented by a lady named Amelia Bloomer. The truth is that Elizabeth Smith stitched up the first pair. She was the daughter of Gerrit Smith, the Utica philanthropist, Abolitionist, friend of John Brown, and foe of liquor, who was quite a fellow in his own right and went mad. After she had married a banker named Miller, Elizabeth ran up a pair of bloomers for herself and began wearing them around the house. They were not like the gym bloomers worn by schoolgirls when I was young and deeply interested in such things. The first bloomers, in fact, were big things—they looked as if a dirigible could be docked in them.

At that time Mrs. Amelia Jenks Bloomer was editor of a publication called *The Lily*, printed at Seneca Falls and dedicated to temperance and the rights of women. One season Elizabeth Smith Miller came to Seneca Falls to visit her cousin, Elizabeth Cady Stanton, and that's how Amelia Bloomer found out about the pants. Mrs. Bloomer wrote a strong piece in *The Lily* on "Sanitary Attire for Women" and praised Elizabeth's invention (the sanitary qualities of the costume escape me; the meaning, perhaps, is that dust couldn't get in). From this article the public got the idea that Amelia was responsible for the new mode and started calling the things bloomers. Mrs. Stanton herself wrote in her memoirs about Elizabeth: "To see my cousin, with a lamp in one hand and a baby in the other, walk upstairs with ease and grace, while, with flowing robes, I pulled myself up with difficulty, lamp and baby out of the question, really convinced me that there was sore need of reform in women's dress."

An inventor from Wayback[1] was Uriah Smith, one of the early leaders of the Seventh-Day Adventists. Uriah was a New Hampshire man who went west to Battle Creek, Michigan. He had a wooden leg and he was handy with tools. While he sat around

[1]The newspapers frequently report changes in the names of towns. I have a suggestion to make. Let some town, dissatisfied with its present name, adopt the name of Wayback. Its people will go forth and blazon that name before the world, saying, "I'm a two-fisted drinker from Wayback," or "I'm a southpaw pitcher from Wayback." It is a name that will bring quick fame to the town that takes it.

arguing religion and politics with his cronies, he had a habit of whittling away at his wooden leg and he became an expert wood carver. He had trouble maneuvering the false leg when it came time to kneel and pray, which was often, so he rigged up a swivel foot and had it patented. Then he invented an automatic folding school seat—the kind that flops back when the pupil stands up. His most spectacular invention, however, was inspired by the automobile, which was beginning to appear on the streets of Battle Creek toward the end of Uriah's life. He recognized the basic reason for public antagonism toward the auto—the dad-burn contraption was forever frightening horses, causing them to rear and bolt. So Uriah invented a false front for automobiles—a large gismo shaped to represent the head and shoulders of a pleasant-looking horse. This contrivance was fitted over the hood of an automobile, and it was Uriah's theory that as it chugged along the street, real horses would regard it with interest rather than fear. I don't know if he ever got into production, if these things actually appeared on the streets; if they did, I imagine there were, in Battle Creek, some deeply chagrined (and contused) stallions.

Let us not, through considering such things as self-cleaning spittoons, bloomers, office ticklers, and smut machines, overlook the fact that there have been some valuable contributions by inventive Smiths. The first cantilever bridge, for example, was designed by Charles Shaler Smith for the Cincinnati Southern Railroad crossing of the Kentucky River. This bridge was built in 1877, and two years later Smith designed the first hanging railroad bridge near Canon City, Colorado.

Horace Smith and Daniel Baird Wesson collaborated on the invention of the Smith & Wesson revolver, which they began manufacturing in Massachusetts in 1857. Hamilton E. Smith of Pittsburgh invented the first practical mechanical washing machine in 1858. Another Hamilton Smith, a professor at Kenyon College in Ohio, patented a tintype camera in 1856.

Sir Francis Pettit Smith took out a patent on a screw propeller in 1836, six weeks ahead of John Ericsson, and built the screw steamer *Archimedes* for the British Navy. This whole business of the screw propeller is confused. In a recent magazine article I said flatly that Sir Francis invented it. You wouldn't think that people could feel so strongly about screw propellers, considering that they're under water and out of sight. Letters of abuse poured in, most of them touting the Swede Ericsson, although one correspondent displayed shimmering originality, claiming the screw propeller was invented by a man named Grimes. The *Encyclopedia Britannica,* for once, is mealymouthed and congressional in reporting on the matter, stating simply that Smith and Ericsson took out patents on screw propellers in the same year. To forestall any further abuse, I want it known right now that I don't give a good goddamn who invented the screw propeller.

A few more inventive brothers have been:

Major O. J. Smith, who invented the newspaper syndicate in 1882 and is therefore partly responsible for comic strips.

Joel West Smith of Connecticut, who invented the Braille typewriter after recasting the whole Braille system. He was himself blind.

Silas G. Smith of Hollis Center, Maine, inventor of the locomotive snowplow.

Angus Smith, discoverer of the Angus Smith Method (in plumbing) of protecting iron pipes from corrosion. The Angus Smith Method consists of dipping the pipes, while hot, into a mixture of coal tar, pitch, resin, and linseed oil. This used to be done to humans.

It is manifestly impossible even to estimate the impact of the Smiths on American commerce, beyond saying that it has been enormous. They range from men like the late James Dickinson Smith, banker, president of the New York Stock Exchange, and commodore of the New York Yacht Club, to Si Smith, who runs the corner grocery. They include genteel citizens like Geoffrey S. Smith, president of the austere Girard Trust Company in Philadelphia, where everyone calls everyone else "Mister" and bows to depositors and bank examiners alike. And they also include such characters as Uncle Billy Smith—the man who really started the oil industry. Uncle Billy was a blacksmith in Titusville, Pennsylvania, in 1859, when a man named Edwin L. Drake came along with an idea that it might be profitable to tap pools of oil beneath the surface of the earth, pipe the stuff aboveground, and invent automobiles. Uncle Billy Smith and his son Sam did the drilling, while the rest of the population stood around and made smart remarks. In the end, of course, Uncle Billy brought in the first oil well. Hence Rockefeller Center.

The Register of Directors and Executives in American business is loaded with Smiths, and the Alger formula fits many of them. Herbert Edward Smith, president of the United States Rubber Company, started as a salesman and now lives on Park Avenue. He went a long way in rubber. Blaine Spray Smith, an Iowa boy who became a cement peddler in Chicago, rose to leadership in several cement companies and even got to be a director of United States Steel and joined a yacht club. He went far in cement.[2]

For brilliant attainment, consider Thomas H. Smith, once the leading importer of tea in the United States. He achieved one of the most magnificent insolvencies in the history of American business. When he went bankrupt in 1828, his New York company owed the government alone more than three million dollars in unpaid duties on tea. Those were the days, remember, when a dollar went a lot farther in bankruptcy than it does today.

Successful Smiths and rich Smiths are scattered over the country and through the pages of our economic history. One of the most colorful was Borax Smith, otherwise Francis Marion Smith, an adventurous man out of Wisconsin. He and a partner named Coleman went West and discovered the borax deposits in Nevada and Death Valley. They monopolized the market, invented the twenty-mule train, and of course got rich. Borax Smith, incidentally, published the only magazine ever put out for mules. It was called *Blue Mule*.

[2]The Alger pattern for success doesn't fit in the case of the eminent editor and general manager of the San Francisco *Chronicle,* Mr. Paul Smith. He achieved the editorship of the *Chronicle* at the age of twenty-seven and attributes his success to the fact that he never sold papers on the streets when he was a boy.

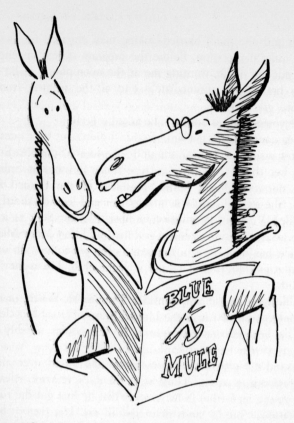

During the nineteenth century the name "George Smith of Coalville" was familiar to everyone in England. George was the son of a bricklayer, educated himself, made a fortune in business, and became a philanthropist. He was naturally unpopular because he worked for the betterment of conditions among laborers and their children. He is not to be confused with George Smith, who lived in England during the same period and who was a famous Assyriologist. An Assyriologist is not a medical man, but a scientist who digs at Nineveh.

Smith as a brand name is prominent in several branches of American merchandising. One day I arrived at an NBC studio to be a guest on the Mary Margaret McBride program. Miss McBride always has a studio audience consisting of about fifty women and one small harried-looking man engaged in leading a life of quiet desperation. Before the program started an engineer called out my name, wanting me at the microphone so he could take a brain level. Immediately one of the women from the audience grabbed me.

"Are you Split Pea Smith?" she asked eagerly.

"I beg your pardon, madam," I said. "I didn't get your question."

"I just wanted to know," she said, "if you are Split Pea Smith." I told her that I was sorry to report that I was not Split Pea Smith, nor was I Mock Turtle Smith, Noodle Smith, or Ox Tail Smith. She immediately lost interest in me. I learned shortly that the Allen V. Smith Company in upstate New York is a large enterprise dealing in wholesale groceries, and that Mary Margaret McBride has done such a thorough sales promotion job on one particular product that when people think of split peas they think of Smith.

Middle-aged people will remember the Smith Wheel—a motorized gadget attached to the rear axle of an ordinary bicycle. The name has been associated with many other products, notably cough drops, typewriters, and rugs.

Alexander Smith carpets are known the world over and are manufactured at a big factory in Yonkers, New York. Alexander was a young man from New Jersey when he first got the rug bug and started a carpet business in the Bronx. His factory burned down. He built another one. It burned down. He moved to Yonkers and started again. Along about this time he made the acquaintance of a young carpenter named Halcyon Skinner. These two invented the Axminster loom and other mechanical aids to greater efficiency in the weaving of carpets. The Smith factory today is geared to turn out fifty miles of carpeting every twenty-four hours. In 1894 it whipped up new carpeting for the Russian Czar's imperial palace in time for the coronation of Nicholas II. It is somewhat famous, too, as the place where Poet John Masefield worked as a mill hand when he was a young man and unable to get his regular work of cleaning spittoons in Greenwich Village bars. In the time of old Alexander himself, he employed a third of the population of Yonkers but couldn't get himself elected mayor of the town. Still and all, he was a good man with a rug.

Lyman Cornelius Smith is the man whose name was given to the L. C. Smith typewriter. He was born in Connecticut, became a commission merchant in New York City, then moved to Syracuse to enter the lumber business. Finally he and his brother Wilbert started a shotgun factory. They were turning out a pretty fair article, but it wasn't as good as they wanted it to be, so they hired a man named Alexander T. Brown, a sort of mechanical genius, and told him to make a better shotgun. Brown went to work on shotguns, but he had another idea knocking around in his mind. He had seen a model of a single-case typewriter and had recognized its shortcomings. He thought that he could make a typewriter that would print both upper and lower case. He talked the Smiths into letting him fool around with this idea, and so he became the man who was really responsible for the L. C. Smith typewriter. A Brown yet! The first machine was called a Smith Premier and was so successful that Lyman and Wilbert brought in two more brothers, Monroe and Hurlbut Smith. Today the firm is known as the L. C. Smith & Corona Typewriter Company and is spread all over the map.

As already suggested in these pages, there are many Smiths who would be just as happy if there never had been a single Smith Brothers cough drop. The Ford joke had its day and died, the Mae West joke flourished and then went away, but the cough-drop joke survives the years and the decades. It is favored by the kind of people who, on meeting a man named Street, will ask, "Don't you have a son named Dead End?" I think it is probable that down through the years the greatest sales resistance to Smith Brothers cough drops has been among people named Smith, who have scorned a product which has brought them so much corny assault from parlor wisecrackers. Nowadays the joke, so called, has even been turned upon a certain variety of non-Smiths, those brash gentlemen such as Rex Stout and Robert St. John, who permit themselves to be seen in public wearing beards and who frequently hear themselves addressed as Trade or Mark.

The company itself is not responsible for the japery that Smiths have had to endure. The company, in fact, has been opposed to any kind of frivolity touching its product. In his vaudeville days Doc Rockwell wrote an act for himself and a partner with a Smith Brothers cough-drop theme, featuring song routines in the manner of Gallagher and Shean in which the names of Trade and Mark were used. Rockwell figured his act would be valuable promotion for the cough drops. He sent the script and sketches of the scenic drop to the company in Poughkeepsie, thinking that perhaps the Smith Brothers would be happy to help finance the act out of their advertising budget. The company responded that it certainly would not and that, moreover, if Doc ever put that extravaganza on a stage they'd take him to court.

A Scottish carpenter named James S. Smith was the founding father of Smith Brothers cough drops. In the beginning, more than a hundred years ago, he cooked the black goulash on an old kitchen stove, made the lozenges by hand, and sent his two boys out to peddle them. After his death the sons, William W. and Andrew Smith, continued turning the drops out in small quantities at the restaurant they operated in Poughkeepsie. When the business prospered they rented a barn for a factory and increased production. In those days the cough drops were sold in bulk, but William (Trade) and Andrew (Mark) now decided to package their product. There was a street of modest homes near their barn-factory, and they made an arrangement to have the families in these houses do the packaging at home. In time that thoroughfare became known as Cough Drop Street.

The increasing success of the enterprise spawned a whole series of imitators and resulted in much litigation. At various times other firms popped up making Schmid Brothers Cough Drops, and Schmitt Brothers, and Original Smith Brothers, and Improved Smith Brothers, and even Smythe Brothers. Possibly because their cough drops were of a better quality, the Smith Brothers of Poughkeepsie won out over all these piratical competitors. Their basic formula is still supposed to be a closely guarded secret, though I suspect the Russians have it. The present heads of the company are another William W. Smith, grandson of old Trade, and his brother Robert. Once every six months William retires

into a secret room and sloshes together a fresh batch of the concentrate. No other human being on earth knows what goes into it. That, at least, is the romantic story—you've probably heard it in connection with other products, notably Coca-Cola. Personally I am an unromantic skeptic, believing that a laboratory chemist who never got better than D on his report card could take one cough drop and in fifteen minutes tell you precisely what went into it. If, however, William actually does go into that secret chamber, he must have one helluva job on his hands, mixing enough concentrate to last six months. The company's present capacity is nineteen million cough drops a day.

Semantic note: When you speak of "Smith Brothers" around Reno, you are not necessarily referring to cough drops. The Smith Brothers operate a plush gambling resort called Harold's Club and are said to clear a million dollars a year. No secret formula needed.

Critique of Pure Smith

> *Mrs. Erminie Adele Smith classified fifteen*
> *thousand words of the Iroquois language. I*
> *know two of them:* how *and* scalp.

The human animal differs from the lesser primates in his passion for lists of Ten Best. We have our ten best-dressed women and our ten best-dressed men. Sloppy dressers of both sexes have their day in the sun, and there are lists devoted to anatomical superiority, such as best lips, best noses, best hair, best shoulders, best lung warts, best elbows, best prats, and best varicose veins. We are assaulted with the Ten Most Beautiful Words, the Ten Best Movies, the Ten Most Exciting Fights in El Morocco, and the Ten Greatest Individuals Who Are Not Known Personally by Elsa Maxwell (maybe it's only five).

Our concern now is with lists of Great Books, and they usually come in job lots of a hundred to a list. There are many to choose from—a book devoted to lists of Great Books came out a few years ago and made money for its publisher.

The Smith most often met with on these lists of Great Books is Adam. He is the only Smith among the authors of the Great Books used in the famous course at St. John's College in Maryland. And Dr. Will Durant includes him on his list of "100 best books for an education."

Arnold Bennett made a list which took in Adam's *The Wealth of Nations* and Alexander Smith's *Dreamthorp*. A Edward Newton compiled a list of "100 Good Novels," and on it was *Colonel Carter of Cartersville,* by F. Hopkinson Smith. This same novel was listed by Frank Thomas, noted bookseller. Christopher Morley's list of great books includes *Dreamthorp* and Logan Pearsall Smith's *Trivia.* And Henry Seidel Canby, choosing a hundred outstanding books out of the period 1924–44, listed both *Betty* and *Lillian Smith.*

Turning from quality to quantity, a number of Smiths have achieved sufficient popularity to get their names on the all-time best-seller lists. The first best-selling Smith in the United States was a forewarning of things to come, a precursor of the present-day rash of books which tell the reader how to feel good even though his back's killing him, his neighbor's after him with an ax, the rent's overdue, and the kids have all just gone up in flames. This cheerful pathfinder was Hannah Whitall Smith, a Philadelphia zealot and mother of Logan Pearsall Smith. Her book, *The Christian's Secret of a Happy Life,* was a best seller in the 1880s. It is possible that the expression, "So help me Hannah!" dates back to her.

Two additional Smiths have books on the all-time best-seller list: Betty, with *A Tree Grows in Brooklyn,* and Thorne, with *Topper.* Four others with high ranking as best sellers were:

1833. *The Life and Writings of Major Jack Downing,* by Seba Smith.

1886. *The Marvel of Nations,* by Uriah Smith. (Could this have been old Swivel-foot Uriah, whom we met in the last chapter?)

1898. *Caleb West,* by F. Hopkinson Smith.

1944. *Strange Fruit,* by Lillian Smith.

Let us now examine some of these writing Smiths more closely. First we have Adam, whose theories are familiar to every student of economics. He was born in Scotland in 1723 and barely escaped bumhood, for when he was three years old he was kidnaped by a party of roving tinkers (tinsmiths) who meant to raise him in their own profession. Somehow his family got him back, and eventually he studied at Glasgow University and, after that, he was a Snell Exhibitioner at Balliol College, Oxford. The meaning of this latter exploit is not clear to me—I suppose he went around exhibiting his snell. He became a professor of logic and moral philosophy and in 1776 published his famous book under its full title, *An Inquiry into the Nature and Causes of the Wealth of Nations*. It is concerned with tariffs and an increased exchange of goods across national borders and international division of labor and all such as that. I have no room in this book for a full explanation of Adam's position, but don't think I don't understand it. If you want it explained, you'll have to send me a self-addressed barrel and I'll write it out for you if I ever get the time.

The Alexander Smith whose *Dreamthorp* appears on two lists of Great Books was a designer of lace patterns in Glasgow. *Dreamthorp*, published in 1863, is a group of essays, although Alexander was best known in his own time as a poet. He was too poor to go to college but had to work in a factory and, between lace patterns, he composed poems which were published in a Glasgow newspaper. He became known as one of the chief representatives of the Spasmodic School of Poetry. This does not imply that he wrote fitfully or intermittently, or that he was subject to outbursts of emotional excitement. The Spasmodic School has been described as "a group of nineteenth-century British authors whose works were in an overstrained style." Alexander is the only Smith in the whole history of writing who was ever guilty of such a thing.

We come next to Logan Pearsall Smith. He was the only son of a pious and prosperous Quaker family in Philadelphia. When he was a youth Logan rebelled against working in the family's bottle factory and in 1888 he deserted and went to England, where eventually he became a British subject. He lived on a farm in Sussex and wrote little short things, usually no more than a paragraph or two at a crack, and these he called *Trivia*. He was a philosopher and a stylist, and some critics have described the book on which his fame rests as one of the few modern volumes that will be read by future generations. Since his recent death there have been some published revelations about him which make him out to have been an old poop. Just to give you an idea about his writing, here is a little forenote to his book *All Trivia*:

THE AUTHOR

These pieces of moral prose have been written, dear Reader, by a large Carnivorous Mammal, belonging to that suborder of the Animal Kingdom which includes also the Orang-outang, the tusked Gorilla, the Baboon with his bright blue and scarlet bottom, and the gentle Chimpanzee.

And one typical item from the same book:

THE QUEST

'We walk alone in the world,' the Moralist writes in his essay on Ideal Friendship, somewhat sadly. 'Friends such as we desire are dreams and fables.' Yet we never quite give up the hope of finding them. But what awful things happen to us, what snubs, what set-downs we experience, what shames and disillusions. We can never really tell what these new unknown persons may do to us. Sometimes they seem nice, and then begin to talk like gramophones. Sometimes they grab at us with moist hands, or breathe hotly on our necks, or make awful confidences, or drench us from sentimental slop-pails. And too often, among the thoughts in the loveliest heads, we come on nests of woolly caterpillars.

And yet we brush our hats, pull on our gloves, and go out and ring door-bells.

The Seba Smith who produced *The Life and Writings of Major Jack Downing* was a New Englander, and almost all disquisitions on American humor begin with him. He was born in Maine in 1792 and died in 1868, and he was a political writer in the sense that Finley Peter Dunne and Will Rogers were political writers. He was the first man bold enough to employ the American vernacular in his writing, and his Major Jack Downing was chiefly occupied in needling Andrew Jackson. His pieces, done in the language of the back-country New Englander, were read throughout the nation for more than a decade. He also wrote some poetry, and if you want a critical estimate of that part of his work, Edgar Allan Poe called him "the worst of all wretched poets." Mention must be made, too, of Seba Smith's wife, Elizabeth Oakes Smith, herself a poet and the first woman of any consequence to hit the lecture platforms screeching for female equality. Seba was against her for this sort of carrying on, though there is no evidence that he ever whipped her for it.

Our nation has had one other Smith operating in Seba's field of letters—the celebrated Bill Arp of the South. He was Charles Henry Smith, a Georgia lawyer, and as Bill Arp he has been called the Will Rogers of the Confederacy. He spoke for the South in the time of the Trouble and afterward. Once a reporter asked him for the details of his career in the Confederate Army. He replied: "Well, I reckon I'll have to give you the gory facts. I killed nearly as many Yankees as they did me."

F. Hopkinson Smith (first name Francis) was a hog of a different wash. He wrote fancy and, as noted, his most famous works were *Colonel Carter of Cartersville* and *Caleb West*. He was a native of Baltimore, served as a clerk in an ironworks, and then became an engineer of some prominence. He built, among other things, the seawall around Governors Island, the Race Rock lighthouse off New London, and the foundation on which the Statue of Liberty stands. He was an artist in water colors and traveled a great deal and got started writing by describing his journeys through foreign lands.

Among the contemporary Smiths in the book world, the most important are Betty from Brooklyn and Lillian from Georgia. Between the two of them, these girls keep the name of Smith pretty consistently on the best-seller lists.

Lillian Smith has addressed herself to the racial problem in the South, and her books have been eloquent and passionate arguments against the traditional but-would-you-want-one-to-marry-yer-sister attitude. National fame arrived for her in 1944 when *Strange Fruit* was published. This book was a novel constructed around a love affair between a white man and a Negro girl in a small Georgia town. Many critics acclaimed it as a work of art, while a few stores refused to handle it on the grounds that it was "dirty." Two and a half million Americans bought it, and it was translated into a dozen languages. Miss Smith's second book, *Killers of the Dream,* came out in 1949. It was just as forthright and just as passionately concerned with the Negro problem, treating of the author's own experiences in the South and pleading for an end to the fumbling. It had nowhere near the success of *Strange Fruit.* By critical estimate *Killers of the Dream* had all the high literary quality of *Strange Fruit.* Could it possibly be that readers stormed the bookstores for the first volume because it had a lot of intimate sex stuff in it? Of course not!

Lillian comes from a family of Smiths that has been in Georgia for generations. Her father was a prosperous lumberman and founded Laurel Falls Camp for girls at Clayton, Georgia. The author now runs the camp and is known to the girls as "Miss Lil." She is a very important Smith.

It happens that I know more about Betty than I know about Lillian. Betty Smith is one of the rare characters of our time. I wrote to her and asked her if she could find time to sit down and ruminate a bit on the matter of her name and jot down some notes. I reminded her that she is not an authentic Smith—her father's name was Wehner and her mother was a Hummel. She married a Smith, had two children named Smith—Nancy Jean and Mary Elisabeth—was divorced, and then married a Jones, Joseph Piper Jones, and they live in Chapel Hill, North Carolina. In my letter I mentioned that she might find my daughter, Nancy Jean Smith, installed as a student in the University of North Carolina at Chapel Hill and living, appropriately, in an establishment called Smith Hall. Here is Betty's response:

DEAR H. ALLEN:
  What do you mean I'm not a Smith? Even after I married a Jones I wouldn't give up the name of Smith.
  Don't brag. I, too, had a daughter named Nancy Jean Smith in the University. She hated the plain name of Nancy Smith and hoped someday she

would marry a name "that not everybody had."
She did. She is now Mrs. Dagobert Pfeiffer.

I have been embarrassed by other women having
the name of Betty Smith. Some woman named Betty
Smith threw her newborn baby out of the window
and killed it. I received many letters from people
saying they understood how my sudden fame may
have unhinged me to the extent of killing my baby,
but that they would have taken the baby off my
hands.

In some big city after a raid on brothels, all the
girls were permitted to testify under the name of
Betty Smith instead of the customary Jane Doe because there was an actual citizen named Jane Doe
living in that town.

Advertisements feature handkerchiefs with the
full name printed on them, rather than a monogram,
and the name is inevitably "Betty Smith." So this
leads people to believe that I lend my name to that
sort of promotion in order to get free handkerchiefs.

In the past year I got six clippings concerning the
marriage of one Betty Smith or another, and this
leads people to believe that I divorce and remarry
several times a year.

At the University here a beauteous doll named
Betty Smith was elected Beauty Queen. There was
much publicity about it in the papers. This girl is
about eighteen or twenty. So, people seeing me on
the street and thinking I had been elected Beauty
Queen, would say: "I wonder how many thousands
of dollars she paid to get elected."

During the war I lived in a small town near my
husband's army base. It so happened that the town's
call girl was also named Betty Smith. Every time a
warship came into port, sailors kept calling me at all
drunken hours inviting me to take carnival with
them. The prostitute was not listed in the phone
book, but I was.

There's a laundress here in town named Betty
Smith, and often some irate citizen phones my

house and asks where the hell his shirts are, and I always say how the hell should I know, which shocks people who are accustomed to laundresses being humble. When other people, trying to be more considerate, call and say, "Are you the Betty Smith who washes?" I always say, "No," and then realize that they must think I am a dirty girl indeed.

So, that's what I get for being named Betty Smith. I cannot tell you all the things that have happened to just "Smith" alone without the "Betty." They would take pages and some days to write.

Trusting the above will do, I *remain*,

BETTY SMITH

(On the very day the above letter arrived, the newspapers were carrying large advertisements featuring Miss Betty Smith, skating star of the show *Howdy, Mr. Ice of 1950*, declaring that she smokes Luckies.)

Betty is popularly regarded as the queen of the Chapel Hill literary colony. Bookish people all over the country have heard about this group, and they picture in their minds a lovely prospect —all these brilliant authors sitting around 'neath the magnolia trees, sipping delicately at mint juleps and discussing beautiful letters and saying "suh" and "ma'am" to one another. It isn't quite that way. Actually the Chapel Hill authors don't get together much at all, because their sessions usually end up with scratching and clawing and fist fighting and cussing, just like writers anywhere else. Under the urging of some of the professors, they used to assemble for the purpose of mutual criticism. One author would then read his or her latest short story, or a chapter from a book manuscript. Having finished the reading, the author would look up expectantly, seeking expressions of approval (he wouldn't ever have read it in the first place if he hadn't thought it to be a goddamn masterpiece). Almost always the responses were, "Good God, what tripe!" Or, "Why don't you go somewhere and commit suicide?" Or, "Why, you dumb son of a bitch, you don't even know syntax!" And then the laying on of hands, amounting almost to gang warfare, and the usual situation of people not speaking to other people for months at a stretch. The last session of the Chapel Hill literary group that I have any news about had a spectacular sort of climax—a lady poet, normally shy and inhibited, walked up to another lady author, snarled, "You filthy bitch, I've always wanted to do this to you!" and flung the contents of her highball glass fair in the lady's face.

There remains one final Betty Smith story. Betty's husband, Joe Jones, is an amiable newspaperman whose hobby is bird watching. Whenever he can find a couple of hours to spare he lights out for the woods and watches birds. Then he comes back to town and talks about the birds he has just watched. I recall a party in Chapel Hill at which Betty and Joe got into a small spat over some trivial matter, something about having a tree taken out of their yard. The argument was upsetting to Betty, and she even shed a few tears and began talking about how Joe didn't really love her. Finally she glared across the room at him and, addressing the rest of the company, said: "If I could lay eggs he'd love me!"

One bright summer day back in the medieval era of 1925 a man was sitting at a small table outside his house in New Jersey. On the table was a typewriter and the man was trying to write a story on it. He was a small, serious man, and he was wearing nothing but sneakers and a pair of shorts. He enjoyed writing, or trying to write, in such a costume.[1]

On this day a black depression was settling down on him, as it often did. The words weren't coming right and he was pretty well disgusted with himself and the notion that he could ever make a living as a writer outside an advertising agency.

In so far as physical exertion was concerned, the little man was a colossal sluggard. Consequently the lawn that stretched in front of him was a mess. The grass was high and wild and nothing but a sharp scythe would have sufficed to get it down.

The little man sat staring out across this weedy jungle and sud-

[1]This little sketch about a writing Smith appeared originally in an anthology of humorous pieces which I compiled in 1945 and which was called *Desert Island Decameron*. I have given myself permission to reprint it here with a few minor alterations.

denly he saw a tail. The tail was a dog's tail, but no dog was visible. It was a short tail, and when the little man first spotted it, it was wagging. Then it stopped, moved a few feet, wiggled some more, moved again, and so on. The little man at the table was fascinated by it. He started thinking in terms of a tail without a dog, and a dog without a tail. His imagination switched to human anatomy, and he thought of legs without a body, and a body without legs, and various other weird manifestations.

He needed money, almost desperately, and he thought that now he had the germ of a short story that might sell. He went to work on it. The short story grew into a novel, and the novel became the first of a series of fantastic tales that made Thorne Smith one of America's most popular humorists.

That first Thorne Smith fantasy, *Topper*, was having a moderate but steady sale when in 1929 his second was published. It was called *The Stray Lamb*. I was a bug-eyed newcomer to Manhattan that year and I remember reading a note in O. O. McIntyre's column, a single sentence saying that the funniest book he had read in years was *The Stray Lamb*. Even in those remote days I was trying to write funny, so I went out and bought the book, and from that moment forward I was one of Thorne Smith's most devoted fans.

Since I was an interviewer there was a clear opportunity for me to meet him. It was arranged, and one afternoon I arrived at the Smith apartment in Greenwich Village. It was a gloomy railroad flat in the basement of an old building, and the furnishings were not only nondescript but shabby. As I came up in front of the house Thorne, who had never been interviewed before, popped out of the entrance and greeted me with an embarrassed sort of violence. He escorted me into his living room, introduced me to his wife, his two young daughters, and Lucy Goldthwaite, who was handling publicity for his publisher. There was a reason for Lucy's presence. They had decided to have a little whisky on hand, and whenever whisky and Thorne Smith got into proximity there were likely to be explosions. Lucy Goldthwaite was there to see that Thorne didn't get his hands on that bottle, even though it was only a pint. He was working on another book, and someone explained to me later that if he took one drink he would be drunk for six months.

After that first meeting we got to be quite friendly and visited back and forth. Much of the time he was off traveling in Europe, or sitting out a contract in Hollywood, where he was a crony of John Barrymore and Roland Young, but whenever he was in New York we managed to get together. He was a caution with the bottle. He told me once that he didn't mind the penalty he had to pay after his long benders, except for one thing. He said that everyone would let him alone, let the thing run its course, until it was time for him to square away and write another book. Then they'd haul him off to a sanitarium somewhere in the country.

"They'd take me out and stand me up against a brick wall, mother-naked," he said, "and they'd turn a fire hose on me. That was a thing I resented bitterly."

Once he decided he would go to France to write a new book. He resolved, at the same time, to show everybody that he possessed will power. He got on one of the big liners and took squatter's rights on a table directly in front of the ship's bar. He put his portable typewriter on the table and every morning he sat down, facing the bar, and worked on his book. He got it more than halfway finished during the crossing and didn't take a drink, and he was so pleased with himself that the first day ashore he got orry-eyed.

In many respects he was a character right out of his own books. He was unpredictable, and in time his publishers were beyond the stage of being surprised at anything he did.

One morning he arrived at the publishers' offices, then on Madison Avenue. He could be dapper when he chose and he was dapper this day. He was carrying a cane and wearing a fairly loud sports jacket with a cornflower at the lapel. He was bright and shining and full of enthusiasm for a new project he was planning. Somebody noticed a bulge on his hip, but so far as his deportment was concerned he hadn't had a drink. After a while he took his merry departure.

Half an hour later a girl in the publishers' office glanced out an open window overlooking Madison Avenue. She saw Thorne, just as he stepped off the curb across the street. She leaned out and yelled a greeting at him. He halted in the middle of the pavement, looked up at her, took off his hat, and bowed. A few feet from where he was standing was an open manhole with a portable iron railing, a red flag, and a "Men Working" sign. Thorne put his hat back on, blew a kiss to the girl in the window, and stepped over to the manhole. He removed his gaudy jacket and hung it, with his cane, on the railing. He blew another kiss toward the girl. Then he disappeared into the manhole.

Thirty minutes or so after that two of the company's editors arrived on the sidewalk, headed for lunch. One of them glanced toward the manhole.

"Hey!" he said. "Isn't that Thorne's coat hanging out there?"

They drew back against the building and decided to wait around for a while and see what happened. They didn't have to wait long. They saw a workman come out of the hole. Then another, and another, until half a dozen grimy laborers had emerged. Last to come up was Thorne. He followed the workmen as they trudged across to the curb. Each man had his lunch bucket, and they sat down in a line on the curbstone. Thorne solemnly took his place at one end of the line. There was little conversation. The workmen seemed to accept him without either suspicion or amusement. One workman handed Thorne half a sandwich and another passed a banana down the line to him. Thorne in turn pulled his half-filled bottle from his hip and each man took a swig from it. Lunch was finished and the bottle killed. Then they sat on the curb staring at traffic, and finally one of the workmen got up, stretched, and headed for the manhole. The others followed him, Thorne again bringing up the rear. He went into the hole without so much as a glance around the street.

The two editors couldn't wait all afternoon, so nobody up above ever knew just when Thorne came up, got his coat and cane, and left. When I asked him about it he said he couldn't remember any of the details.

During that first interview with him I asked him where he was born and he replied, "In college." He wasn't lying. His father was

Commodore James Thorne Smith of the United States Navy, and James Thorne Smith, Jr., was born at the Naval Academy at a time when the commodore was an instructor there. Thorne went to school in Virginia, Pennsylvania, and at Dartmouth, then became a bohemian in Greenwich Village, writing poetry and drinking gin out of a tomato can. Off and on he worked as an advertising copywriter, but he never achieved anything resembling prosperity.

In my own opinion he is at his best in *Turnabout* and *Topper Takes a Trip,* and maybe *The Night Life of the Gods, The Stray Lamb,* and *The Bishop's Jaegers.* I don't know how long people will continue to read him. I do know that today, sixteen years after his death, booksellers say there is a steady demand for his works. Thorne certainly had no delusions of grandeur, even when John Barrymore saluted him with, "You are the American Dean Swift!" He considered himself little more than a hack, and such popularity as he had during the closing years of his life didn't impress him. The income from his work didn't reach large proportions until it was too late for him to enjoy it. He got out of that basement apartment, but the last place he lived in New York differed from it only in that it was upstairs. He had so little faith in the future earnings of his books that he neglected to write a will, with the usual consequence that his estate was in a snarl for years.

If, in this brief attempt to give you a picture of Thorne Smith, I have made him out to be a depraved sort of person, I haven't intended it. He was the kindliest of men. He loved dogs and cats and children. His conversation was brilliant, for he was a man of excellent education, acute perception, and flaring imagination. When he talked, whether in casual chitchat or in telling a story, his conversation carried much of the sharp flavor that went into his writing.

Read any good books lately? There's a new one out, *Practical Nut Growing,* by Gilbert L. Smith of Millerton, New York. Quite good. Or perhaps you don't go for the new stuff. In that case let me recommend *The Fishes of the Fresh and Brackish Waters in the Vicinity of New York City,* written by Eugene Smith. A compelling work.

It is almost astonishing—some of the things that have been written by Smiths. The poem, *If I Should Die Tonight,* was the work of Arabella Eugenia Smith. And Dexter Smith whipped up the lyrical *Ring the Bell Softly, There's Crepe on the Door.* The poem, *Address to the Mummy at Belzoni's Exhibition,* was the work of an Englishman, Horace Smith. And Gertrude Smith, a preacher's daughter out of California, wrote the Arabella and Araminta stories, the Roggie and Reggie stories, and *The Boo Boo Book.* Among the works of Laura Rountree Smith of Platteville, Wisconsin, were *The Pixie in the House, The Pixie Out Doors, The Pixie in School, The Pixie on the Farm, The Pixie in Bunnyland,* and *Three Little Kittens Who Lost Their Mittens.*

Dr. Hugh Smith was author of *Letters to Married Women on Nursing and the Management of Children,* the first maternity book ever published in the United States. It came out in 1792 and dealt with birthmarks, miscarriages, mothers' milk, suckling, weaning, and whipping.

One of the most celebrated of writing Smiths was Kate Douglas Wiggin, whose maiden name was Smith. She spent her childhood in Maine and when she was a little girl met Charles Dickens. She told him that she had read all his stuff and liked it, but that she skipped the dull parts. Dickens didn't live long enough to skip all of her stuff. Kate was enormously successful as a writer in later years and knew everybody worth knowing. Her most famous book was *Rebecca of Sunnybrook Farm.* I suppose there is some merit to writing of this sort, although there isn't.

Certain Smiths have been good at writing history. Goldwin Smith, who died in 1910, was a British historian and publicist whose pamphleteering on behalf of the North during the Civil War helped sway the British Government to support the Yankee cause. In 1864 Smith came over for a lecture tour and was given a hero's reception. He liked America so well that he uprooted himself from England and accepted a professorship at Cornell University. Later he moved to Toronto, where he became an editor. He was one of the chief proponents of the theory that Canada and the United States belong together as one great nation. He was against imperialism, against orthodox religion, opposed to home rule for Ireland, against the Boer War, and so he was heartily despised by a great many people, including Disraeli, who denounced him as a parasite.

This Goldwin Smith became, in spite of his enemies, a widely admired man in Canada, with the consequence that quite a few other Canadian Smiths named their offspring for him. Hence we have a paradox to report. In 1949 another Canadian named Goldwin Smith, who, incidentally, was educated at Cornell, appeared on the lists with *A History of England* which other historians saluted as an exceptionally able piece of work. He is not related to Old Goldwin.

The only Smith ever to get a Pulitzer award in literature was a historian—Justin Harvey Smith, a professor at Dartmouth. His book, *The War with Mexico,* took the history prize in 1920.

Again I must say how impossible it would be for me to enumerate and describe all the Smiths who have contributed to the enrichment or the impoverishment of literature; yet there remain several more whose accomplishments have been such as to demand a place in this Syllabus of Smiths.

The nasty controversy in which certain wobbleheads argue that Sir Francis Bacon wrote the works of Shakespeare while certain other lardnoggins insist that Shakespeare wrote the works of Shakespeare is still very much alive in this country as well as in England. Who started it in the first place? That honor belongs to William Henry Smith, who in 1856 wrote a letter to Lord Ellsmere suggesting that Bacon was the boy, and in the following year expanded the letter into a small book with a big title: *Bacon and Shakespeare: An Enquiry Touching Players, Playhouses and Play-Writers in the Days of Elizabeth.* (The British have made a vast improvement in the naming of books; compare the foregoing title with that of a recent English novel, *Nothing.*)

Richard Penn Smith was a leading literary figure in Philadelphia a hundred years ago. He was a lawyer, an editor, an author, and a playwright, and turned out one of the earliest American plays, *The Triumph of Plattsburg.* There is reason to believe that this Philadelphia Smith is to blame for the literary enormities committed in the name of Davy Crockett; he is said to have composed many of the basic fables on which most subsequent Crockett stories were constructed. A cruel charge, even against a Philadelphia lawyer!

Dr. Elihu Hubbard Smith was a literary character at an earlier time than Richard Penn Smith. The doctor flourished as one of the Hartford Wits, then transferred from Connecticut to New York in the 1790s and formed a little literary group—people interested in the higher things of life, or at least in sitting around and talking about them. They designated themselves the Friendly Club, but I have no doubt that on occasion they called each other sawneys, gowks, dunderpates, and clot-polls. Dr. Smith himself is remembered as the man who compiled the first anthology ever published in America, a collection of poems; and as one of the founders of the first American medical magazine.

Returning to England, we find at least three Smith girls whose works are known to contemporary audiences. Lady Eleanor Smith's novels had a wide popularity in the United States a decade or so ago. If any of her American readers pictured Lady Eleanor as resembling a bloomin' bloated duchess, they were in error. She was the daughter of that same Earl of Birkenhead, mentioned earlier in this book, who was the grandson of a gypsy. His daughter reflected her Romany ancestry both in her personal life and in her writing. She was a vagabond at heart, loved to travel with circuses, and worked for a while as a newspaper reporter. Like her father, she scorned the pretensions of the aristocracy, and her behavior was sometimes shocking to the more sedate shills in Vanity Fair. Once when a particularly stuffy old nanny goat asked Lady Eleanor something about her birth, the Smith girl replied: "It happens, muhlady, that I was born dead. Stone dead. They grabbed me up and threw a slug of brandy into me and I came to life. Wonderful stuff, brandy!"

Dodie Smith has been for some years one of England's leading playwrights, and her name is as well known in America as in her homeland. Among her notable productions were *Dear Octopus* and *Autumn Crocus,* and she is no stranger to the script sheds of Hollywood. Dodie was a buyer in a department store until 1931, when she turned to full-time writing. At one time she rebelled against the mud-commonness of her surname and signed "C. L. Anthony" to her work. Then she went back to Dodie Smith and still writes under that name, though she is entitled to use another. The example of Betty Smith's daughter, fretting against the name Smith and hoping to improve matters through marriage, is repeated here. Dodie Smith, who clearly wasn't too fond of her name, married a man named Alec Macbeth Beesley. And still another case is that of the novelist Sheila Kaye-Smith, who bought a ticket in the matrimonial sweepstakes and came out with the legal name of Mrs. T. Penrose Fry.

In North Carolina when they talk of Old Charlie Smith they could mean, of course, any one of hundreds of Charlie Smiths, black and white, but usually they have reference to a literary man named C. Alphonso Smith. He was a professor who taught at the University of Virginia, the Naval Academy, and at Chapel Hill, and as a writer he is probably best known as author of the first biography of O. Henry. I have no strong opinions about that biography, but Rufus Blair, an amateur authority on O. Henry, has described it feelingly as "the worst book written since the first human began to chip stone." C. Alphonso Smith was celebrated as a storyteller from Wayback, and old-timers say he had no equal as a raconteur. They remember him sitting perhaps on a stump, stroking his chin, and saying, "Now, did I ever tell you about the time that . . ." The epitaph on his tombstone reads: "He gave back as rain what he received as mist."

Let us not try to pass over the name of Alfred Aloysius Smith. He was the white-whiskered old boy whose memoirs were jiggered together by Mrs. Ethelreda Lewis in a book called *Trader Horn* which made a big splash in 1927. The story was loaded with African adventures, and the American public went for it and made it a huge success—such a success, in fact, that the old man was brought to our shores and placed on public view. Then came the repercussions; the book was branded as a fraud. Trader Horn wasn't Trader Horn at all, but Trader Smith. And Mrs. Ethelreda Lewis was accused of having faked a large part of the story. Trader

Horn himself was called a colossal fibber, and his book was described as slightly less authentic than a seven-dollar bill. All of the people were fooled some of the time and some of the people were fooled all of the time, and the longer that book was attacked, the better it sold. A. D. Peters of London, who knew Alfred Aloysius Smith, tells me that the old man was not a fraud. "He did a great many of the things that were in the book," says Mr. Peters. "After the book had run its course and the old man's name was a byword, I used to see him sitting around the lobby of his hotel in London. He sat there all day, fanning his beard, and tourists paraded by to have a look at him. He'd have gone upstairs and got in bed except for one thing—he knew that one out of every ten or so tourists would offer to buy him a drink at the bar, and he was never known to turn down such an invitation."

The late Henry Justin Smith of Chicago deserves a place on our honor roll not so much as a writer but as an editor. He was editor of the Chicago Daily News, and under his tutelage the famous Chicago literary gang was turned loose on the country. His stable of writers included Ben Hecht, Carl Sandburg, Lloyd Lewis, Robert J. Casey, Leland Stowe, and Raymond Swing, among others.

We have already met Chard Powers Smith of Connecticut. In Los Angeles, Paul Jordan Smith has long been literary editor of the Times and is the author of A Key to Ulysses, among other solid works. At one time he wore a hyphen in his name, explaining that when he first landed in Los Angeles there were at least three other Paul Smiths engaged in the writing dodge, so he signed himself Paul Jordan-Smith. Later on he discarded the little connecting rod.

Here are a few additional Smiths who write:

Edgar W. Smith, a General Motors executive and one of the leading figures in the Baker Street Irregulars—a slightly daffy organization devoted to the worship of Sherlock Holmes. Edgar has written extensively about the great detective.

William Gardner Smith, a Negro novelist whose Last of the Conquerors attracted considerable attention a couple of years ago.

Beverly Smith, Washington editor for the *Saturday Evening Post*, certainly one of the most brilliant writers operating today in the capital. He was one of Stanley Walker's boys on the New York *Herald Tribune* in the early thirties, but he has managed to live it down.

Robert Aura Smith, a Denver-born Rhodes scholar, long a foreign correspondent for the New York *Times* and author of various books on international matters.

Howard K. Smith of the Columbia Broadcasting System, whose middle name is Kingsbury, and Kingsbury Smith of International News Service, both distinguished foreign correspondents and authors.

One category in which the Smiths fall short of their usual quotient is fiction. For a novelist or a playwright to name one of his principal characters Smith would seemingly denote poverty of imagination. That rule has held true for so long that nowadays a writer who does call an important character Smith is showing remarkable originality. As a usual thing the name is employed in fiction either for comedy effect or as a disguise.

In the theater there are occasional walk-on Smiths, played by the versatile George Spelvin. A notable exception, however, is found in the comedy *Dulcy*, by George S. Kaufman and Marc Connelly, which bears upon the confusions wrought by Dulcy Smith when she tries to better her husband's business career. A check through the casts of *Sixteen Famous American Plays*, edited by Bennett Cerf and Van Cartmell, reveals not a single character named Smith. The hero of *The Front Page* is a Johnson, and *Ah, Wilderness!* is about a family of Millers. At the time this book is being assembled Kenny Delmar is playing the role of Hominy Smith in the Broadway production *Texas Li'l Darlin'*. Hominy Smith is a gallus-snappin' politician whose principles are just a shade higher than those of the average politician. Let it be noted that one of the chief supporting roles in this same production was given to a first-rate actor named Loring Smith; and Loring Smith has a daughter named Sydney Smith who is a regular performer on TV (not to be confused with T. V. Smith, the erudite professor of philosophy who served awhile in Congress and knows about Euclid and sitch).

Smiths do sometimes appear as characters in novels. A heroic party whose name is generally given as Henry Smith or Gow was an armorer in *The Fair Maid of Perth*, by Sir Walter Scott. And in the first decade of the present century a New York novelist named Henry Wallace Phillips (whose mother was Adelaide Smith) wrote a book called *Plain Mary Smith*. One of the chief characters in Virginia Woolf's *Mrs. Dalloway* was named Septimus Smith. He commits suicide. And Aldous Huxley, in *Crome Yellow*, has a character named Mr. Barbecue Smith, an author of books of comfort and spiritual teaching, described as a "short and corpulent man, with a very large head and no neck."

Janet Ayer Fairbank wrote a novel called *The Smiths* in 1925, and ten years later Branch Cabell came up with a book called simply *Smith*. This latter novel came out during the period when its author couldn't make up his mind about his own name. He had achieved a reputation as James Branch Cabell but dropped the James for several years and as Branch Cabell (or Gow) turned out a trilogy called *Smirt*, *Smith*, and *Smire*. Any book bearing the single magniloquent word *Smith* for a title should get more than passing mention here. I have had to read it in a hurry, during a couple of evenings when other people insisted on having the television set going, and it may be that I haven't got out of it all that Branch intended. The book has to do with a Mr. Smith who rules over the Forest of Branlon although he really doesn't, being in actuality a Mr. Smirt who is only dreaming that he is Mr. Smith and who, when he *was* Mr. Smirt, was dreaming that he was that, too, I think. I never did quite figure out exactly who he was and I assume that in the book that came after *Smith* he (who?) was dreaming that he was Mr. Smire. I'd try to find out, but my back hurts. As for Mr. Smith, during the period when he was dreaming that he was Mr. Smirt, he begot four children by four different women, to wit: Tana, who worked for a sinister white rabbit on the moon; Airel, who lived on a glass mountain; Rani, daughter of the South Wind who lived in a paper palace erected on a weather vane; and Arachne, the Spider Woman who devours her mate (Smirt, maybe?). The book *Smith* is largely about Mr. Smith's magical adventures in getting his four sons out of the dream world of Smirt and into the Forest of Branlon, which is itself a dream world. While he is doing it Mr. Smith smokes Virginia cigarettes—even while he's having a talk with Charlemagne. Some book.

Rachel Crothers wrote a book called *Expressing Willie* in which the hero was Willie Smith, and then there is *Clarence* by Booth Tarkington. The Tarkington novel doesn't identify Clarence as a Smith until along toward the end of the story. Clarence is a bug bug, or entomologist.

One of the most interesting Smiths ever to appear in a fictional work is found in *Orphan Island*, a novel by Rose Macaulay, published in 1924. The story has its beginning in London in 1855 when a governess named Miss Charlotte Smith assembles a group of East End orphans on a ship bound for San Francisco, where they are to enter an asylum. In the Pacific the ship is wrecked. All the orphans, Miss Smith, a Scottish nurse named Jean, and the ship's doctor, O'Malley, are cast ashore on a small uninhabited tropical island. Now we jump ahead to the year 1922 and meet a Cambridge don named Thinkwell who gets a tip on the location of the island and is attracted by the idea that the shipwrecked party may have survived. Thinkwell sets out to locate the island and when he reaches it finds a remarkable state of affairs existing on it. Miss Charlotte Smith is now ninety-eight years old and reigns over a community of more than a thousand subjects. Her empire is called Smith Island, and the social order is that of Victorian England—just the way it was in 1855. She had married the doctor, O'Malley, and had ten children by him, and these children had become the landed gentry of the island while the orphans and their progeny made up the working class. Adhering to the Victorian pattern, Miss Smith called her house "Balmoral" and named her eldest son Albert Edward. The Church of England was the state religion, and off in one corner of the island was a dissident group providing a condition tantamount to the Irish problem.[2] So,

[2]This is the first time in all history that the word *tantamount* has ever been used without being followed by *to election*.

along comes this Thinkwell from England. His arrival is not welcomed by Old Charlotte Smith, for she is by now completely satisfied with her position and the leadership she will pass on to her
children. She warns Thinkwell that he is not to agitate the lower
classes—she doesn't want them even to know about England. The
word gets around, however, and there are stirrings of revolt. Old
Jean, the Scottish nurse, sets off the fuse. She is so disappointed at
the thought of not getting back to her native land that she blabs a
secret she had kept all those years: Miss Charlotte and Dr. O'Malley were never legally married, for the reason that O'Malley
already had a wife back in Ireland. This news is so shocking to
Miss Smith that she throws a superb fit and dies. Whereupon
the orphans raise a rebellion, throw off the Smith yoke, declare
a republic, and change the name of their country to Orphan
Island. That's the story in broad outline, though one important
point is missing—we lost track of Dr. O'Malley somewhere back
there. He seems to me to have been the strong character of the
book—not telling Old Charlotte Smith about his wife in Ireland.
Moreover, he drank. Such a man deserved better than the fate
allotted to him by the novelist: a shark ate him.

In Western fiction one of the more celebrated characters was
Whispering Smith, who appeared originally in a novel by Frank
H. Spearman. At my time of life I find myself in no mood to go
out and dig it up and read it. Remembering, however, that a
motion picture was made of it not so long ago, I took occasion
one day in Hollywood to approach Alan Ladd about it. Mr. Ladd
played the title role.

"What sort of a guy was this Whispering Smith?" I asked him.
"Well," said the actor, "he whispered."

The village blacksmith was a yuck. That word has several defi-
nitions. Fred Allen describes a yuck as a faulty human who rushes
around trying to get on radio quiz shows. The Irish actor Arthur
Shields says a yuck "is what they call somebody in Ireland too
low to kick and too wet to step on." In a broad sense, a yuck is
simply an individual we dislike ardently and for cause. I dislike
the village blacksmith. Whole generations of Americans learned

to yammer Longfellow's poem in school and then went out into the world to yawp bits of it at anyone they met who happened to be named Smith. "Why don't you go somewhere and stand under a spreading chestnut tree?" they ask, and I'm tempted to request that they in turn go somewhere and flyingly embrace a galloping goose. I may be overly sensitive about the village smithy because of the fact that at least once a year he leads me into a vexatious argument. The Huguenot publishing house which has put up with me for ten years has on its staff an executive who, when my first book was handed in, thought of a splendid title for it. He wanted to call it *A Mighty Man Is He*. With my assistance he was voted down. He fought hard to have that title go on the next book, but failed. He was in there yelling when the third book arrived. He tried variations, such as *The Smith a Mighty Man* and *Smith Is a Mighty Man*. When he heard about *this* book and its subject matter, he concluded that his day had come at last, that he could no longer be denied; but he was denied, and at last reports he was being seen standing alone at bars, late into the night, brooding.

A pox, then, on the yuck with his large and sinewy hands. His name was not Smith in the first place. In poetry, even though Chesterton salutes it as the most poetic of names, Smiths are seldom mentioned by name. When Edgar Allan Poe wrote *For Annie* in tribute to a schoolteacher who was his friend in Richmond, he didn't bother to give us her full name, which was Annie Maria Smith. A man named David L. Proudfit, who was known as Peleg Arkwright, once turned out a poem called *Prehistoric Smith*, but it was not too flattering. This particular Smith was pictured with a tail, sitting on a rock and sucking his thumb. He would have been sucking his tail if he could have reached it.

Thomas Hardy wrote *Epitaph on a Pessimist*, which serves nicely to close out this section of our book:

> *I'm Smith of Stoke, aged sixty-odd,*
> *I've lived without a dame*
> *From youth-time on; and would to God*
> *My dad had done the same.*

Good Night, Sweet Smith

In 1844 John Rowson Smith was one of the country's leading panoramists—artists who painted on long strips of canvas which were then placed on rollers and exhibited by unwinding before paying audiences. John Rowson did one job that was four miles long, showing scenes along the Mississippi. That's painting.

There is, says the song, no business like show business. Let's all shake hands with our neighbor on the left and agree that the statement is correct. It is, however, open to widely divergent interpretations. When he wrote his song Mr. Irving Berlin appears to have been saying that show business is a punctilious and inspirational branch of human striving. It is clearly implied that if the noblest of all King Arthur's knights were alive today he'd be chewing scenery on a Broadway stage, or whinnying into a night club microphone, or playing guessing games before the television cameras. Yet there is another school of thought which holds that there is, in truth, no business like show business because, in every one of its several divisions—the movies, the stage, radio, television, the circus, the opera, the cabarets—there is a greater proportion of immature and unalloyed bastards than in any other field on earth, with the possible exception of politics.

This second school of thought argues that the common coin of show business is an amalgam of malicious gossip, backbiting, hypocrisy, cheap and maudlin sentiment, addiction to religious quackery, lying, conniving, cheating, intellectual numbness, and classic depravity.

Such an indictment seems farfetched. If it's true that there's a broken heart for every light on Broadway, it's probably also true that there's a broken heart for every ball bearing in Detroit. The difficulty in show business is that you are dealing with actors, and an actor who is at heart a scurvy villain can go along for years fooling even his close friends into believing he is a kindly soul with humanitarian instincts—the best of all possible fellows. Anyone who attempts to write about people in the entertainment world is therefore usually treading uncertain ground. All he can say for sure is that—there's no business like show business.

Among the inhabitants of this weird world are, to be sure, many Smiths. Some are of major importance while others are of whimsical interest. There was Patricia Smith, a sword swallower with the circus who once got into difficulties with the law for walloping the fat lady with a bottle. And Mr. George Jean Nathan informs me that one of the most important members of our tribe in the whole history of the American theater was Casimir Benvenuto Smith. He was the first theater usher ever to wear a dress suit on the job—at the old Walnut Street Theater in Philadelphia.

Damon Runyon used to tell about an acquaintance in show business named George Smith who had a custom of sending a calendar each year to all of his friends—a calendar which featured a long list of names under the heading: "I Am Not Speaking to the Following Persons." The list was revised each year, and Runyon looked forward to receiving his calendar and checking the new list against the old, seeing which individuals had been restored to grace by George Smith and which had been nominated for the silent treatment. Runyon believed that George Smith had a good and sensible thing—that his formal list prevented many embarrassing situations in the corner booth at Lindy's and in the lobby at the Garden. This George Smith is not to be impugned because his list was long. The I'm-not-speaking-to-him tradition is as much a part of show business as is the incredibly childish tradition that the-show-must-go-on. It is not uncommon for an actor and actress to appear on stage night after night in torrid love scenes when elsewhere they are not on speaking terms and have a strong distaste for each other's tripes. Two of the most prominent performers currently appearing on Broadway broke off conversational relations at the start of their association because one had been assigned a nicer dressing room than the other. And one season at the opera whole groups of people quit speaking to other groups of people after a lady singer got into an argument with a stage director over whether or not she would wear a purple dress.

For present purposes I have grouped all branches of show business into this single chapter, including music—all music, even the type that needs a haircut. I have a special report from Celebrity Service, an organization which traffics in information concerning famous personalities of the American scene. Forty-five Smiths are listed as celebrities in the company's master file, and of these twenty-one are in one branch or another of show business. Show business, in fact, provides us with perhaps a thousand celebrities for every one we get from the world of science.

In music we find an almost incredible association of the name Smith with our national airs and anthems. Consider first the song "America." The words for it were written by Samuel Francis Smith, a New England Baptist clergyman and poet. On occasion it has been charged that the Reverend Sam stole the music from the British, for the air is the same as in "God Save the King." Sam never claimed that he composed the music, but one thing is certain—he didn't borrow it from Britain. Musicologists have traced the air back to an old St. Cyr melody and have found that at one time or another it was in use in nine different countries with nine different sets of words. The German composer Handel is said to have copied it from the St. Cyr melody and made it into the Prussian national hymn, *"Heil dir im Siegerkranz."* It was in that incarnation that the British themselves appropriated it. Sam Smith, the Boston clergyman, was a writer of hymns, such as "The Morning Light Is Breaking," and one day in 1832, while prowling through a stack of old German music books, he came upon the Prussian song. He hummed the tune and liked it and decided he'd try to make a little American song out of it. One authority says he was not aware that it was the tune of the British anthem. In any event, he sat down and scratched out "My country 'tis of thee" as a beginning line and went on from there and in half an hour had the whole thing finished. He didn't think much of it at the moment, and some years later, after it had become the nation's patriotic hymn, he said: "If I had anticipated the future of it, doubtless I would have taken more pains with it." He was, incidentally, the Smith about whom Oliver Wendell Holmes wrote the much-quoted line, "Fate tried to conceal him by naming him Smith."

The music to which Francis Scott Key wrote the words of "The Star-Spangled Banner" is generally credited to John Stafford Smith, an English organist and composer. There has long been controversy over it, but the best authorities say that Smith composed the song for the Anacreontic Society of London—an organization formed to honor a Greek poet who wrote largely about wine and women and who choked to death on a grape seed when he was eighty-five. The original song was "To Anacreon in Heaven" and it became widely popular; soon it was even being warbled and bellowed by the people of that brash new republic, the United States of America. Sigmund Spaeth has noted that almost everyone who decided to write a patriotic song in the America of George Washington's time used that same tune. One of the most popular of these songs was "Adams and Liberty," which was nothing more than "To Anacreon in Heaven" with a fresh set of words. Francis Scott Key himself used the tune first for a song salute to the hero Stephen Decatur, calling it "The Warrior's Return." Key was a Washington lawyer at the time the British fleet was preparing to bombard Baltimore. One of his friends, a Maryland doctor, was being held prisoner on one of the British ships, and Key got permission to go aboard under a flag of truce and plead for his friend. He was on one of the ships, then, when the fleet proceeded against Fort McHenry, and stood on the deck and watched the bombardment, and when daylight came and he saw the star-spangled banner still waving over the fort, he decided there ought to be a song about it. He began writing it on the back of a letter, fitting the words to the Anacreontic tune, and when he had finished it called it "The Defense of Fort McHenry." This led eventually to Lucy Monroe.

At the risk of being hauled up for trying to overthrow the government, I must report that there are a lot of people who are dissatisfied with "The Star-Spangled Banner." They argue that it's not a good song because the average citizen can't handle it; that the words are somewhat archaic and that the whole thing compares unfavorably, from a musical point of view, with the French national anthem or even the musical battle cries of most of our colleges. These critics say that we ought to try to get a new national anthem, but they are unwilling to utter a public criticism of the old, on the grounds that they might be slapped in the pokey or even lynched. Well, *I'm* not going to be the one that says it.

The name of Kate Smith is closely associated with the more recent patriotic anthem, "God Bless America," yet it was written when Kate was about eight years old. Irving Berlin wrote it during World War I but didn't publish it—stuck it away in his files (he is the only man living who sticks such things away in files rather than in old trunks) and forgot about it, until 1939. That year the radio singer asked him to write a real stirring patriotic song for her, and he remembered the old composition, dug it out, and gave it to her for her free use on the air, stipulating that all royalties from it should go to the Boy and Girl Scouts. Kate Smith went to work with it, and before long "God Bless America" had all but supplanted "The Star-Spangled Banner" as our national anthem.

Victor Herbert had a weakness for Smiths when he went looking for collaborators. One of these was Edgar Smith, who arrived at a sort of eminence from having composed the song "Heaven Will Protect the Working Girl." Another was the more famous librettist, Harry Bache Smith, who worked with Herbert on many scores and who also collaborated with De Koven, Berlin, Kern, and Romberg. Harry, who came originally from Buffalo, turned out many hits, including "The Sheik of Araby." In the history of American song writing Kate Smith is credited with a part in the composition of her theme song, "When the Moon Comes over the Mountain." Clay Smith, a Hoosier trombone soloist, composed a batch of popular songs, the best known of which was "Sorter Miss You." And the Negro team of Cecil Mack and Chris Smith has turned out such things as "Down among the Sugar Cane" and "You're in the Right Church but the Wrong Pew." Chris Smith also wrote "Ballin' the Jack" and "Beans, Beans, Beans!" The song "Little Sir Echo" was the work of Laura R. Smith, and Dick Smith wrote "Winter Wonderland."

A genuine dearth of Smiths exists in classical music, yet one of the most distinguished figures in American music was David Stanley Smith, composer, conductor, and former dean of the Yale University School of Music, who died late in 1949. He spent forty-three years on the Yale faculty and was composer of many well-known orchestral and choral works. For twenty-six years he was conductor of the New Haven Symphony Orchestra and had been guest conductor for all the major symphony groups in other cities.

We come now to the Carleton Smiths. Two of these are prominent in American music. Dr. Carleton Sprague Smith, who fools around with the flute, is chief of the New York Public Library's Music Division, former president of the American Musicological Society, a director of the Metropolitan Opera Company, a lecturer on music, and father of a girl Smith named Damaris. Years ago Dr. Smith was a music critic on a Boston newspaper. There is reason to believe that nobody in Boston is permitted by law to criticize music unless his name is Smith. Moses Smith, who today is associated with the recording business, built his reputation as a music critic on the Boston *Transcript*; and Warren Storey Smith of the Boston *Post* is today one of the leading music critics of the nation (he's the same fellow who confessed the crime of having once used a hyphen in his name).

The second Carleton Smith is a lecturer and writer chiefly on music and other cultural matters and is director of the National Arts Foundation. He is also an authority on foreign affairs, having once been a newspaper and radio correspondent in Europe. He has lectured at all the principal music centers in the United States and abroad, he has written books, he has collected and recorded folk songs from Afghanistan to Chile—he has, in fact, done real well for a boy out of Bement, Illinois.

There remains yet another Carleton Smith of prominence. I must confess that after I got Carleton Sprague Smith isolated from the other Carleton Smith I shoved the whole business of Carleton Smiths aside on the theory that the field was covered. Yet there remained an itchy memory of a Carleton Smith who didn't quite fit the pattern of the other two. The name was somehow associated with that dinner, years ago, of the Benevolent and Protective and Completely Universal Order of Fred Smiths of America. At last I got him pinned down. He is Carleton D. Smith, presently director of television operations for the National Broadcasting Company. He has been with NBC for nineteen years, having started as an announcer in Washington.

"I have been Carleton Smith for forty-five years," he informed me. "I am the one you met at the dinner of Fred Smiths. I became Fred Carleton Smith for the occasion since I was the only announcer NBC had by the name of Smith. I know of Carleton Sprague Smith. I haven't met him. Carleton Smith from Bement, Illinois, has frequently been confused with myself and vice versa. He has been given to lecturing and travel, so his path has frequently crossed mine. I think we both visited South America about the same time in 1936 and again in 1938. He is frequently seen in the company of Mary Garden and he is known as the individual who sends cigars to Sibelius. My friends frequently think that I am the person publicized as doing those things."

Whereas the Smiths enjoy a low rating in the classical spheres, we are easily the dominating clan in that branch of music which is indigenous to America—the hot and blue department. A large proportion of the experts who write on the subject of jazz are named Smith, and they have many performing Smiths to write about.

Consider these arresting facts: According to the historians, the first blues singer in history was Mamie Smith. The greatest blues singer of all time was Bessie Smith. And the five greatest blues singers of all time were Mamie Smith, Bessie Smith, Laura Smith, Clara Smith, and Trixie Smith. The critics long ago crowned

Bessie as "Empress of the Blues" and they regard her "Empty Bed Blues" as a classic.

The blues as a musical form has been described as midway "between a holler and a spiritual" and can be blown into a jug as well as sung. *The Standard Dictionary of Folklore* gives us the following definition:

> The poetry of the blues—the tender, ironic, bitter, humorous, or topical expression of a deprived people—tells of "careless love," of the woman who has lost her man or the no-good woman a man can't forget, of the train whistle in the night and the longing to go with it, of floods and cyclones, of jails and chain gangs and levee camps, of lonesome roads, river boats, back alleys, and barrel houses, of hard times and hard work.

That's the kind of business the Smiths excel in—the sorrowful gripe.

In a single book by the Frenchman Hugues Panassié, considered one of the best authorities on le jazz hot, we find words of acclaim not only for the blues-singing Smiths but for:

Joe Smith, great New Orleans-style trumpet player who died in 1937.

Jabbo Smith, trumpet, "who would be marvelous had he greater control over himself." (Nature of wildness not stated.)

Willie Smith, one of the "three greatest" alto sax players.

Tab Smith and Buster Smith, both saxophonists.

Stuff Smith, violinist and band leader.

Willie the Lion Smith, calypso singer and hot piano player. (I may have two Willie Smiths confused here, but certainly Willie the Lion is not Willie the alto sax player.)

Pine Top Smith, greatest of the boogie-woogie performers.

Floyd Smith and James Smith, both hot guitarists.

Carl Smith, trumpeter in the early Count Basie band.

There are others, but my inclination is to get away from this subject because it is a sort of religion, with an army of adherents who cannot tolerate talk from the non-hep. Just to illustrate the complexity of the thinking that goes on behind hot music, I'd like to quote from one of *Esquire's* yearbooks on jazz. Joe Smith, the trumpet player, and several other performers are cited as reflecting the following:

> *Emotional attitude II*: The Romantic. The essence of individualism: the ego giving out over all. This attitude is characterized by big, lugubrious, fabulous sweeps of sound; the outlook is one of breadth, picturesqueness, a reassertion of the imagination and sentiment (but not sentimentality, at which level it deteriorates to artistic insignificance). The music which reflects this attitude is expansive, full of buoyant, happy tones and dramatic pauses and arpeggios.

I wonder if Joe Smith knew that was what he was up to.

The Queen Smith of radio is Kate, who has progressed from songster to become one of the nation's most popular cracker-barrel philosophers. She is cracker-barrel not in the sense of using a rural dialect, nor because she has the general contours of one, but because she is a philosopher of homespun wisdom, able to convince her legions of followers that there is nothing nicer on earth than just folks. Since the vast majority of people hold this same belief, Kate has maintained and even increased her fame and popularity twenty years after her introduction to show business. In a recent magazine poll the nation's leading newspaperwomen selected the twenty most influential women in the United States, and Kate made the list. (Senator Margaret Chase Smith ranked Number 6 in the voting.)

Kate was born in Washington, D.C., while at the same time she was born in the little town of Greenville, Virginia. She has at various times given both places as her point of origin, and Greenville has a highway sign announcing to the tourist that he is about to arrive in the community where Kate Smith was born. We do know that Kate's father was a news dealer in Washington when she was a child and was ambitious for her to become a nurse. She began singing about the time she began walking, performing in

choir lofts and in army camps around Washington. When she was sixteen she started her training as a nurse, but after six months of it the lure of show business took hold of her and she headed for New York, where she got a job singing in a show called *Honeymoon Lane*. Next came a part in the musical hit *Flying High* and her meeting with Ted Collins, who has been her manager and associate ever since. Collins took this large, cheerful girl by the hand and led her into radio in 1931. For seven years she was a singer, enjoying an enormous popularity, and in 1938 she began branching out as a talker. Her patriotic enterprises during World War II revealed her as a woman of remarkable durability—in addition to her regular schedule of performances she made more than six thousand personal appearances. She was responsible for the sale of two billion dollars' worth of war bonds, and one of her wartime campaigns brought twenty-five thousand people named Smith to the blood banks.

Kate is a person who rejoices in what she calls her plain, simple, common-sense Americanism, and tells a story on herself to illustrate her position. Once she was invited to sing with the Philadelphia Orchestra with Leopold Stokowski conducting. Arriving for rehearsal, she was introduced to the maestro, who said, "And now, Miss Smith, you intend to sing *'Mon coeur s'ouvre à ta voix,'* *n'est-ce pas?"*

"Well," said Kate, "I don't know about all that. I just came here to sing 'My Heart at Thy Sweet Voice.' "

Kate Smith is a glad talker rather than a glad singer. The gladdest of the glad singers is Jack Smith, who got his start in 1931 but who has only reached national popularity in the last few years. He has a peculiar singing style, a voice which convinces listeners that he is so God-dern happy he can't hold still. He began his professional career at the Cocoanut Grove in Los Angeles after a young fellow named Crosby had moved out of the spot to have a try at radio. Jack went along as a journeyman singer for quite a few years until one day a big chance arrived—an opportunity to exhibit his happy pipes on an established program—the Kate Smith show. That guest shot gave him the boost he needed, and he was soon on the radio networks himself. Before leaving him I must mention that he is by no means the same man as Whispering Jack Smith who was a recording star in the early 1920s, just before radio hit big and brought with it the likes of Rudy Vallee. Whispering Jack Smith's records, such as "When the Red, Red Robin Comes Bob, Bob, Bobbin' Along" and "Cecelia," were widely popular in the period when Gene Austin reigned as America's favorite balladier. Then radio came in and these established singing stars chose to ignore it, with the consequence that a new crop of crooners took over. By the time the recording stars awoke to what was happening, the public had acquired new idols. Much the same sort of thing may be happening today in television.[1]

Going back into radio history, we find a Smith who may properly be called a pioneer. On August 3, 1922, the first deliberate sound effect ever heard on a radio show was produced by a Smith. This historic event occurred at Station WGY in Schenectady during the broadcast of a dramatic production, *The Wolf.* Midway in the drama the show's director, Edward H. Smith, stepped up to the microphone and slapped a couple of boards together to simu-

[1]Just as this manuscript was being sent off to the printer Whispering Jack Smith died unexpectedly in New York while watching a telecast of a ball game.

late the slamming of a door. Director Smith never was accorded proper recognition for this portentous act, forerunner of a tidal wave of sounds that would soon overrun the country. In my own opinion he was a greater man than Johnny Appleseed.

During the war years a Smith with an uncommon talent had a long run in radio. He was Dr. Henry Lee Smith, a Princeton man who could pluck a human being out of a crowd, ask a few questions, and from that person's speech mannerisms tell him where he came from and where he had been and the brand of tobacco his uncle chewed. Dr. Smith's peculiar art is best illustrated with a story. He was riding one day in a New York taxicab, listening to the driver talk, and finally he spoke up: "After coming from Hamburg, did you spend much time in Cleveland before moving to New York?" He was able to explain to the startled driver that "you have some very definite traces of a Hamburg area dialect, with a Cleveland overlay that breaks through the New York characteristics." On occasion Dr. Smith was able to tell a person not only what city he came from, but name the section of the city where the subject had lived. During the war he listened to the infamous Lord Haw Haw broadcasting from Berlin at a time when the identity of the traitor was a complete mystery. Dr. Smith identified the voice as being that of a man with an Irish origin who had spent some time in the United States—an exact description, as it turned out, of William Joyce, alias Lord Haw Haw. After the war Dr. Smith became head of the State Department's language school. Asked once to state his own definition of language, he had a ready answer. "Language," he said, "is nothing more than a bunch of noises made by the face."

Roaming around in other areas of show business we find Ethel Smith, probably the most prominent organist in the country, and Joe Smith, half of the veteran vaudeville team of Smith and Dale. And in television we have, of course, the creator and boss of the Howdy Doody show, Bob Smith. Just a few years ago Bob was a disk jockey in Buffalo; today his puppet, Howdy Doody, has become such a delight to the juvenile television audience that his income is estimated at something over $350,000 a year. In addition to bossing and performing on the Howdy Doody show, Bob for several years had a two-hour early-morning radio show on NBC each weekday. He is one of the few people in radio who broadcast from their own homes. He has a fully equipped studio in the basement of his New Rochelle house. He is, it may be added, a musical moke—a term out of minstrel-show days designating an artist who performs on several instruments. Bob plays the piano, drums, guitar, accordion, organ, saxophone, ukulele, clarinet, trombone, trumpet, bass fiddle, tuba, zither, and hums good.

In the history of the legitimate theater the name of Sol Smith is important largely because of the reminiscences he wrote. Sol was born in New York State in 1801 and ran away from home to join a wandering theatrical troupe traveling through the upper Mississippi Valley. He was a man of prodigious energies—a sort of everything moke. He learned the printer's trade in Louisville and studied law in Cincinnati. He became a partner in the firm of Ludlow & Smith, managing theatrical road companies in the South and Midwest. In his spare time he taught singing, edited and wrote for newspapers, acted in his own productions, practiced medicine, and, just for a hobby, went around organizing volunteer fire companies. He settled finally in St. Louis, where he wrote the memoirs which have been of great value to historians of the American theater.

Winchell Smith is another name of consequence in theatrical history. A native of Connecticut and a relative of John Brown, he became one of the important American playwrights of his time. He was an actor from 1892 to 1904, when he became associated with Arnold Daly in the production of George Bernard Shaw's plays. In 1906 he turned to writing, and his dramatizations included both *Brewster's Millions* and *Lightnin'*. His play *The Fortune Hunter,* produced in 1909, marked the coming to stardom of John Barrymore. George Jean Nathan says that Winchell Smith was, somewhat secretly, a play doctor who had a hand in many major theatrical successes without the public's ever knowing it. He died in 1933.

Elsewhere we have met with Edgar McPhail Smith as one of Victor Herbert's collaborators. Edgar was a playwright as well as a librettist and from 1896 to 1904 wrote the scripts for Weber and Fields. His theatrical productions included *Tillie's Nightmare, Pousse Café, Barbara Fidgety, Robinson Crusoe, Jr.,* and *Red Pepper.* A more recent theatrical writer is Paul Gerard Smith, who has been turning out stage comedy material for years. He has written extensively in musical comedy, for vaudeville acts, and for the movies. And newly arrived in the legitimate theater is a young genius named Oliver Smith, Wisconsin-born stage designer who has blossomed into a producer of such invigorating matters as *Gentlemen Prefer Blondes* and the Ballet Theatre.

A shortage of Smiths exists in the upper brackets of Hollywood, though it is not quite a famine. The beautiful Alexis would seem to be the top Smith among the movie performers, and everyone knows what you're talking about when you mention the name of Pete Smith. A handful of lesser actors and a scattering of business and technical personnel constitute our contribution to the Hollywood scene as of this moment. Among the front-office bashaws, perhaps the most important is Andrew W. Smith, Jr., a former newspaper reporter who moved into the picture business in 1914 and is now a top executive with Twentieth Century-Fox.

Sir C. Aubrey Smith helped carry the clan banner for many years in Hollywood, but he is dead now. He was one of the immigrants who kept the "British colony" alive in the picture capital. In his younger days Sir C. had been a championship cricket player and he organized cricket matches in California and rallied other imported actors into a group dedicated to nurturing British traditions in the midst of this howling and savage wilderness. Their activities and attitudes were given adequate treatment by Evelyn Waugh in his little book about the big graveyard.

Pete Smith, as the producer of short subjects, copped an Academy Award for his work. He was once a stenographer in New York City, then a film reviewer, and later a publicity director in the Hollywood studios. Charles Smith, a young character actor who attracted attention in the Henry Aldrich pictures, is still working in pictures, and other names familiar to the casting directors include Stanley Smith and Gerald Oliver Smith.

Audiences in both the legitimate theater and film houses have

recently become increasingly aware of the talents of Kent Smith. He has been around as an able actor for years, always on the upgrade, and 1950 finds him playing opposite Joan Crawford in pictures and opposite Helen Hayes on the stage. His background has been chiefly stage, though he is in demand as a picture actor and makes his permanent home in Beverly Hills.

He was born Frank Kent Smith, but when he began play acting he discarded the Frank. He used to tell interviewers that he was a Smith from Smithville, identifying his birthplace as Smithville, Maine. The town is the seat of a long line of Smiths, including the actor's father, but Kent was born in New York City. He attended Phillips Exeter and then entered Harvard, but he didn't get his degree from the latter plant because of his habit of wandering off and joining theatrical groups. He was a member of the University Players at West Falmouth, a company which also included Henry Fonda, Margaret Sullavan, James Stewart, Bretaigne Windust, and Mildred Natwick. He can remember playing his part on stage at the summer theater, then scurrying over to a little night club where he doubled as headwaiter and adagio dancer.

From Cape Cod he moved on to New York, playing bits at first, and when he was twenty-two he was cast opposite Helen Hayes in *Antony and Cleopatra* at a summer theater in Suffern, New York. He trouped around the country and came back to Broadway to play in *Dodsworth* with Walter Huston and Fay Bainter. He appeared opposite Katharine Cornell in *Candida* and was with Miss Cornell again in *The Wingless Victory*. He reached the peak of his career early in 1950 in Joshua Logan's *The Wisteria Trees* opposite Helen Hayes.

The two most illustrious Smiths in the history of motion pictures have been women, and both came out of Canada. There is, of course, the world-famous Gladys Smith (sometimes called Mary Pickford) and there is Alexis.

Alexis is an adornment to the name. She is beautiful, she is talented, she is intelligent, and she is friendly. The adventure of attaining stardom under her true name makes such a pleasant little story that I asked her to write it out for me, and here it is:

> Alexis Smith is my real name—even the Alexis.
>
> As a matter of fact, I have had more hassles over the name Alexis than over the Smith.
>
> I was born June 8, 1921, in Penticon, British Columbia, the daughter of Alexander Smith and Gladys Fitz-simmons Smith. One of my grandfathers was a gold miner in South Africa. The other was a gold miner in Alaska.
>
> My family wanted to name me for my father, and had heard the name Alexis. I don't think they realized it was masculine when they bestowed it on me.
>
> As it turned out, I was to experience much more provocation over Alexis than Smith. With shudders I recall my days in grade school. When the roll was called and I chirped my name, the teacher would feign surprise and say, "Alexis? Why, I thought you were a little boy! Alexis is a little boy's name." And the other kids would howl and point their nasty

little fingers at me. The name Smith didn't worry me at all in those days—it was that Alexis part that brought the strong blush to my cheeks.

But eventually the name of Smith caught up to me.

In my Hollywood High School days I was a tall, gawky, skinny kid who had escaped the horrible fate of becoming a child prodigy at the piano. My ambition was to be a ballet dancer and I studied under good teachers, but nature ruined any hope of such a career for me by growing me too big. I had a fair singing voice and had won a declamation contest, so now I decided on acting. In Los Angeles City College I played the lead in a student production of *The Night of January 16th,* and a Warner Brothers talent scout saw me, arranged a test for me, and suddenly I was in pictures.

Now comes the most interesting part about my name. I was given a lead role opposite Errol Flynn in *Dive Bomber,* and there was immediate talk around the studio about a new name for me. Everyone took it for granted that Alexis Smith would never do. The story is printed occasionally that I resisted—that I fought the studio, insisting on retaining my real name. That's not true. I assumed, along with all the others, that a new name was inevitable and I spent a lot of time (and almost went crazy) babbling names to myself. I was so ga-ga over my incredible luck that I didn't care if they changed my name to Alexis Astor or Luana Lurline or Primrose Stubbs.

Somehow the experts in charge of changing names at the studio let the matter slide and I went ahead with the picture, operating under what you might call the working title of Alexis Smith. Still no decision had been reached, and finally a rough cut of the picture was run in the projection room and they had to call me something in the cast credits and there it was—Alexis Smith. It happened that one of the studio promotion geniuses was present, and when he saw that name on the screen he let out a yell.

"Alexis Smith!" he cried. "What an inspiration! What a magnificent name for a girl! Alexis is different! It's glamorous! It's exotic! And just plain everyday good-ole-honest Smith! Men, this is IT!"

So that's the way it was—and lucky for me. My name is easy to remember, and it fits nicely in lights.

I have had my share of mistreatment from miserable amateur comedians around the studios because my name is Smith. I remember an assistant director on the picture *The Constant Nymph* and how he would call out: "Mr. Boyer, Miss Fontaine—and THE SMITH BROTHER!" Studio regulations say actors are not allowed to strangle assistant directors or he would have got it, for he had a whole repertoire of corny gags about the name Smith. There have been others.

In all honesty I can say that I am thankful that I have the name Smith. I'm proud of it—I think it is fun being a Smith.

Miss Mary Pickford, according to a report, is writing the story of her life. If the report be true, then she is at work on one of the most bizarre woman stories of modern times—a story that ought to be done by someone like Irving Stone. Miss Pickford has written other books, notably *Why Not Try God?* But I doubt that she has the correct perspective on her own fabulous career.

She was born Gladys Marie Smith in Toronto. Her mother, left a widow with three small children to support, found work as a character actress. The children trouped with her, and their earliest memories were of backstage life. Of the children, Little Gladys was the most proficient as a performer and was playing child roles when she was six. This little band of Smiths (they were really quite forlorn) eventually arrived in New York and somehow, when she was thirteen, Gladys caught the professional eye of David Belasco and she went into one of his productions. This is the point at which she changed her name.

In 1909 D. W. Griffith had joined the Biograph Company and was making crude motion pictures in the Fourteenth Street establishment which was known as the Biograph Factory. One day Mrs. Griffith entered the hall of the factory and saw a prim little girl who was waiting for a chance to see her husband. The child had on a plain blue serge suit, a blue and white striped shirtwaist, and a straw sailor hat with a blue ribbon bow. Mrs. Griffith talked to her and then called her husband, and he said he would use her in a picture, paying her five dollars a day, but he'd have to decide later about taking her on as a regular employee. He put her into a film called *The Violin Maker of Cremona* and was pleased with what she did and hired her for further work at twenty-five a week. In those beginning days of motion pictures the identities of the actors were kept a deep secret, mainly because the actors themselves didn't want their names associated with this shabby upstart in the world of entertainment. One of the little girl's early pictures was *The New York Hat*. The script had been bought from a Los Angeles schoolgirl named Anita Loos for fifteen dollars, and one of the principal performers was a young actor named Lionel Barrymore. After a while Biograph began to get many letters from the public demanding to know the name of the girl with the curls who was usually cast in the role of "Little Mary" in the films. The company refused to give out her name, and for several years she was known to an increasing audience of admirers only as Little Mary.

Something about her took the public's fancy, and as the movies grew she became more and more popular and, before very long, she was famous. In 1910 her mother called on Griffith, made mention of Mary's growth in the public esteem, and said the child's salary would have to be doubled. Griffith turned her down, and Mrs. Pickford (as Mrs. Smith now called herself) took Mary to Carl Laemmle. The public knew by now that the girl with the curls was Mary Pickford, and her skyrocket ride to national celebrity put her in a position to demand and get incredible rewards. Soon she was making a thousand dollars a week; later she would be paid ten thousand a week.

Her most successful pictures were confections like *Tess of the*

Storm Country, Stella Maris, Daddy Long Legs, Pollyanna, Rebecca of Sunnybrook Farm, Poor Little Rich Girl, and *Little Lord Fauntleroy.* She became, in a label dreamed up by a press agent, America's Sweetheart.

The years passed and the former Gladys Smith grew wealthy and now she tried to escape from those saccharin dramas that had made her famous. She yearned to prove herself in more substantial roles and she tried it, but the public didn't want her any other way —the public wanted her as Tess and Rebecca and Pollyanna, in stories that were loaded with mawkish sentiment, portraying the American girl as the public wanted her to be—sweet and innocent and virtuous, a trifle better than the seraphim, a shade purer than Ivory soap. I'm not trying to say the American girl wasn't that way, although there is an authenticated case of a young lady in Boston around 1912 who bore a child out of wedlock, and another case of a girl in Omaha who stuck a butcher knife in a young man who had been her sweetheart from childhood on and who offended her by dropping to his knees and imploring her to wed him.

Miss Pickford's divorce from her first husband, Owen Moore, was one of the first of the Hollywood matrimonial scandals, widely publicized because of her fame and because of official charges that the divorce itself was irregular. Her marriage to Douglas Fairbanks brought into being the Most Famous Couple on Earth, and life at Pickfair, their celebrated residence, grew into a beautiful legend. Following her divorce from Fairbanks she married Charles (Buddy) Rogers who, appropriately, had in his time as a screen star acquired the title of America's Boy Friend.

Meanwhile this wondrous lady whose screen portrayals had reflected a banal view of life held by multitudes of American citizens, who had grown to immense fame and fortune through such portrayals, was becoming eminently successful in another direction —the world of business and finance. Winsome Little Mary grew up to become one of the shrewdest and canniest businesswomen in the country. Some say she has no equal, in her sex, as a bargainer.

That, in essence, is her story as it looks to me. What interests us here is that she is a Smith, born and bred, and easily the greatest of all Smiths in the world of entertainment. After some urging

on my part, Miss Pickford wrote down the story of her Smith
background and the circumstances under which she changed her
name. So far as I know, this is the first account of the whole
business; most sketches of her life say that her mother, on becoming an actress, took the name of Pickford. Here is Mary's own
version:

> My father's name, believe it or not, was John
> Smith, and I remember as a tiny girl hearing him
> say that he would never risk being arrested, for if
> the judge asked him his name and he replied,
> "John Smith," he would surely be held in contempt
> of court.
>
> His mother, Sarah Keye, and his father, Joseph
> Smith, were both English and came to Canada at a
> very early age. I believe Sarah was six and Joseph
> an infant. They had twelve children, nine girls and
> three boys, so you can see it was a lusty clan. Of
> those three boys, my uncle Bill remained a bachelor
> while Uncle Joseph had two children, both girls.
> That left only my brother Jack to carry on the name
> of Smith in the male line, and the name of our
> branch of Smiths died out with the passing of my
> brother. Grandmother Smith, who used to say she
> was certain that Adam's name was Smith, was a
> devout Methodist and attended the same church in
> Toronto for eighty years. Heaven knows how many
> generations of Sunday-school pupils she taught.
>
> I was christened Gladys Marie. My mother's sis-
> ter had been reading a highly romantic novel in
> which the heroine was named Lady Gladys—hence
> the Gladys, which was soon shortened to "Glad."
> The handbills announcing my earliest appearances
> in the theater read, "Baby Gladys Is a Wonder,"
> which at the age of six gave me a highly inflated
> opinion of my own importance which, I might add,
> a wise mother nipped in the bud.
>
> When David Belasco gave me a part in a play
> and learned my name was Gladys Smith he said
> something would have to be done about it and for

me and my mother to think it over. There have been many explanations of why Pickford was chosen; actually it is an old family name. My mother's father's mother was an Englishwoman by the name of Elizabeth Pickford. She married a Hennessey and their son, John Pickford Hennessey, is buried in the family plot in the Catholic cemetery in Toronto. Mr. Belasco liked the name Pickford when it was suggested, so we took that as a surname, retaining the Mary (Marie) and dropping the Gladys.

The Smith Is My Undoing

> *Jack the Ripper was loose in London in 1888.*
> *He killed about twenty persons and was never*
> *caught. He brought high distinction to an other-*
> *wise drab sort of Smith. The first of all his muti-*
> *lated victims was a prostitute named Emma*
> *Smith.*

Save in the most obvious circumstances an author can never be
certain when he is going to offend his readers. A few years ago I
fabricated a novel which had a cat as its principal character.
Several of my friends warned me that I was laying myself open to
vilification and perhaps even physical danger. I could not, they
said, write an entire book about a cat without enraging either the
cat lovers of the world or the cat haters of the same world. The
feeling seemed to be that I would be assaulted from both camps.
So the book was published and I sat back with a carbine across my
lap waiting for the enemy. Nothing happened. One forlorn little
letter came from a lady who happened to be a cat lover and who
decreed that I was *en rapport* with cats and had done well by
them.

The next book I wrote was about an unsentimental excursion
into the Midwest, and in it was a brief account of a visit to a soda
fountain where I had jerked syrup as a boy. I complained in print
about the degeneration of the banana split, describing how the girl
at the fountain went about composing the dish and then recalling

the magnificence of the banana split as it was constructed around 1920.

I never got so much abuse over anything in my life. People wrote from all over the country denouncing me for a barbarian, a quack, and a bungler of crushed nuts.

During the preliminary maneuvers leading up to the writing of this book I put together some of the Smith material to make a magazine article, and it appeared in *Cosmopolitan*. The theme of that essay was: The Smiths, who have been the Number One clan in our nation almost from the time Captain John set foot on the soil of Virginia, who have been right up near the top in almost every other field of human endeavor, are strangely absent from leadership in sports.

The Smiths of the country rose in arms, howling for my scalp. I was a traitor to my tribe. I was ignorant. I should change my name to Poophead and get somebody to inject some plain air into my veins. This storm of protest didn't distress me, but had an exhilarating effect. It demonstrated clearly that the Smiths, like all other minority groups, have more than a little pride and that they will go forth to battle when their good name is besmirched. And like all other minority groups, they will go forth to battle whether the besmirchment is grounded in fact or not. In this case it *was* grounded in fact.

There are scores of Smiths, of course, in baseball, football, basketball, boxing, golf, tennis, and all the other athletic pursuits; yet candor compels me to insist that they are usually the players who fumble the ball, kill the caddy with a faulty backswing, fall off the horse, kayo the referee, or strike out with the bases loaded. There is a saving circumstance, however, in the fact that they excel as professional kibitzers. The Smiths are the most skillful of all onlookers at sports events. The top sports writer in the country today is Red Smith. The profession he graces is, in fact, aswarm with Smiths—from Ken Smith on the East Side of Manhattan to Harry Smith, who has been at the trade for fifty years or more in San Francisco. Pick up any of the recent anthologies devoted to sports stories and note the prevalence of Smiths among the writers, and the absence of Smiths among the performers written about.

Some time ago I found myself involved in a collaboration, the end result of which was a book of anecdotes taken from the history of baseball. My collaborator was a Virginian, a complete stranger to me—the same Ira L. Smith who appears elsewhere in this volume as Watch-the-Thumb Smith. When the first printed copy of our book came into my hands I thumbed through it (actually I forefingered through it), and a singular fact presented itself. Two Smiths had produced a book on baseball, and the only Smith of any consequence whose name appeared in the text was not a ballplayer but a fan—one H. C. Smith of Chicago, whose admiration for Iron Man McGinnity was of such magnitude that, when he heard that the aging pitcher was out of a job, he bought the Newark club and installed his hero as its manager. The only ballplayer named Smith who got into our book was included not for any heroic performance but because he swallowed a chew of tobacco while running from first to second and became so sick that he had to be taken out of the game.

Coming upon Grantland Rice one evening in Manhattan, I backed the sports authority against a wall and gave him a brief word-association test. I called out certain surnames and asked him to designate the sports personalities that popped into his mind as each name was spoken.

"*Robinson,*" I said.

"That would be Jackie," said Mr. Rice, "or Wilbert, or——"

"*Jones,*" I interrupted.

"Bobby . . . Ben . . . Available . . . Wah Wah," he responded, covering four sports quickly.

"*Johnson.*"

"Walter . . . Ban . . . Jack."

"*Miller.*"

"Eddie . . . Don . . ."

"*Young.*"

"Buddy . . . Babe . . . Cy."

"*Brown.*"

"Three-fingered . . . Bobby . . . Tommy."

"*Smith.*"

CATFISH
SMITH

Mr. Rice tipped his head back, ruminated for a moment, and then said:

"Well, now, there are lots of Smiths, of course. . . . Let me see —there's Red Smith——"

"Who's he?" I asked quickly.

"Sports writer," said Mr. Rice. "But then there's also Red Smith the coach—was a guard at Notre Dame, coaches baseball, used to be with the Cubs, used to be with the New York Giants football team, works down in Texas now.

"I'm trying to think," said Mr. Rice, "if I ever named a Smith on an All-American team. Must have. Oh yes. Catfish Smith. He was an end at Georgia around 1931. But come to think of it, I believe he was as famous for that name as he was for playing football."

"Did he get the name," I asked, "from the fact that he darted around in the manner of a catfish?"

"No," said Mr. Rice. "He got the name one day when he bit the head off a catfish for a dollar."

This little experiment with Grantland Rice proves, I think, my contention that the name Smith never leaps to the tongue when one contemplates the field of athletics. We have been there in numbers, but none of our boys has ever quite made the list of the so-called immortals in sports. And if you didn't know it already, there are more immortals in sports than there are in heaven.

No Smith has ever been given a place on the all-time all-star baseball teams which sports writers occasionally assemble on paper. And the name Smith is unknown in the Baseball Hall of Fame at Cooperstown. No Smith ever won a "most-valuable player" award in the big leagues. No Smith has ever led either of the big leagues in pitching, batting, base stealing, or home runs, and these are the categories in which great heroes are made.

Mr. Rice, if he had thought further, would have remembered other Smiths from his All-American teams—he gave nine Smiths the nod at one time or another. Yet I have examined a dozen or so *all-time* All-American football teams and can find the name Smith mentioned but once. Orland F. Smith, a guard at Brown, was included on a list that was restricted to players who were in action during the ten-year period from 1918 to 1928. I am informed that Orland, who was called Orlando Furioso under the tradition that all Smiths must be given fantastic nicknames, was a second-stringer at Brown until his senior year. And while there have been these other Smiths on the All-American lists since 1903, they were never stars of the first magnitude, never performers to be remembered as the names of Thorpe, Gipp, Heffelfinger, Grange, Nagurski, Nevers, Baugh, and Blanchard are remembered.

The best year for the Smiths in football was 1935, when three members of the clan made All-American. They were I. Smith, guard from Ohio State; R. Smith, a tackle from Minnesota, and Alabama's Riley Smith, who was a brilliant quarterback and placement kicker.

Recognition must be given to:

Andy Smith, star fullback at Penn State, who made Walter Camp's All-American team in 1903 and who coached California's "Wonder Team" in 1920.

Maurice Smith of Notre Dame, who cleared the path for the great George Gipp.

Bruce Smith, backfield star whose name will long be remembered at Minnesota.

Ernie Smith, a great tackle for Southern California in the early 1930s.

Harry "Blackjack" Smith, USC guard in 1938–39.

Then there was Earthquake Smith, still considered the best linesman North Carolina ever had. One of the Southern schools, too, had a backfield star named Smith whose exploits are said to have inspired many of the legends reflecting academic ignorance among subsidized football players. This particular Smith reputedly missed one game when a naïve and uninformed professor made the mistake of asking him to repeat the alphabet. In class the football star was given a seat behind the star scholar. Once during a written examination the scholar answered the first nine questions correctly but wrote under the tenth: "I do not know the answer to this question." The football star also answered the first nine, but under the tenth he wrote: "I don't either."

It would seem inevitable that one of these days a Smith is going to come along and perform so brilliantly in one of our major sports that he will join the company of such individuals as Babe Ruth, Jack Dempsey, Bill Tilden, Ty Cobb, Gil Dodds, George Gipp, Christy Mathewson, Bobby Jones, Earl Sande, Joe Louis, Red Grange, Honus Wagner, Jim Thorpe, Nat Holman, Tris Speaker, Helen Wills, and all the others. It hasn't happened yet, though certain polo fans have threatened to dent my skull with mallets for neglecting Cecil Smith. Cecil came off a Texas ranch in the 1930s and is probably the greatest polo player in the world today.

Both Clair Bee and Nat Holman have compiled lists of the greatest basketball players of all time, collegiate and professional, and the name Smith appears on none of those lists; yet LeRoy

Smith of Long Island University has been one of the standouts in college basketball for the last year or so. No Smith has ever won the Indianapolis Speedway race. In golf Horton Smith, Macdonald Smith, and Alex Smith have been prominent, but their names do not appear on the lists of the greatest golfers of all time. Lately there has been a swimming star named Bill Smith, nicknamed "Flying Fish" Smith. We have had a lady duck-pin bowling champion in the person of Doris Smith, but none in fly casting. Dorothy Smith was a star in archery, but there's never been a champion pool shooter named Smith. Among the six-day bicycle racers, Ted Smith appears to be one of the top stars of the present crop; and in ice hockey both Don Smith and Sid Smith are coming along. A boy named Bobby Smith from San Diego turned up in 1950 as a pole-vaulting sensation, but he wasn't quite as sensational as his advance billing.

Returning to baseball, the 1950 season found a single Smith wearing a big-league uniform—Frank Smith, a relief pitcher for the Cincinnati Reds. Leo Durocher was high on a Negro pitcher named Ford Smith during spring training, but when the season opened, Ford was back with Jersey City.

In baseball the nearest approach to immortality, among the Smiths, belongs either to Elmer, who was the first man ever to hit a home run with the bases loaded during a World Series (1920), or to Germany Smith.

The information on Germany Smith was passed along to me by Robert Smith, the baseball historian. Germany's story begins with another Smith—John "Phenomenal" Smith, a prominent pitcher in the early days of baseball. Back in 1885 Phenomenal Smith pitched for the Flatbushers against Brooklyn and lost, 18 to 5, although not one of the eighteen runs was earned. There were nineteen errors behind him, seven being committed by the shortstop. That shortstop was Germany Smith, and his seven bonehead plays established a record for shortstops engaged in professional play. He retained that record for fifteen years, and then it was tied, in Buffalo, by another shortstop—fellow by the name of Jud Smith.

Robert Smith speaks feelingly, too, of Piano Legs Smith, who was with the Giants in 1900 and who had the distinction of committing ninety-one errors in 118 games. Robert also mentions Sherry Smith, a capable pitcher for Brooklyn, and J. Carlisle Smith, a third baseman who wore a luxuriant red pompadour and was popular with the ladies. This J. Carlisle Smith played originally for Auburn College and had set himself the goal of one day performing in a World Series. In 1914 he was signed with the Boston Braves, the Braves clinched the pennant in September, and J. Carlisle's goal was in sight. Then in the ninth inning of the last game of the regular season J. Carlisle Smith broke his leg sliding into second.

Says Robert Smith:

"Don't forget Pacer Smith, who played for Decatur in 1887 and who got his name from the peculiar gait he used on the base paths. He was a good pitcher. He murdered his wife with a butcher knife and was hanged."

And where, you may well wonder, does this Robert Smith get all his baseball information? He gets much of it from Guy McI. Smith of Danville, Illinois. Guy is close to eighty and is an important figure in baseball though he never played a lick in his life. He's said to be the nation's greatest authority on statistical matters and old-time ballplayers.

The only Smith whose name appears on the lists of world champions in boxing (disregarding one Jem Smith who dates back to bare-knuckle times) is Mysterious Billy Smith, the first welterweight champion. He lost the title, I understand, by fouling his opponent. Gunboat Smith never got to the championship. Do I hear you whisper the name of Sugar Ray Robinson? Yes, I know. His real name is Walker Smith, but nobody ever uses it, and he will go into the books as Robinson. He has often been described as the finest all-around fighting man in the ring today. He was a skinny little crapshooter answering to the nickname "Smitty" when a fight manager got hold of him, gave him a little schooling, and threw him into a ring. The manager had so little faith in him as a boxer that he hadn't bothered about getting him a permit to fight. At the moment Smitty was getting ready to climb into the ring for his first fight the manager reached in his pocket and found

a card belonging to another kid named Ray Robinson and used that one for his new boy, and the name stuck.

In racing, the Kentucky Derby winners have been ridden by people named Swim, Simms, Winkfield, Pickens, Perkins, Shilling, and Goose, but never by a Smith. There have been several jockeys named Smith, but the only one who ever achieved any notice worth mentioning was F. A. Smith, whose front initials plus a certain chubbiness around the hips brought him the affectionate nickname, among racing fans, of "Fat." There have been outstanding trainers, to be sure, such as Whistlin' Bob Smith and Silent Tom Smith. Silent Tom is the man who developed Seabiscuit, loudly. But there have not—— Wup! Just a moment! Hold the phone! What's this? Right here in the list of——

Yes, it's true. A bit sadly I must report that a Smith *did* reach the top, did soar to immortality in the world of sports.

His name? George Smith. And who was George Smith? He was a horse—and he won the Kentucky Derby in 1916.

If no Smith, other than a horse, has attained to immortality in sports, we can still take satisfaction from the knowledge that we have contributed more than our just proportion of sports writers, and that some of the performing Smiths have brought color and drama and even high comedy to the playing fields.

We could argue all night and still wind up with a hung jury if we tackled the proposition: Is Red Smith as great a man as Joe DiMaggio? Few would dispute my assumption that Red Smith is the best sports writer named Smith in the whole world; many would agree that Red is the best sports writer on earth named anything. Yet you need travel only a few blocks to the east from Red's little coop in the *Herald Tribune* building to find Jack Smith and Stan Smith turning out first-rate sports copy at the *Daily News,* and Ken Smith performing expertly on the sports staff of the *Daily Mirror,* and Marshall Smith serving as sports editor of *Life* magazine. All across the country Smiths are thumping typewriters in sports departments of our daily newspapers; they write on sports in the magazines, and they turn out books. It was Shirley W. Smith, an executive at the University of Michigan, who invented the fable which became the motion picture *It Happens Every Spring.*

Red Smith of the *Herald Tribune* and other papers has a more formal name, but few people know about it. It is Walter Wellesley Smith. He was born in Green Bay, Wisconsin, in 1905, attended Notre Dame, and after working on newspapers in Milwaukee, St. Louis, and Philadelphia arrived at his present location in 1945. He takes genuine pleasure from the confusions that sometimes arise out of his being known as plain Red Smith. He insists that it would be the same if he operated under the name of Walter, and recalls that in his St. Louis days the president of the First National Bank was Walter W. Smith, an important man nationally as well as Missourily. Red was in the phone book as Walter W. Smith and remembers the delight he had in getting, each Christmas, a case of Texas grapefruit from Jesse Jones, and how holiday greetings arrived regularly from such people as Secretary and Mrs. Henry Morgenthau.

Walter Wellesley is a little sad that the other Red Smith, whom he calls the Impostor, has removed himself from the big leagues. Richard (Red) Smith maintained himself for some years in a double-barreled position as a coach and scout for the Chicago Cubs in baseball and as assistant coach of the Giants in the National Football League. In 1950 he resigned both jobs and joined the

Dallas club in the Texas league as a coach. The presence of two important Red Smiths around major sports events sometimes led to bewildering episodes. Let Red (The True) Smith tell it:

> In Boston during the 1948 World Series—Braves versus Indians—the phone wrenched me out of the weeds and a faintly familiar voice said:
> "Red?"
> "Yeah."
> "Leo."
> "Who?"
> "Leo." Then I recognized it.
> "You coming up to see me?" he said, and he went on to say he'd been with Bob (Hannegan of the Cardinals) last night and that he'd seen Horace (Stoneham), who was worried, and so on. I said I'd be up to see him. After a while the fog cleared and I called Durocher's room.
> "You called the wrong Red Smith," I told him.
> "Oh, Jesus!" he said, although he hadn't really told me anything. "Oh, God!" et cetera. I told him to stop worrying and start getting his phone calls straight, and I went to sleep.
> That night on the train for Cleveland Joe Reardon, head of the Phillies' farm system, said, "I was on the phone with you the other day." It didn't seem worth disputing the point and the train was making a good deal of noise, so I shrugged. But he persisted, "I know. I know you made that Nicholson deal. I was listening in on another phone."
> Slowly, because of that morning call, I realized he was talking about the Impostor and the recent trade for Bill Nicholson of the Cubs. I explained.
> "So that was it," Joe said, light dawning. "When they told me they were dealing with Red Smith I thought, 'How far can they trust him? He'll put it in the paper.'"
> Afterwards I urged Phil Wrigley and Jim Gallagher to find out who was making their deals for 'em and please to have him get his phone calls

straight. I don't mind being disturbed early—the hell I don't—but I do not wish to wind up owning one of the Cubs' pitchers. Or, even worse, one of the Giants.

Did no good, though. I've been hounded for World Series tickets by people I've never heard of, and I once received a telegram in Chicago from Wellington Mar authorizing me to go hire a big tackle from Iowa.

Trouble is, the spurious Smith and I were classmates at Notre Dame and he makes the utterly false claim of coming from Green Bay. Actually he comes from Combined Locks, a paper mill up the Fox River, and only played guard for the Packers and managed the baseball team in Green Bay.

Two or three falls ago Red and I met regularly at the Monday football writers' luncheons in Shor's. The Associated Press man always collected ballots there for the AP's weekly poll naming the top ten teams in the country. Nobody ever knows ten top teams, of course; usually one guy at a table will fill out ballots for everybody, just groping blindly as soon as he gets past the first name—Notre Dame.

One day the Impostor brought news that our friend and classmate, Red Hearden, was having an undefeated season at St. Norbert's College, De Pere, Wisconsin, which is five miles up the river from Green Bay. In my time St. Norbert's was a junior college and we at East High could lick 'em at anything.

Nevertheless, each Monday during that season the Impostor and I saw to it that St. Norbert's was listed no worse than tenth on the ballots at Shor's. By sheer weight of numbers this put our pal's team pretty high up on the national lists.

In Green Bay for a visit the next summer, I mentioned Hearden to a friend. "He had a great season," the guy said, awed. "Had an unbeaten team, and do you know? It was rated twenty-second in the whole country!"

I tell this as evidence of the Impostor's coaching genius. At a distance of a thousand miles, he put St. Norbert's up there on a par with the Penns and Californias and Tulanes and Alabamas, and far ahead of the Yales.

Thus Red Smith's account of his relationship with Red Smith. As for other Smiths, he has this to say:

Many years ago when I was traveling with the Cardinals a broad arrived in my room in the Alamac Hotel here in New York, obviously under the impression that the room belonged to a certain ballplayer named Smith. She was large, unwashed, and skunk drunk, which made for complications; I think I finally sent her to a fashionable infielder's room, doubting that she would be welcomed by the other Smith, whose wife happened to be traveling with him.

I haven't heard any real good Smith stories since the time my great-uncles, Sile and Howard, were boys chopping wood on the Wisconsin farm. "Howard," says Sile, "put your finger on that block and I'll chop it off." Howard did and Sile did. Case of overdoing mutual respect; Howard didn't think Sile would chop and Sile didn't think Howard would leave his finger there.

Out of the lore and legend of American baseball come stories about three characters named Smith.

Mayo Smith, playing with Buffalo, led all International League hitters in 1944 with a batting average of .341 and gave all the credit for this performance to his two-year-old daughter.

One day early in that season Mayo was leaving his home for the ball park and his tiny daughter raised her arm, gurgled "Goo-by, Daddy," and waved her hand in a peculiar sort of waggle. That afternoon Mayo got four hits out of four times at bat. In the time-honored tradition of ballplayers, he sat down and tried to figure out what had caused him to have such a good day. A ballplayer almost always attributes favorable performance not to his own talent but to some extraneous influence, such as the necktie he wore to the park, or the hard knot in his shoelaces, or the presence of a billy goat in the vicinity of the stadium. At last Mayo got it— the kid, and the way she said goo-by, and the way she waved that hand. On the following day Mayo had the child stand in the same spot, drilled her until she was able to repeat the performance, making the hand waggle the way it had waggled yesterday, coaching her to say "Goo-by, Daddy" with the same intonation she had used before. And Mayo Smith was invincible that afternoon. Each day thereafter the little girl went through that farewell routine, and when the season was over her daddy unblushingly gave her full credit for his beautiful batting average.

"I'd a hit over .400," said Mayo, "if they'd-a let me take the kid on road trips."

Many years ago there was a clever southpaw pitcher playing with a college team, named Rufus Smith (not to be confused with my dog, whose name is Rufus Smith, nor with Rufus Smith, provost of New York University). A scout for the Detroit Tigers got a look at this Rufus and sent a glowing letter about him to Frank J. Navin, then boss of the Detroit club. Navin signed the boy, sight unseen and sent him to a minor-league club for seasoning.

Toward the end of the season Rufus was brought up to Detroit for his big tryout against major-league hitting. Navin was seated in his box at the Detroit park when this little squirt of a guy came out, wearing a Tiger uniform, and began warming up.

"Who's that?" asked Navin.

"Why, boss, that's Rufus Smith," someone told him, "the kid we got out of that college."

Navin took another look at the boy, frowning darkly, then stood up and said: "Well, I'm not going to sit around here and look at *him* all afternoon." He left the ball park and Rufus Smith went on to win the game, showing a lot of class in doing it. But the following day Rufus got word from the business office that he wasn't needed around Detroit, and he disappeared into the bushes. It was quite a while before anyone found out why this promising prospect had been sent away. Navin owned, in addition to the ball club, a string of race horses, and those horses had not been performing adequately. Navin was convinced that his contract rider,. a jockey named DuBois, was responsible, and he had worked up a dudgeon against DuBois. That day when he looked out and saw Rufus Smith he thought the college boy was the jockey—that Du-Bois had come in from the track, donned a Tiger uniform, and was now preparing to sabotage the ball club, as he had, in Navin's opinion, sabotaged the racing stable. And because Rufus Smith bore a striking resemblance to a jockey who was in disfavor, he lost his chance with the Tigers.

My own favorite among baseball players named Smith is old Slow-Eye. Even though it belongs to pure mythology, there are fans on the Pacific coast who will tell you the story of Slow-Eye Smith and swear it is God's own truth. I suspect that it originated as fiction, perhaps a short story in some magazine; if that is so, I haven't been able to locate the owner who deserves credit for his creation.

Slow-Eye Smith came by his name because of the way he saw things—slow. So far as he was concerned everything in the nature of movement appeared in slow motion. An automobile doing fifty miles an hour looked to Slow-Eye to be going about five.

One day this remarkable gentleman was sitting at a lunch counter in Los Angeles, waiting for a sandwich. Nearby sat a man who happened to be a ballplayer with a local club. This second man saw a fly whiz down the counter and then saw Slow-Eye reach out casually and pluck the insect from the air. Another fly zipped past, and Slow-Eye nipped it deftly between thumb and forefinger.

"How in the world did you do that?" spoke up the ballplayer. "That fly was goin' like a bullet."

Slow-Eye slowly turned his head and looked at his neighbor.

"I never been able to understand," he said, "why it is folks think a fly goes fast. Why, to me it seems like they just sorta drift along."

The ballplayer gave some thought to this ocular phenomenon and then had an idea.

"You ever play baseball?" he asked.

"Sure," said Slow-Eye. "Played baseball in school. You oughta see me hit that ball. Don't make any difference how hard the pitcher throws it, it's just glidin' along like a canoe by the time it gets to me. Only thing I don't like about playin' baseball is all that waitin' around I got to do, standin' there and waitin' for the ball to get up to me so's I can knock it over the fence. Never could stand waitin'."

"Godamighty sakes!" exclaimed the other man. He questioned Slow-Eye some more about his reduced-speed vision. Then he told him to stay right in that restaurant, to wait for an hour, and Slow-Eye said he would. The ballplayer raced down to the offices of his club and poured out his story and was called a crank, an idiot, a drunk, and a con man. He persisted, however, and finally got the club manager sufficiently aroused to go back to the restaurant with him. But Slow-Eye wasn't there. Nor were they ever able to find him. He had said, hadn't he, that he never liked waitin'?

Joe Williams, star of the Scripps-Howard sports pages and a man with whom I used to play a game called The-Hell-with-Eatin'-Anything, gave some thought to the matter of Smiths in professional athletics. He thought of this one and then that one and finally he said:

"I can tell you a negative sort of story, but it's about a Smith who had more influence on a major sporting event than any other Smith in history."

So here is that story, hot from the typewriter of the estimable Colonel himself:

> In the spring of '42 Mike Jacobs made a con-
> nection with the War Department and arranged for
> Billy Conn and Joe Louis, both in the Army, to box
> for Army relief. This was to be a return bout. The
> two men had met in '41 and it was a thriller. Conn
> had the title won going into the thirteenth. All he
> had to do to win was coast the rest of the distance.
> But the donkey Irish in him came out; he tried to
> slug with Louis, and he was stiffened. Nevertheless,
> the stage was set for a million-dollar return bout,
> and this was the bout Mike Jacobs had arranged.
> As the day for the match approached Conn got a

furlough to attend the christening of his first-born
in Pittsburgh. After the christening there was a gala
at Conn's house with both families attending. This
is where the Smiths come in. Conn's father-in-law
was and is Jimmy Smith, an old-time ballplayer.
In the beginning Smith took a dim view of Conn
as a son-in-law. After the christening that day, one
word led to another and presently Smith was chal-
lenging the young man who had given Louis his
hardest fight since he had become champion. The
scene was the kitchen, where the aristocracy of the
Irish usually gather. There was a blurred flurry of
movement. Whether anyone hit anyone else depo-
nent knoweth not. But in the tumult there came
a shriek from Conn. Something grievous had happened to his left hand—his best hand. X rays showed
it was broken. The big fight had to be called off.
Army relief lost half a million dollars. That, my boy,
is what a Smith can do on a fast track with a favoring wind.

Colonel Williams, in a postscript, points out that when Conn
and Louis finally did meet after the war, the customers paid
$1,925,564—the second largest gate in the history of the game
(topped only by the second Tunney-Dempsey thing in Chicago).

George Ellsworth Smith was rarely called by any one of his
three proper names but was known far and wide as Pittsburgh
Phil. He started life as a cork cutter in a factory, but he had a
mathematical flair plus a certain daring plus also a coldly unemo-
tional attitude toward life. In time he became one of the most
famous gamblers this country has ever known. He is said to have
been the first man to try to make an exact science out of horse-race
forecasting. He would select a single race, giving himself plenty of
time for study, and then he'd figure that race. He figured everything. He traced the blood lines of the competing horses back to
Eohippus. He studied the anatomy of each animal and then,
having satisfied himself as to hocks and pasterns, he examined
their minds, performing a sort of psychoanalysis on them. He

studied the dirt or the turf of the track and the weather forecasts and the personal quirks of the jockeys and the sleeping habits of the grooms and the love life of the trainers and the nature and quality of the wood the quarter poles were made from. And when he was through and had chosen his horse—that horse couldn't lose even if he was shot dead in the back stretch.

Damon Runyon was the guy who repeatedly sang the old refrain—horse players always die broke. Runyon surely must have known about Pittsburgh Phil. He was a widely celebrated character in his day. Lillian Russell, when she was introduced to him, exclaimed: "Why, you're more famous than John L. Sullivan or Buffalo Bill." When he died he was worth something over two million dollars.

Peace of Smith

The American Association for the Advancement of Atheism was organized in New York City in 1925. Its first president was Charles Smith.

In the history of religion the name of Smith enjoys a position of high frequency, although the individual voltage has been low. No Smith has ever reigned as Pope, or as Archbishop of Canterbury, or even become whatever it is the Aga Khan is. It is possible, of course, that someday one of our name will reach the top at the Vatican, although the chances are quite slim at the moment—there is no Smith in the College of Cardinals, no archbishop named Smith, nor do I find the name in the current list of Roman Catholic bishops in the United States. The House of Bishops of the Protestant Episcopal Church, Smithless for years, began to show signs of progress and enlightenment in the spring of 1950, when the Right Reverend Gordon V. Smith became Bishop for Iowa.

Nonetheless, we have contributed some imposing personalities to the religious scene. One of our men had a series of hot flashes and founded a sizable church. We have produced one of the world's greatest evangelistic shouters. And the postwar spate of inspirational literature is nothing new to the Smiths, who have been turning it out for years. We have already met Hannah Smith, who wrote of the happy life; there have been many others, such as Roy Lemon Smith, a Kansas-born Methodist minister whose published works include: *Moving Pictures in the Church,*

Capturing Crowds, Four Wheel Brakes, Some Wild Notions I Have Known, Spare Tires, Pantomimes and Pageants for Pulpit Use, Two Years of Sunday Nights, Winning Ways for Working Churches, and *Suburban Christians.*

The Methodist Church lists two Smiths among its bishops. One is A. Frank Smith of Houston, board chairman of Southern Methodist University and a leader in the Boy Scout movement; the other is W. Angie Smith of Oklahoma City. A few years back Bishop H. Lester Smith of Cincinnati was president of the Methodist Council of Bishops. He was quite a fellow, having once been an oilman in Pennsylvania and a tiger hunter in India. Let it be noted, parenthetically, that it would seem to be required of a Methodist Smith that he part his name on the side if he wants to reach the top.

One of the most prominent Smiths in religious history was John the Se-baptist, an English non-conformist clergyman who was bounced out of the Established Church in 1602 for having radical views on the subject of baptism. He didn't like the way they did their baptizing in England and in a loud voice he said so, and then fled to Holland. When he got over there he baptized himself, the way he believed a man ought to be baptized in order to make it stick, and that's why he was called John Smith the Se-baptist. He is of further importance to us because he figured prominently in the religious rebellion which led, in the end, to the emigration of the Pilgrim Fathers to New England. Contemporaries of the Se-baptist were Henry Smith, a Puritan divine who was called "Silver Tongue" Smith, and Richard Smith, described as "the greatest pillar of the Roman Catholic Church in his time."

John the Se-baptist should not be confused with the Reverend John Smith who arrived in Massachusetts in 1630 and was one of the founders of Barnstable and Sandwich. He sired thirteen Smiths, and their descendants, scattered over the nation, are beyond counting.

Gipsy Smith, whose real name was Rodney, ranks among the great evangelists of modern times and occupied in England the same position that Billy Sunday held in the United States. He started out as a member of General Booth's Christian Mission, which later became the Salvation Army. He was expelled from the organization for a breach of discipline, but he went right on preaching. Occasionally he came over to this country and traveled up and down the land whooping like a Comanche. He turned up in Chicago, for example, in 1909 at a time when sin was flourishing more than usual. Old-timers in Chicago still talk about that visitation. Gipsy went after sinners in every category, but his big guns were trained on commercialized love. One March day he led a thousand hosannah-shouters into the very center of the red-light district, and while hundreds of whores trembled at the upper windows, the invaders fell to their knees on the pavement and sang in thunderous accents, "Where Is My Wandering Boy Tonight?"

The rise of Father Divine to a position where His followers believe Him to be God is, of course, one of the wonders of modern times. If you are one who doesn't believe Him to be God, please remember that He caused the 1950 water shortage in New York City. He said so Himself. He said that the people of the city didn't love Him as they should, and He shouted: "I will dry up your rivers and I will dry up your streams! This water shortage in New York City has been just a slight sketch and a reflection of what I will do."

Now, you've got to be a little careful about a man (or God) who goes around doing things like that; nevertheless, at the risk of having Him dry *me* up, I must call attention to a few facts out of Father Divine's past which suggest that a man named Smith was largely responsible for His rise to divinity. Let us go back to 1931 when this little Negro had a mere handful of followers in a couple of houses at Sayville on Long Island. In the fall of that year the Sayville police became alarmed over the doings on Macon Street, especially on Sundays, when Father Divine's free chicken dinners were attracting crowds from Manhattan. So they arrested Him on a charge of maintaining a public nuisance. He was brought to trial before Justice Lewis J. Smith in Nassau County, and Justice Smith charged the jury in such a manner that a verdict of guilty was a virtual certainty. God was hopping mad about this, and the story goes that He uttered a curse on the head of Justice Smith. The judge was to all appearances a man in robust health, but four days after Father Divine's conviction he was dead of a heart attack. Thousands now flocked to this new leader, convinced that He had struck down His enemy, and the newspapers began to take an interest in Him. He was ready for them. When they asked Him where He was born he replied that He was not born. "I was combusted," he said, "at the corner of Lenox Avenue and Forty-second Street." When they pointed out that Lenox Avenue and Forty-second Street don't intersect, God replied, "They did when I was combusted there."

Diligent search is bound to turn up Smiths of some importance in every branch of the Christian religion. They have been leaders in Christian Science, in Seventh-Day Adventism, in Moral Rearmament, and among those who roll holy. There have been Smiths, no doubt, among the Two-Seed-in-the-Spirit Predestinarian Baptists, a cult mentioned recently in the writings of the Reverend Alson J. Smith. A Milwaukee businessman, Charles R. Smith, was at last report president of the National Spiritualist Association—the largest group of Over Yonderites in the country.

Mention should be made of the Reverend Clustor Q. Smith, president of Oklahoma City University and a Methodist, because of his unusual first name, and the Reverend Blake Smith, Arkansas Baptist writer and broadcaster, because of his father's name, which was Other Smith. And among the clerical Smiths of colonial times—there were dozens of them—we note the name of the Reverend Cotton Mather Smith, a fighting preacher under General Philip Schuyler during the Revolution. It was said of him that he could preach a sermon an hour long in less than twenty minutes.

Concerning the career of Joseph Smith, founder of the Church of Jesus Christ of Latter-Day Saints, there can be no beating around the burning bush. If you are one of the million adherents to the present-day Mormon Church, you believe that God and Christ and John the Baptist and Elijah and several angels actually appeared before Joe for purposes of divine revelation. If you are not a follower of the Mormon religion, you believe that Joe was daft. Or, to be charitable, that he was just a fellow who saw things.

Joseph Smith was born in 1805 in Vermont, and when he was eleven his family moved to Palmyra in New York. According to a biography written by his mother, Lucy Smith, Joe's paternal grandfather was known as "Crooked Neck" Smith and had fits. His other grandfather was a beggar and a devout follower of faith healers. His father, Joe, Sr., was a jack-of-all-trades who believed in demons and witchcraft. The York State region where he settled was teeming with queer religious groups—spiritualism would soon have its origin there.

When Joe was about fourteen he went into the woods one day to do some praying and there had his first vision. Two vague sort of presences appeared before him and told him that all existing religions were in error—that Joe should hold himself in readiness to receive the truth. Three years later an angel by the name of Moroni visited Joe and notified him that the time of revelation was at hand. There followed seven more visions in seven years. On September 22, 1827, Moroni told Joe that he would find the sacred book at a certain spot on Cumorah Hill. Joe went up there and dug, and came up with a series of plates of gold, each about six inches wide and eight inches long, with Egyptian writing on them. The plates were held together with golden rings, making a sort of unwieldy book, and along with the book came a device called Urim and Thummim, described as "two transparent stones set in a rim on a bow fastened to a breastplate." I'd hate to have to draw a picture of it from that description.

Urim and Thummim were the magical instruments which made it possible for Joe, who was practically illiterate, to translate the sacred book. The actual translation turned into a fanciful sort of operation. Joe hung a blanket from the ceiling and then hid himself behind it with the plates and the Urim and Thummim gadget. By looking at the plates through the Urim and Thummim he was able to dictate in English what was written in Egyptian, and on the other side of the curtain some of his friends took turns writing it down. The Mormons themselves believe that when Joe looked at the plates through the transparent stones the sacred text translated itself one sentence at a time and Joe would holler that sentence through the blanket. If the copyists on the other side

made a mistake putting it down, the next sentence would no⁺
pear until the error had been corrected.

The book that emerged from this intricate operation proved to
be a history of two races which inhabited ancient America—the
Jaredites who came from the Tower of Babel, and the Nephites
who left Jerusalem six hundred years before the birth of Christ.
These Jaredites and Nephites achieved a degree of civilization
comparable to our own, in that they engaged in incessant warfare
with each other, killing themselves off until only a few scattered
tribes remained, and these were the American Indians.

The sacred writing tells further how Jesus appeared in America
after his resurrection and how the people grew wicked and how
finally everyone of importance was exterminated, save for one
prophet named Mormon, who was allowed to live in order that he
might write down this very history and hide it on Cumorah Hill
so that it would be there waiting for our Joe when he got on earth.
There are some angles of this story, as I have it here, that don't
seem to parse; I've put it down to the best of my ability, without
the services of a Urim and Thummim, and if any canonical error
has crept in, I can only plead that I'm a lousy theologian.

It took Joe two years to get the Book of Mormon translated, and
it was published in 1830 at a buck twenty-five and peddled over
the York State countryside. In that same year at Fayette the
Church of Jesus Christ of Latter-Day Saints was organized. It
didn't prosper, largely because the people of that region had such
a wide assortment of daffy cults to choose from, so in the following
year Joe had a new revelation which told him to move West. He
went to Kirtland, Ohio, where he fell in with a former Baptist
preacher named Sidney Rigdon. Joe talked Rigdon around to ac-
ceptance of his new religion, and Rigdon brought about two
thousand of his personal followers into the fold—people who had
accepted his theology before and now were willing to switch over,
on his say-so, to devout belief in Joe Smith, Moroni, the golden
plates, and Urim and Thummim. Sometimes I am consumed by
sinful envy when I think of the clergy. Whatever they say, by
God, that's the law. All they have to do is say the world is flat, or
round, or upside down, and the people say amen. All they have to

do is say the world is really an oyster, and the people nod and get out the horse-radish. If I had it to do over again, I think I'd go for holy orders. Get a little more respect for my opinions around here.

From Ohio the Mormons moved on to Independence, Missouri, where they met with vigorous opposition from the Pukes, so they back-tracked, and in 1838 on the east bank of the Mississippi Joe and his people founded a new town which they called Nauvoo. Before long Nauvoo had become the biggest town in Illinois. Then in 1843 Prophet Joe came up with a fresh revelation providing for celestial marriage, or polygamy. The leaders kept this one to themselves for nine years before letting the general membership have it.

The Mormons of Nauvoo were not exactly a peaceable people, but quarreled among themselves and had a few riots, so that the non-Mormons of Illinois took to hating them, shooting them and burning down their houses. Trouble piled up and led eventually to the arrest of the Prophet and his brother Hyrum. They were charged with treason and put in jail at Carthage, Illinois. On a June day in 1844 a mob broke into the jail and slaughtered the two Smiths.

The Mormons disputed bitterly over choice of a successor to the prophet, and out of the dispute came Brigham Young, a strong man and brilliant organizer. It was Brigham who planned and led the great exodus from Illinois to the outer world—taking the tribe to a place then beyond the boundaries of the United States, where they could escape the persecution that seemed to follow them everywhere under the Bill of Rights.

Millions of words have been written about this church, its founder, and especially about the migration across the plains and the mountains. That heroic march into the wilderness remains one of the great epics in the history of America, no matter what you may think of the theological motivation behind it.

As for Joseph Smith, he gets some rough handling from the historians. Charles Francis Potter, in *The Story of Religion,* opens his account of the Mormon Church with this sentence: "The incredible thing about Mormonism is that such a respectable religion could have derived from such a disreputable person."

Dr. Potter says that the Prophet was a psychopath who, notwithstanding his warped mind and his poorly developed ethical sense, was a shrewd schemer. *The Cambridge History of American Literature* suggests that the Book of Mormon was an inferior grade of sheep-dip.

Among the many critical assaults on Mormon theology is one in which Sidney Rigdon, the man who joined Joseph Smith in Ohio, is made out to be the real founder of Mormonism. According to this story, a Presbyterian clergyman named Spaulding wrote a historical novel which he called *The Manuscript Found in the Wilds of Mormon; or Unearthed Records of the Nephites.* Preacher Spaulding took his manuscript, which he had produced as a work of pure fiction, to a printer in Pennsylvania and ordered it made into a book. The manuscript disappeared from the print shop on the same day that a young man employed there also disappeared. The young man was this same Sidney Rigdon. It was Rigdon, according to the story, who decided to use the imaginative work of the Reverend Mr. Spaulding as the rock upon which he would construct a new religion. He went around looking for a likely prophet, preferably one with a weak mind and an inclination toward hallucinations. He found his boy in Joe Smith and used Joe as the instrument for adapting the novel into scripture.

The Mormon Church today has close to a million members. Through the years its achievements in organization and planning have been praiseworthy. Its theologians can argue brilliantly against any criticism you might direct against their Prophet and his teachings. Some of the Mormon writers, for example, say that the Book simply *had* to be of divine origin, considering the all-around dumbness of our boy Joe. Members of the Church believe in Joe Smith, in Moroni, in the Jaredites and Nephites and the coming of Christ to North America, in the golden plates, and in Urim and Thummim. It is all right for them to believe these things because it makes them happy and contented.

Smiths who descended from Joseph and Hyrum have been eminent in the councils of the Mormon Church down to the present day. One of these, Joseph Smith, son of the Prophet, didn't go West with Brigham Young. He stayed in Illinois and

Missouri, becoming a hotelkeeper and a farmer and, in 1860, he formed the Reorganized Church of Jesus Christ of Latter-Day Saints. His church opposed polygamy and had no connection with the main body in Utah. It is still a going concern in Independence.

Joseph Fielding Smith was president of the Church in Salt Lake City from 1880 to his death in 1918. He was Hyrum's son and drove an ox team in the great exodus. His grandson, also Joseph Fielding, was made Presiding Patriarch of the Church in 1942, serving also as head of the University of Utah.

At this distant point, nearing the end of our book, we arrive at the Smith of Smiths. That is the phrase Lord Macaulay used to describe him, and that is the title of Hesketh Pearson's biography of Sydney Smith.

We are not referring to Sir Sidney Smith, the British naval hero who beat the behind off Napoleon at Acre and who brought from Bonaparte the bitter comment, "That man made me miss my destiny."

Nor are we speaking of Sidney Smith, president of the University of Toronto, or of Sidney Smith, the Illinois boy who became famous as creator of the Gumps and Old Doc Yak in the funny papers—a handsome and convivial man who created a sensation in 1928 when he signed a million-dollar contract, giving him $100,000 a year for ten years with a brand-new Rolls-Royce thrown in each year.

This one spelled it Sydney, and if I, as a Smith, had to name my favorite of all the Smiths in history, this is the man I think I'd choose. Charles Dickens thought enough of him to name one of his children Sydney Smith Dickens. Morris Bishop calls him history's greatest exponent of diner-out humor (and adds that its foremost representative in a later era was Logan Pearsall Smith).

Said Sir Henry Holland: "The power and diversity of Sydney Smith's wit was greater than that of any man I have ever known." He was acclaimed by Sir Walter Scott, Thomas Moore, Disraeli, Carlyle, Sheridan, and Ruskin. Queen Victoria is said to have busted her viscera laughing at the sayings of Sydney. And Abraham Lincoln read him and quoted him constantly.

Sydney Smith was a preacher. He was born in 1771 and died in 1845. His father, Robert Smith, was a merchant and somewhat of a character in his own right. Robert chose a pretty Huguenot for his wife, and the wedding took place at St. George's, Bloomsbury. When the final words had been spoken and the happy couple reached the door of the church, Robert announced that all of a sudden an urge had come over him to see America, at once and alone. He kissed his bride and walked away from her and did go to America and was gone for quite a few years. That's how close the Smith of Smiths came to not being born at all. In time Robert did come back and rejoined his wife and begat five children, including Sydney.

Sydney had a good education and was ordained in 1796, becoming first a curate in the village of Nether Avon. Soon he was engaged as tutor to the son of the local squire and traveled to Edinburgh with the boy. Here Sydney became a member of a small group of lively intellects, which included Francis Jeffrey and Henry Brougham. At the suggestion of Sydney they founded a journal of opinion and criticism which became the celebrated *Edinburgh Review*. It is said that modern journalism had its origin in the *Review*, which struck boldly and vigorously against sham and hypocrisy and stupid tradition. Sydney was among the most effective of the journal's anonymous writers for a quarter of a century. He fought for parliamentary reform and for many another cause, but his most famous fight was the one he, a clergyman of the Established Church, waged in favor of emancipation of the Catholics in England. In time he became canon of St. Paul's in London, but he never rose higher in the Church because of his criticisms of the Church itself and because his wit brought the allegation that he lacked sufficient dignity to become a bishop. He was called the English Voltaire and once described himself as belonging to the family of Falstaff. If you can imagine H. L. Mencken behaving as H. L. Mencken while serving as a country parson, then you have an approximate idea of what Sydney Smith was in nineteenth-century England.

Sydney is the man who said: "It requires a surgical operation to get a joke well into a Scotch understanding." He invented, in a sermon, the classical definition of human misfits—square pegs in round holes. As an experimental farmer he once fed his pigs on fermented grain and reported that they were quite happy in their sty, grunting the national anthem. Fred Allen, in his early days as a musical-comedy performer on Broadway, dropped a line from Sydney's writings into his monologue one warm day and brought down the house. "It's so hot," he said, "that I feel like taking off my skin and sitting around in my bones." As one of the great wits of our own time, Fred acknowledges a debt to Sydney Smith and quotes him often, taking joy from such lines as, "The whole of my life has been passed like a razor—in hot water or a scrape."

While living in Edinburgh, Sydney confessed himself mystified by the theology of the Scots. "It is in vain," he wrote, "that I study the subject of the Scotch Church. I have heard it ten times over from Murray, and twenty times from Jeffrey, and I have not the smallest conception what it is about. I know it has something to do with oatmeal, but beyond that I am in utter darkness."

When he married Catharine Pybus at the parish church of Cheam in Surrey, Sidney's conduct was not quite as radical as that of his father. However, at the conclusion of the ceremony Sydney flung six worn teaspoons into his bride's lap. He then explained that he was an honest churchman and that one of his marriage vows could be accomplished on the spot—he was endowing his wife with all his worldly goods.

He was a great hand for applying mathematics to the problems of everyday life. In his old age, for example, he wrote:

"If you wish for anything like happiness in the fifth act of life, eat and drink about one half what you *could* eat and drink. Did I ever tell you my calculation about eating and drinking? Having ascertained the weight of what I could live upon, so as to preserve health and strength, and what I did live upon, I found that, between ten and seventy years of age, I had eaten and drunk forty four-horse wagon-loads of meat and drink more than would have preserved me in life and health! The value of this mass of nourishment I considered to be worth seven thousand pounds sterling. It occurred to me that I must, by my voracity, have starved to death fully a hundred persons."

To Lady Grey, who was disturbed about the spread of cholera, he wrote:

"The cholera will have killed by the end of the year about one person in every thousand. Therefore it is a thousand to one that any person does not die of the cholera in any one year. This calculation is for the mass; but if you are prudent, temperate and rich, your chance is at least five times as good that you do not die of the cholera—in other words, five thousand to one that you do not die of cholera in a year; it is not far from two million to one that you do not die any one day from cholera. It is only seven hundred and thirty thousand to one that your house is not burnt down any one day. Therefore it is nearly three times as likely that your house should be burnt down any one day, as that you should die of cholera; or, it is as probable that your house should be burnt down three times in any one year, as that you should die of cholera."

His Edinburgh associate, Jeffrey, was an extraordinarily small man, standing scarcely five feet in height, and Sydney often joked about his size. Once he wrote to Jeffrey: "Magnitude to you must be such an intoxicating idea, that I have no doubt you would rather be gigantic in your errors than immense in no respect whatever." When his friend took his seat on the bench as Lord Jeffrey in 1834, Sydney commented: "His robes, God knows, will cost him little; one buck rabbit will clothe him to the heels."

Criticizing a review written by his other friend, Brougham, Sydney said he found the article to be in poor taste. "But," he added, "it is very able. It is long yet vigorous like the penis of a jackass."

A letter to Lady Holland included this paragraph:

"I am concerned to hear of Lord Holland's gout. I observe that gout loves ancestors and genealogy. It needs five or six generations of gentlemen or noblemen to give it its full vigor."

He disliked life in the country, where he was compelled to spend many of his years, preferring the salons of London, where he sparkled. At one of his country places a lady suggested that his paddock would be improved by the presence of deer, so

Sydney fitted his two donkeys with antlers and scandalized the neighborhood.

For a long time this man who has been described by Hesketh Pearson as "the greatest of English wits and the most humorous wit in English" was vilified by patriotic Americans because of a slurring passage in one of his essays. It went:

"In the four quarters of the globe, who reads an American book? Or goes to an American play? Or looks at an American picture or statue? What does the world yet owe to American physicians or surgeons? What new substances have their chemists discovered or what old ones have they analyzed? What new constellations have been discovered by the telescopes of Americans? What have they done in mathematics? Who drinks out of American glasses? Or eats from American plates? Or wears American coats or gowns? Or sleeps in American blankets? Finally, under which of the old tyrannical governments of Europe is every sixth man a slave, whom his fellow-creatures may buy and sell and torture?"

He was hated in America for raising those questions, even though there was truth in them—they were written when the new nation was scarcely thirty years old. Moreover, they were usually taken out of context from an essay in which Sydney expressed admiration, as he usually did, for the new country across the water. As a citizen of an old civilization he enjoyed giving advice to the raw young republic. On one occasion, warning America against being led into war by a love of glory, he wrote feelingly:

"We can inform Jonathan what are the inevitable consequences of being too fond of glory: Taxes upon every article which enters into the mouth, or covers the back, or is placed under the foot—taxes upon everything which it is pleasant to see, hear, feel, smell, or taste—taxes upon warmth, light, and locomotion—taxes on everything on earth, and the waters under the earth—on everything that comes from abroad, or is grown at home—taxes on the raw material—taxes on every fresh value that is added to it by the industry of man—taxes on the sauce which pampers man's appetite, and the drug that restores him to health—on the ermine

which decorates the judge, and the rope which hangs the criminal
—on the poor man's salt and the rich man's spice—on the brass
nails of the coffin, and the ribands of the bride—at bed or board,
couchant or levant, we must pay. The schoolboy whips his taxed
top—the beardless youth manages his taxed horse, with a taxed
bridle on a taxed road—and the dying Englishman, pouring his
medicine, which has paid 7 per cent, into a spoon that has paid
15 per cent—flings himself back upon his chintz bed, which has
paid 22 per cent—and expires in the arms of an apothecary who
has paid a license of a hundred pounds for the privilege of putting
him to death. His whole property is then immediately taxed from 2
to 10 per cent. Besides the probate, large fees are demanded for
burying him in the chancel; his virtues are handed down to
posterity on taxed marble; and he is then gathered to his fathers—
to be taxed no more."

Sydney could and did wound people with his wit. Chided for
his cruelty, he excused himself by saying that he had a weak
voice and that no one would ever hear him at all unless he spoke
insultingly. He was fond of Macaulay but resented the celebrated
author's garrulity. He described Macaulay on one occasion as "a
book in breeches" and again said that "he not only overflowed
with learning but stood in the slops." Sydney proposed building
a round table with a raised, revolving platform in the center, so
he could put Macaulay on it "and distribute his talk fairly to the
company." One day he visited Macaulay when the author was
ill in bed, and found him "more agreeable than I have ever seen
him—there were some gorgeous flashes of silence."

He wrote about anything and everything that was of concern
to the nation. Defending female education, he scoffed at those who
argued that educated women would neglect their natural duties,
saying it was highly improbable that any mother would "desert
an infant for a quadratic equation."

Reporting once on a visit he had from the famous Thomas
Robert Malthus, the man who worried about world population,
Sydney wrote: "Philosopher Malthus came here last week. I got an
agreeable party for him of unmarried people. There was only one
lady who had a child; but he is a good-natured man, and, if

there are no appearances of approaching fertility, is civil to every lady."

He suffered from hay fever and spoke of the membrane in his nostrils as being so irritable "that light, dust, contradiction, an absurb remark, the sight of a Dissenter—anything, sets me a sneezing, and if I begin sneezing at 12, I don't leave off till 2 o'clock—and am heard distinctly in Taunton when the wind sets that way, at a distance of six miles."

Of the January weather he once wrote to Lady Grey:

"We have had the mildest weather possible. A great part of the vegetable world is deceived and beginning to blossom—not merely foolish young plants without experience, but old plants that have been deceived before by premature springs; and for such, one has no pity. It is as if Lady Blessington were to complain of being seduced and betrayed."

The process known to modern comedy as "milking a gag"—dragging every possible laugh or chuckle or snicker from it before finally giving it up, was not unknown to Sydney. For example, when he heard that a young Scot of his acquaintance was going to marry an Irish widow of tremendous physical bulk, he exclaimed:

"Going to marry her! Impossible! You mean a part of her; he could not marry her all himself. It would be a case, not of bigamy, but of trigamy; the neighborhood or the magistrates should interfere. There is enough of her to furnish wives for a whole parish. One man marry her!—it is monstrous! You might people a colony with her; or give an assembly with her; or perhaps take your morning's walk around her, always provided there were frequent resting-places, and you were in rude health . . . Or you might read the Riot Act and disperse her; in short, you might do anything with her but marry her."

Sydney sometimes joked about his surname. A certain statesman was accused of nepotism, and Sydney leaped to his defense.

"Such a disposition of patronage," he said, "is one of the highest inducements to a man of high rank and large fortune to abandon the comforts of private life for the turmoils and disappointments of a political career. Nor does the country suffer by it; on the contrary, a man is much more likely to be able to judge of the competence of his relatives for office than of anyone else. Indeed, I feel so strongly on this point that if by any conceivable freak of fortune I were placed in such a position, I should think myself not only authorized but compelled to give a post to every man of my name in the country."

His witticisms were not always studied, and he enjoyed uttering as well as hearing a clever pun. Walking one day with a friend, he observed two women quarreling from opposite windows in a narrow street. "They will never agree," said Sydney, "for they argue from different premises."

Speaking of the futility of arguing with a certain prejudiced citizen, he remarked that "you might as well attempt to poultice the humps off a camel's back." After meeting Daniel Webster he described the American statesman as "much like a steam-engine in trousers."

"I don't like dogs," said Sydney on another occasion. "I always expect them to go mad. A lady asked me once for a motto for her dog Spot. I proposed 'Out, damned Spot!' but strange to say she did not think it sentimental enough."

His warm friend Lady Holland was among the most eminent females in England, and when at last he persuaded her to visit his home in the country, he announced feverish plans for her reception:

"I have spoken to the sheriff," he reported, "and mentioned it to the magistrates. They have agreed to address her, and she is to be escorted from the station by the yeomanry. The clergy are rather backward; but I think that, after a little bashfulness, they will wait upon her. Brunel, assisted by the ablest philosophers, is to accompany her upon the railroad; and they have been so good as to say that the steam shall be generated from soft water, with a slight infusion of chamomile flowers."

As for his religion, he has been described as a devout man who despised and fought against all forms of orthodoxy. Many of his quips reflected his distaste for the austerities of formalized worship, and he was usually in disfavor with the higher clergy, who refused to be amused. A friend once expressed a desire to hear him preach, and he warned: "To go to St. Paul's is certain death. The thermometer is several degrees below zero. My sentences are frozen as they come out of my mouth, and are thawed in the course of the summer, making strange noises and unexpected assertions in various parts of the church."

Sydney once got into an argument with an irascible country squire who lost his temper and shouted: "If I had a son who was an idiot, I'd make him a parson!" To which Sydney replied: "Very probably—but I see that your father was of a different mind."

One day he came upon a child who was stroking the shell back of a pet turtle, and Sydney asked why he was doing it. "To please the turtle," said the child. "Why," said Sydney, "you might as well stroke the dome of St. Paul's to please the Dean and Chapter."

In his fading years Sydney turned his wit upon the infirmities that were overtaking him. He reported to a friend that "I feel so weak both in body and mind that I verily believe, if the knife were put into my hand, I should not have strength or energy enough to slide it into a Dissenter." He was put on a slim diet and remarked to General Fox: "Ah, Charles, I wish I were allowed even the wing of a roasted butterfly." His loss of weight caused him to write to another friend: "If you hear of sixteen or eighteen pounds of human flesh, they belong to me. I look as if a curate had been taken out of me." He grew philosophical about death and said he was studying deathbed utterances. "It seems necessary," he wrote, "that great people should die with some sonorous and quotable saying. Mr. Pitt said something not intelligible in his last moments. G. Rose made it out to be, 'Save my country, Heaven!' The nurse, on being interrogated, said that he asked for barley water."

On his own deathbed Sydney roused himself to ask for his medicine. His nurse found a half bottle of ink standing on the bed table where the medicine should have been, and said to her dying patient, "You must have taken a dose of ink by mistake." And the Smith of Smiths gasped out his final joke: "Well, then, bring me all the blotting paper there is in the house."

Arms and the Smith

The Smiths never had any arms and have invariably sealed their letters with their thumbs.
—Sydney Smith

This Enquiry into the Nature and Causes of the Wealth of Smiths has been, in some respects, one long rodomontade. We can be as vain and complacent as any of our neighbors; it would go against the law of Nature for us to be otherwise. Our name has even been installed in a proverbial expression which is applied to people of enormous conceit. Such an one (whoops!) is called a Smith of Nottingham—a person who imagines that no one on earth is able to compete with him. The saying derives from an old English verse which goes:

> *The Little Smith of Nottingham*
> *Who doth the work that no man can.*

Our individual conceits are of great diversity. On the outskirts of Omaha lives a man named Smith who has for some months been displaying a willingness to have himself memorialized in these pages. I informed him that the mere fact of being named Smith was not sufficient, that only Smiths of noteworthy achievement were eligible—that if he had accomplished in his life something far out of the ordinary, and if that accomplishment struck me as being worth reporting to the world, then I would be happy to include his name in the Blue Book of Smiths. Several weeks

passed and another letter came from him. He said that in the fall of 1941 he laid in a supply of popcorn, consisting of thirty-six one-pound bags. Without the assistance of another person he popped and ate those thirty-six pounds of popcorn in three and a half months, consuming one dishpanful each evening until the last grain was gone. Had anyone else ever eaten so much popcorn in so short a period? Had *anyone named Smith* ever done it? I think not. His name is Sam Smith.

The official register of personal or family conceit is the coat of arms. The science of heraldry had its origin in the Middle Ages, when men were walking wash boilers, indistinguishable one from another because of their armor. A turtle could quickly identify another turtle, but when knighthood was in flower a warrior, once the visors were down and the beavers up, could not distinguish friend from foe. Each knight therefore adorned his shield with some identifying insignia and fastened a distinctive crest to his helmet. In the thirteenth century, when it was stylish to wear mail, the armorial insignia was embroidered on a cloth surcoat which was worn over the mail, and out of this custom came the expression *coat of arms*.

In time a highly complex system of heraldry arose, similar in many respects to the registry operations of the American Kennel Club and possessing a language all its own. In the jargon of heraldry, for example, colors are not colors but *tinctures;* red is *gules,* and black is *sable,* and purple is *purpure.* Great Christ! The positions of the various figures (charges or bearings) on the shield, called the escutcheon, have definite significance. The urdee, the embattled grady, the nowy, the brisure, the bordure, the mullet, and the martlet—all these items and many more help to tell a little story of family life. A person versed in heraldry can look at a specific coat of arms and read it the way an architect reads a blueprint, uttering heraldic gobbledegook about the birth, marriage, home town, hobbies, susceptibility to head colds, and even sinfulness of the proprietor.

The Smiths would appear to have no great need for coats of arms to distinguish one individual from another. We have achieved separate identification when it was wanted through our baptismal names, by calling ourselves Okay, Other, Another, ⅝, Oceanwave, Millage, Wanton, Ai, and so on. What we do need is a tribal coat of arms, an insignia that will serve the whole Diaspora of Smiths.

There exists a massive work called *The General Armory of England, Scotland, Ireland and Wales* in which eight pages of small type are devoted to Smiths and their coats of arms. Checking through this list of prideful Smiths, I find that the most commonly recurrent charges are the stork, the horseshoe, and the ostrich. There are frequent mermaids, greyhounds, goats, falcon wings, beavers, leopards, unicorns, lions, bulls, eagles, peacocks, crows, ravens, quill pens, and daggers.

Employing some of these heraldic devices, Leo Hershfield has blazoned a coat of arms for the use of the Congress of People Named Smith. In his original sketch Mr. Hershfield missed a main point, and it had to be sent back for revision (he turned purpure with embarrassment). There was no *abatement* on it.

An *abatement* is a figure added to the escutcheon to denote degradation of one kind or another. The *abatement* signifying illegitimacy is the *baton sinister* (not the *bar sinister* as it is usually and erroneously denominated). Examining that first draught of our coat of arms and thinking back over the motley assortment of Smiths with whom I've been dealing in these long months of scholarly endeavor, I recognized that a *baton sinister* was needed on our shield. So Mr. Hershfield put one on—the strip running diagonally across the escutcheon. He must have sensed what I had in mind, for he worked in a *baton sinister* with a dog on it. If this last-minute addition to the escutcheon is not clear, let me explain. There are many Smiths to whom actual illegitimacy cannot be charged but who are, nonetheless, entitled to the name, in variation.

If the truth be told, I'm a horrible bastard myself.